# CAMBRIDGE LIBRARY COLLECTION

*Books of enduring scholarly value*

## Education

This series focuses on educational theory and practice, particularly in the context of eighteenth- and nineteenth-century Europe and its colonies, and America. During this period, the questions of who should be educated, to what age, to what standard and using what curriculum, were widely debated. The reform of schools and universities, the drive towards improving women's education, and the movement for free (or at least low-cost) schools for the poor were all major concerns both for governments and for society at large. The books selected for reissue in this series discuss key issues of their time, including the 'appropriate' levels of instruction for the children of the working classes, the emergence of adult education movements, and proposals for the higher education of women. They also cover topics that still resonate today, such as the nature of education, the role of universities in the diffusion of knowledge, and the involvement of religious groups in establishing and running schools.

## Conversations on Arithmetic

In this 1835 work, Sarah Porter, née Ricardo (1790–1862) shows her enthusiasm for arithmetic, and her concern for teaching it in a way that will develop the pupil's mind: 'There is no branch of early education so admirably adapted to call forth and strengthen the reasoning powers.' She uses the device of a conversation between pupil and teacher, popularised by Jane Marcet (several of whose works are reissued in the Cambridge Library Collection), to guide young Edmund from the written symbols for numbers through addition, subtraction, multiplication and division, fractions and decimals, proportion, and square and cube roots. Answers to the questions are provided at the end of the book. A member of the Central Society of Education, which promoted imaginative theories of education instead of rote learning, Mrs Porter reworked her book in 1852 as *Rational Arithmetic*, a more conventional and less entertaining textbook for use in schools.

# Conversations on Arithmetic

SARAH PORTER

# CAMBRIDGE
## UNIVERSITY PRESS

University Printing House, Cambridge, CB2 8BS, United Kingdom

Cambridge University Press is part of the University of Cambridge.
It furthers the University's mission by disseminating knowledge in the pursuit of
education, learning and research at the highest international levels of excellence.

www.cambridge.org
Information on this title: www.cambridge.org/9781108075350

This edition first published 1835
This digitally printed version 2015

ISBN 978-1-108-07535-0 Paperback

# CONVERSATIONS

## ON

# ARITHMETIC.

BY

Mrs. G. R. PORTER,

AUTHOR OF "ALFRED DUDLEY,"
&c.

LONDON:

CHARLES KNIGHT, 22, LUDGATE STREET.

MDCCCXXXV.

# PREFACE.

An author should not, perhaps, offer to the public a new elementary work, without assigning some reason for thus swelling the already numerous list of books written for the purposes of education.

Every writer hopes that his individual work will not be found one of supererogation, and believes that what he has to propose will correct established errors in practice, or afford new facilities for acquiring knowledge. However little may be accomplished in these respects, there is, perhaps, sufficient reason for attempting that little. In this hope, and influenced by this belief, I have written the following work.

Having had my attention early awakened to the beauties of the study which forms the subject of these pages, it has ever been a matter of regret with me that arithmetic should be acquired in the unsatisfactory manner in which it is generally taught. There is no branch of early education so admirably adapted to call forth and strengthen the reasoning powers; this object,

therefore, independent of the advantages attendant on
the thorough knowledge of arithmetic, offers in itself a
sufficient motive for engaging the young mind in the
pursuit.   If its end and aim were only to exercise these
mental faculties, the time thus employed in the education of youth would be well bestowed, " not so much to
make them mathematicians as to make them reasonable
creatures."*

   To assist in rescuing arithmetic from the degraded
rank it at present occupies among intellectual pursuits,
is a principal object of the following work.   I have endeavoured so to simplify the subject, that mothers or
instructors, who have not previously turned their attention to this interesting and important branch of education, may be enabled by its help to teach their pupils
the *rationale* of the science, and to lead them gently
and almost imperceptibly, step by step, to the full
understanding of the subject—thus imparting to them
a clear insight into the science of arithmetic, at the
same time calling into action their reasoning powers,
and " preparing them for those difficult and knotty
parts of knowledge which try the strength of thought."*
Whether or not I have succeeded in my attempt can
only be discovered by the test of experiment, and from
the verdict of enlightened preceptors.

   Rules should never usurp the place of reasons, and
particular cases should not be confounded with general

---

* Locke's Conduct of the Understanding.

principles. The pupil should be led to think for himself, and then he will, as he feels his own strength, be
glad to exercise his new-found power, provided it be
not crushed while in its first infancy by the imposition
of an overwhelming weight. Very young children can
better understand the first rudiments of arithmetic than
they can engage in the mere mechanical operations of
numbers; they will be interested in exercising their ingenuity by answering simple questions while yet they
would be perplexed with the management of many
figures; and if they be early tried with the latter, they
become hopeless of understanding what is set before
them;—they learn by rote what is necessary to the working of a sum, and continue to have vague and obscure
ideas on the subject ever after, or until self-education, if
that ever should take place, at length dispels the cloud.

It is particularly hurtful to the mind to be hurried
into knowledge, and it cannot be too strongly urged,
that but little should be proposed at once, and till this
is thoroughly understood and mastered, nothing new on
the same subject should be offered;—the advantages
attendant on this manner of instructing cannot be more
forcibly put, than in the words, and on the authority of
Locke. " This distinct gradual growth in knowledge is
firm and sure; it carries its own light with it in every
step of its progression in an easy and orderly train, than
which there is nothing of more use to the understanding.
And though this, perhaps, may seem a very slow and
lingering way to knowledge, yet I dare confidently

*a* 3

affirm that whoever will try it in himself or any one he
will teach, shall find the advances greater in this
method than they would in the same space of time have
been in any other he could have taken."

I am aware that the manner in which it is here proposed that arithmetic should be taught, differs materially
from the usual practice. But it must be recollected
that a two-fold object is sought to be attained—that
of teaching the science, in combination with the cul-
tivation of the reason.. To this end I have studiously
avoided giving any rule without having first called upon
the pupil's ingenuity to seek one for himself, or without having clearly explained to him wherefore the
method is followed, or on what principles the rule is
founded. Many children would rather acquiesce than
inquire; and if they can seize upon and apply a rule
to practice, will not pause to ask why the required
results are produced. I have therefore endeavoured
throughout to awaken the attention of the pupil, and
incite him to the use of his understanding, before any
general rule has been given for performing what was to
be done.

In the arrangement made, I have wished that the
easy should be placed before the difficult, and that the
successive propositions should as much as possible depend on what has preceded them. Perhaps the chapters
on the properties of numbers, and the method of cancelling may meet with some objections. But I believe

these to be quite requisite as preliminaries to the
proper understanding and application of fractions, while
the method of cancelling may be advantageously applied to the solution of almost all intricate questions in
arithmetic. This has been found to be no unpleasing
mental exertion to children; they who have practised it
like thus to shorten their work by their own ingenuity,
while it initiates them into an acquaintance with the
nature of numbers, better than any of those routine sums
with which pupils are ordinarily exercised.

I shall not, I trust, incur the charge of presumption
for thus putting forth a method which differs from that
which is usually practised. My views are not the fanciful speculations of a mere theorist, nor would I have
ventured to offer this work to the public, had it not been
the result of a conviction, gained by practical experi-
ence, that arithmetic can be taught thus with advantage
and success.

The form of conversation has been chosen, since it
affords a greater facility for explanation and familiar
illustration than any other. In the first part I have
been desirous, while addressing the pupil, of avoiding
all terms or even words, but those which it might be
supposed a young child can well understand. It was
at the same time desirable to make some observations
suited to a more advanced age, and occasionally to
offer to the instructor reasons for a departure from
established methods. To meet this difficulty all such

matter as is not intended for the very young pupil
is placed within brackets, thus [   ], and therefore need
not in any way interfere with, or perplex the explanations necessary for the young beginner.  In the latter
parts these interruptions will be found less frequent,
since it is taken for granted that when the pupil has
arrived at more advanced stages, he will readily comprehend most of the observations which each particular
rule has drawn forth.

# TABLE OF CONTENTS.

## PART I.

# PART II.

---

# PART III.

COMMERCIAL ARITHMETIC.

CHAPTER III.

-----

PART IV.

CHAPTER I.

CHAPTER II.

CHAPTER III.

# CONVERSATIONS ON ARITHMETIC.

## CHAPTER I.

## NOTATION AND NUMERATION.

*Mrs. D.* I THINK you are now old enough, my little boy, to be taught arithmetic; in learning which you see Alfred and Emily take so much pleasure.

*Edmund.* That means, I suppose, to answer questions about nuts and apples on my slate, instead of counting on my fingers?—I shall be very glad of that.

*Mrs. D.* As the first step, you must learn to write the figures, which are the signs of numbers. In the mean time these little fingers must again serve our purpose.

The figure which denotes, or is the sign for,

| | |
|---|---:|
| One, is written thus . . . . | 1 |
| One and one more, or two, are written . | 2 |
| Two and one more, or three, are written . | 3 |
| Three and one more, or four, are written . | 4 |
| Four and one more, or five, are written . | 5 |
| Five and one more, or six, are written . | 6 |
| Six and one more, or seven, are written . | 7 |
| Seven and one more, or eight, are written . | 8 |
| Eight and one more, or nine, are written . | 9 |
| Nought, or nothing, is expressed by a cipher, which is written . . . . | 0 |

Now, when you have copied these on your slate, and can count each number on your fingers, you shall have another lesson.

*Edmund.* Mother, I can write all these figures now; and I want you to show me the signs for ten, eleven, and so on.

*Mrs. D.* Not so fast, my little man. Before you learn these, we must have a little conversation, according to our old method. Remember, my dear child, when I tell you anything, and you do not see clearly what I mean, you must ask me again and again, till you *quite* understand it. You must be attentive and patient, and not say you know when you do not know. Now, let me see you write your figures. Tolerably done.— These nine figures are called digits.

[*Alfred.* From the Latin word *digitus,* a finger.

*Mrs. D.* True; which is a corroborative proof that in the infancy of arithmetic the fingers were the principal reckoners. When men first began to cast up their accounts, there is little doubt that this method was adopted, as being the readiest and simplest.]

To count, and to recollect the number we have counted, with the help of our fingers, is certainly a very convenient plan, as long as our numbers do not exceed the number of our fingers; but when they are beyond these, we are obliged to have recourse to some other contrivance. You know, Edmund, you have often found that you have not nearly fingers enough to reckon the various things which you wish to count, and we have felt the want of some better way of finding out answers to the many questions you have asked. Thus, to express any number beyond ten, we must count your fingers a second time, and recollect that we have already used them once; unless, indeed, Emily will lend us one of her fingers, to show that we have counted yours once over. Each of your fingers will then represent one, or an unit, and each of hers ten ones, or ten units; so you can express ten units with yours, and she ten tens with hers. But let me see in what situation our accounts stand at present. You have none of your fingers held up, and Emily has one of hers, to show that one ten has been counted.

*Emily.* While I am holding up my poor finger all this time, recollect, Edmund, that every one of my fingers are worth ten of yours.

*Mrs. D.* In order to express this in writing, we put down the sign for nothing, or nought, to show that there are no units, and the sign for one is put in what is called the place of tens, at the left-hand side of the place of units—the tens going before the units, as being of greater value: thus, one ten and no units are expressed in this manner, 10.

*Edmund.* Well, now we have Emily's little finger put down on the slate, let us go on counting. Here is another of my fingers held up.

*Mrs. D.* This will show that we have counted

Ten and one, or eleven, we therefore write 11. In like manner,

Ten and two, or twelve, are written   . 12
Ten and three, or thirteen, are written . 13
Ten and four, or fourteen, are written   . 14
Ten and five, or fifteen, are written   . 15
Ten and six, or sixteen, are written   . 16
Ten and seven, or seventeen, are written 17
Ten and eight, or eighteen, are written . 18
Ten and nine, or nineteen, are written . 19

Now you have got to hold up your last finger, and then Emily must let us have another of hers, to show that you have counted two tens, or that you have reckoned your fingers twice over. Then there will be two tens and no units or twenty, written  .  .  . 20

In like manner,

Two tens and one unit, or twenty-one, are written .   21

Two tens and two units, or twenty-two, are written    22

And so on, till we have counted your fingers over three times, and then your sister's hand will show us three tens, or thirty, written   .    .    .    .   30

In like manner,

Three tens and one unit, or thirty-one, are written    31
    and so on.

Four tens, or forty, are written  .    .    .    .  40

Four tens and one unit, or forty-one, are written  .  41
    and so on.

Five tens, or fifty, are written    .    .    .    .  50

Five tens and one unit, or fifty-one, are written   .  51
    and so on.

Six tens, or sixty, are written   .    .    .    .  60

Six tens and one unit, or sixty-one, are written   .  61
    and so on.

Seven tens, or seventy, are written   .    .    .  70

Seven tens and one unit, or seventy-one, are written  71
    and so on.

Eight tens, or eighty, are written .    .    .    .  80

Eight tens and one unit, or eighty-one, are written    81
    and so on.

Nine tens, or ninety, are written  .    .    .    .  90

Nine tens and one unit, or ninety-one, are written    91
    and so on.

*Edmund.* But when we have used all Emily's fingers, what shall we do then?—we must certainly take Alfred's, and after he has no more to lend us, we must have yours, mother.

*Mrs. D.* Alfred's fingers may then be made each to represent ten tens, or one hundred, and each of mine may represent ten hundreds, or one thousand; but I suspect your brother and sister would not always be quite ready to form part of your calculating machine, and as I think, likewise, that I can employ my own hands more advantageously, we must henceforth find some substitute for our digits. And now, Edmund, you have learnt enough for this morning; in the afternoon you shall write down some tens and units, and show me whether you remember what I have said to you.

[*Emily.* Why do we not say ten one and ten two, instead of eleven and twelve, they would be so much better understood by a beginner? Ten three, ten four, &c., would be better than thirteen, fourteen, and all the rest of the teens: these, however, are so like three and ten, four and ten, that there is no difficulty in recollecting that they mean the same thing; but eleven and twelve are barbarous words, and completely spoil the uniformity of numbers.

*Mrs. D.* Only of their names, Emily; and for this we must thank our Saxon ancestors, from whose language we have derived our numeral words. Eleven signifies one left, and twelve two left (after ten is taken away being understood). But though you may think these names of numbers capable of amendment, you cannot, I am sure, fail to give your unqualified admiration to the present system of notation; we are so accustomed to it from our earliest childhood, that we scarcely know how to appreciate its perfect beauty and simplicity—by which we are enabled, with only ten characters, to express any number whatever, and to work out the most difficult questions, merely by knowing how to marshal our men in their proper places, and to assign to each its due rank.

*Alfred.* There certainly seems little reason to doubt that this manner of reckoning by tens arose from the practice of counting with the fingers. Accordingly, if we had happened to have been made with a smaller or a greater number of fingers, eight or twelve, for example, the system of notation would have been entirely different.

*Mrs. D.* The signs, but not the system, would have been different. In the one case we should only have had eight characters, and these would have recurred at intervals of eight numbers instead of ten ; while in the other case we should have had twelve characters, recurring at every twelfth interval.

*Alfred.* How could these changes be managed, mother, and how would they affect the value of the present numbers ?

*Mrs. D.* In no other way than by altering the signs or symbols of those numbers—the aggregate of units would have been exactly the same. If we count those sheep we now see grazing in the park, and find there are twenty, their number would still be the same, whether this were represented by 24, 20, or 18.

*Alfred.* It would be curious to follow this up, and find what these signs would be if the number of digits were different from what they are at present. Could I do this ? Do I know enough to make this transformation ?

*Mrs. D.* Yes, quite enough ; but the inquiry is more curious than useful. It cannot by possibility lead to any practical good, and I advise you to dismiss it from your mind, as tending to confuse and bewilder you to no useful purpose. When you are " unco wise," in these matters, and like to indulge in fanciful speculations, from the mere love of the pursuit, then you may in this respect follow the example of many eminent mathematicians who have gone before you. Recollect, however, it is but a whim, and I own I should be better pleased to see my boy exercise his powers in a higher and more useful path of mathematics. It would be just as sensible to transpose the characters of the alphabet at your arbitrary pleasure, and then to form words and sentences on the supposition. But enough, and perhaps too much, of this. It is well Edmund is gone to his play, or the discussion might have frightened him out of his love of arithmetic.]

*Mrs. D.* Here is a box full of white counters, and another box containing counters of all the colours of the rainbow. Now with these we shall be able to express more numbers than we shall have patience to reckon. The white counters we will call units, or unit-counters; the red, tens, or ten-counters; the blue, hundreds, or hundred-counters; the green, thousands, or thousand-counters, and so on. These seventeen white counters will therefore express the same number as this one red and seven white counters; these two red counters will mean the same as these twenty white; and these ten red, or tens, will be the same as this one blue, or hundred-counter.

*Edmund.* How am I to show on my slate one hundred?

*Mrs. D.* The hundreds, as being of a higher value, take precedence or stand before the tens, in the same manner as the tens stand before the units : thus, one hundred is written 100, the two noughts showing that there are no tens and no units. One hundred and one unit are written 101; one hundred and one ten, 110.

*Emily.* So, though we profess to consider these noughts as Mr. Nobodies, yet they act an important part in keeping the places of the different figures ; without them, there would be a sad confusion. See, Edmund, you have written one unit and one ten, instead of one hundred and one unit : put the cipher between them, to show the place of tens.

*Mrs. D.* Now express two hundred and one ten—two hundred and one unit—one hundred and two tens, or twenty—one hundred and two units.

*Edmund (writes).* 210, 201, 120, 102.

*Mrs. D.* You perceive that, by using the same three figures, we can express four different numbers, and you can understand of how much importance it is that you should put each figure in its proper place.

Express the following numbers :—Three hundred and seventy-five; nine hundred and eighty-three; six hundred and forty-seven.  Read 863; 740; 509.

---

*Mrs. D.* Tens of hundreds, or thousands, are placed before the hundreds, and occupy the fourth place on the left: thus, one thousand is expressed 1000, the noughts showing that there are no units, no tens, and no hundreds.

So two thousand three hundred and forty-one are expressed thus . . . . . . 2341

Three thousand two hundred and forty-one are expressed . . . . . . . 3241

Two thousand four hundred and thirty-one . 2431

Read 2134; 1234: 1243.

*Mrs. D.* I think you now clearly understand that every number increases its value ten times by having a nought placed after it: thus, 20 are ten times more than 2; 200 ten times more than 20, and so on, whatever higher number we may use; and always every figure expresses ten times higher value than the same figure placed immediately on the right of it: this is called Notation.  Numeration is the method of reading Notation.  You now have been shown the first step in the knowledge of arithmetic; and the proper understanding of Notation is of great importance to all that comes after it. The subject of your next lesson will be Addition.

[*Alfred.* But, mother, you have taught Edmund to enumerate only as far as thousands; you have forgotten to introduce to his notice all the *illions.*

*Mrs. D.* I think, for the present, we had better leave our little pupil to con over his thousands, and allow him to become quite familiar with them before we bewilder his tender mind with higher numbers. It is enough that he knows the principle of their increase; he can easily be made acquainted by slow degrees with the mere names, without requiring any further explanation. I have not, however, been so deficient in my enumeration lesson as you imagine, having prepared a table which will complete his education in this part of arithmetic, but which should not and must not be shown to him just at present. The value of figures, according to their places, and the names of these, will be readily seen from the following table.

| 9 | 3 | 4 | 5 | 7 | 8 | 9 | 1 | 0 | 5 | 6 | 2 | 8 |
|---|---|---|---|---|---|---|---|---|---|---|---|---|
| Billions | Hundred thousands of millions | Ten thousands of millions | Thousands of millions | Hundreds of millions | Tens of millions | Millions | Hundreds of thousands | Tens of thousands | Thousands | Hundreds | Tens | Units |

It is usual, when a number is composed of many places of figures, to break it into periods and half periods of six and of three figures. The first period em-

braces from units to hundreds of thousands; the second is
the million period; the third the billion; the fourth the
trillion; the fifth the quadrillion, &c.:—the above number
would accordingly be written thus, 9,345,789,105,628.

*Alfred.* Will not your lesson on Notation and Numeration be incomplete, unless you take some notice of the
Roman numerals?

*Mrs. D.* Very true. Be it your care, then, to teach
these to Edmund as soon as he is a little more familiar
with our own numbers.

*Emily.* Surely, mother, the Romans used our figures
as well as their own, for they could not possibly multiply and divide with their strange numerals.

*Mrs. D.* They certainly could not accomplish these
operations with as much simplicity as we perform them
with our present Notation. But it is certain that both
the Grecians and Romans were unacquainted with the
characters now in so general use. The former made the
letters of their alphabet to serve them also as signs for
numbers; and the figures of the latter people are still
generally known and used under the name of Roman
numerals. In consequence of this imperfect mode of
Notation, the operations in arithmetic were laborious
and tedious, and could not well be performed to any
extent without the aid of pebbles or counters: hence our
word calculate, from the Latin word calculus, a small
pebble. To the Roman accountant, as well as to the
pupil in arithmetic, the *abacus* and *calculi*, or cipher-
ing-board and counters, were as necessary aids as are the
slates and pencils of the present day to our schoolboys.

*Emily.* When and how, then, did we obtain our numeral characters? It seems to me scarcely possible
that any intricate calculations can be made without such
a system.

*Mrs. D.* Antiquarians are disagreed as to the exact

date when these characters were first introduced into Europe; but it appears probable, from many well-authenticated records, that they were very little used or known before the fourteenth century. They are usually called Arabic figures, because they were first brought from Arabia into Spain by the Moors and Saracens; but whether this valuable invention originated in Arabia, or whether it was derived from India, is a matter of some doubt, which has given rise to many learned discussions. The result of these seems, however, to be in favour of the latter supposition.

---

*A Table of Roman Numerals answering to our numbers.*

| | | | |
|---|---|---|---|
| 1 | I. | 11 | XI. |
| 2 | II. | 12 | XII. |
| 3 | III. | and so on to | |
| 4 | IIII. or IV. | 40 | XL. |
| 5 | V. | 50 | L. |
| 6 | VI. | 90 | XC. |
| 7 | VII. | 100 | C. |
| 8 | VIII. | 500 | D. or IƆ—for every Ɔ an- |
| 9 | IX. | | nexed, this becomes ten times |
| 10 | X. | | as many. |

1000    M. or CIƆ—for every C and Ɔ placed one at each end, it becomes ten times as much.

5000    V̄. or IƆƆ—a bar over any number increases it a thousandfold.

6000    V̄I.

10000    X̄. or CCIƆƆ.]

CHAPTER II.

ADDITION.

*Mrs. D.* If you put three counters in one parcel and two counters in another, you can readily tell me how many there are when the two parcels are added together.

*Edmund.* Five, to be sure; but this is not a sum on my slate.

*Mrs. D.* Well, then, put down the number 3, and 2 under it, then draw a line, and put 5 under the line, and exactly in a row with the other figures, thus,
$$\begin{array}{c} 3 \\ 2 \\ \hline 5 \end{array}$$
Now you have done an Addition sum; you have found that 2 and 3 are 5, and you have expressed this by figures on your slate, the 5 below the line being your answer.

*Edmund.* But this is so very easy, I want something much more difficult.

*Mrs. D.* Here are two other figures, 6 and 4; now add these together, and put down your answer under the line.

*Edmund.* I do not know how to do that; I do not recollect what 6 added to 4 are.

*Mrs. D.* But cannot you find out? How did you know that 2 added to 3 are 5.

*Edmund.* By reckoning them with the counters.

*Mrs. D.* Cannot you do the same with these higher numbers? Take 6 counters and 4 counters.

*Edmund.* These together make 10; so I write 10 under the line.

*Mrs. D.* Are you quite sure this is right, my love?

*Edmund.* Yes, *quite* sure.

*Mrs. D.* And what makes you so very sure?

*Edmund.* Because I have counted 6 and 4 together, and know they make 10.

*Mrs. D.* Very true;—with any degree of care you may be always certain that you are right; and, little boy as you are, you need not ask any one to teach you what number any one number added to or taken from another number will be; you can always find this out for yourself. But neither you nor I, Edmund, could have known that 6 and 4 are 10, without having previously found this out by trial. It is the recollection of knowledge thus obtained, which enables us to perform sums in Addition with facility.

In writing down the 6 and 4 to be added up, it is exactly the same whether we put the 6 or the 4 first, their change of place does not at all alter their sum; for if we put the six counters to the four, or the four to the six, there still would be ten counters, reckon them which way you will. 6 and 4 are therefore exactly the same as 4 and 6; 2 and 3 the same as 3 and 2. Do you quite understand this?

*Edmund.* Yes; 2 and 1 are 3, and 1 and 2 are 3.

---

*Mrs. D.* Your next lesson must be to learn, by means of your counters, that

| | | |
|---|---|---|
| 1 and 4 are 5 | 1 and 5 are 6 | 1 and 6 are 7 |
| 2 and 3 are 5 | 2 and 4 are 6 | 2 and 5 are 7 |
| | 3 and 3 are 6 | 3 and 4 are 7 |
| 1 and 7 are 8 | 1 and 8 are 9 | 1 and 9 are 10 |
| 2 and 6 are 8 | 2 and 7 are 9 | 2 and 8 are 10 |
| 3 and 5 are 8 | 3 and 6 are 9 | 3 and 7 are 10 |
| 4 and 4 are 8 | 4 and 5 are 9 | 4 and 6 are 10 |
| | | 5 and 5 are 10 |

c

When you know these, and have counted them so often as perfectly to recollect them, I will teach you something new.

----

*Mrs. D.* If from these five counters you were to take three away, how many would remain?

*Edmund.* Two.

*Mrs. D.* This is called Subtraction. Now, I dare say, if you recollect the addition or sum of any two numbers, you can without any difficulty, or without trying with the counters, subtract or take away one of these numbers from their sum. For example, if you take 4 from 7, what remain?

*Edmund.* Three.

*Mrs. D.* Take 3 from 5, 6 from 8, 7 from 10.

What number added to $\begin{Bmatrix} 9 \\ 8 \\ 7 \\ 6 \\ 5 \\ 4 \\ 3 \\ 2 \\ 1 \end{Bmatrix}$ will make 10? Answer. $\begin{Bmatrix} 1 \\ 2 \\ 3 \\ 4 \\ 5 \\ 6 \\ 7 \\ 8 \\ 9 \end{Bmatrix}$

You must make yourself sufficiently familiar with this, to know immediately when you see a figure what you must add to it to make 10. You will then be enabled very readily to do any simple Addition and Subtraction sums without the assistance of your counters.

----

*Mrs. D.* If you have nine counters in this heap, and eight in another, how many will there be together?

*Edmund.* I must then still use my counters. I take one from the parcel containing 8, and add it to the heap of nine; as 9 and one more are 10, I will change these ten units for a ten-counter, and now, besides the one ten, I have seven units remaining in the other heap; and one ten and seven are seventeen.

*Mrs. D.* Write this answer down on your slate. Now add 6 and 7 together.

*Edmund.* I must take 3 from the 6 and add them to the 7, to make one ten, and then there will be 3 units left; and so there will be one ten and three units, or 13. Now I see how I can do real sums on my slate without reckoning with counters; because I know what number added to another will make 10, and I see directly how many units will be left after the ten is made; and then I put down the ten and the units neatly under the line. Give me a great many more sums, mother.

*Mrs. D.* Add 5 and 8, likewise 7 and 9, 6 and 8, 5 and 9, 7 and 7, 7 and 8, 6 and 9.

---

*Mrs. D.* If, when you were reckoning 8 and 9 with the counters, I had told you instead to add 18 and 19 together, you would have had no difficulty in finding the answer?

*Edmund.* No, it would have been very easy; I should have put a ten-counter to each of the heaps, and then, instead of one ten and seven units, there would have been three tens and seven units, or 37.

*Mrs. D.* Exactly so; and if we put any number of tens to the units, you could, in like manner, as readily have added these together, as units alone. What are 27 and 89?

*Edmund.* Eleven tens (or one hundred and one tens) and six units; and so the whole is written 116.

*Mrs. D.* Add together 56 and 73, 34 and 48, 93 and 61.

---

*Mrs. D.* I think if we were now to introduce hundreds, you would be able to master their addition without any further explanation. Let us try; can you tell me the amount of 356 added to 443?

*Edmund.* First, here is one parcel with three hundreds, five tens, and six units; and here is another with four hundreds, four tens, and three units; and added together there are seven hundreds, nine tens, and nine units, or 799.

*Mrs. D.* Add 597 to 359.

*Edmund.* The units added together make one ten and six units, the tens added together are ten tens (or one hundred) and four tens; the hundreds are eight; therefore there are altogether nine hundreds, five tens, and six units, or 956.

*Mrs. D.* Add together, and write down the answers, 426 and 339, 783 and 647, 972 and 854. Recollect, in your additions, that when you have more than ten hundreds, you exchange ten hundreds for a thousand-counter in the same manner as you exchange every ten units for a ten, and every ten tens for a hundred.

*Edmund.* And when I write it down, I must put it at the left side of the hundreds?

*Mrs. D.* Quite right. In putting down your figures for addition, be careful to place the units exactly under the units, the tens under the tens, &c., otherwise you will make a sad confusion among your numbers. Recollect, it is the places they occupy which give to figures their value, and therefore these must be clearly marked out to enable us to be correct in obtaining our answers.

*Emily.* When I write a long row of figures to add up, I can never place them even, but the numbers extend in a zigzag direction from one corner of the slate to the other. Sometimes my hundreds jostle my tens, and at others they are wide apart; and unless I inclose them in perpendicular lines I can never keep them in their respective places.

*Mrs. D.* If you attend to one simple rule, your figures will no longer play truant, and each will retain its proper rank. Always begin the figure you wish to put underneath another, *rather* to the right of the upper one, the slope of the figure then brings it quite to its proper place below this.

---

*Mrs. D.* I think now my little boy can so readily cast up or add together two numbers, that he may attempt a longer sum. How shall we proceed if we have three or more heaps of counters to add up?

*Edmund.* Reckon them altogether, to be sure.

*Mrs. D.* We should do precisely the same with a hundred heaps as we should do with two. First add all the units together, changing every ten units into ten, and putting these to the other tens, and so on with the tens and the hundreds, exactly in the same manner. Here are nine counters and eight counters; these we have already found are 17, or one ten and seven units; here is another heap, containing six counters, to add to them; then seven added to six make one ten and three units, and so the sum of the three heaps is two tens and three units, or 23. Again, let us add 8 more to these, then 8 and 3 are one ten and one unit; so the sum of the four numbers are three tens and one unit, and you would write the whole thus, 8

9

6

8

—

31

In like manner you might go on adding one number after another, till you had an Addition sum as long as the row of figures in my account book. You can now at once understand how several numbers, consisting of

c 3

tens, hundreds, &c., as well as units, can be added together.   Try the following sums :

|      |     |      |
|------|-----|------|
| 23   |     |      |
| 478  | 597 | 3586 |
| 549  | 403 | 7407 |
| 386  | 860 | 6375 |
| 657  | 736 | 8070 |
|      | 975 | 9587 |
| 2070 |     |      |

*Edmund.* Mother, when I add with the counters, all
seems very easy, but with the sum on my slate I get
confused, and I cannot recollect the many tens my units
have made, or the many hundreds my tens have made.

*Mrs. D.* At every step you must repeat the tens with
the units : thus, 7 and 6 are one ten and three, 9 more
are two tens and two, and 8 more are just three tens and
no units ; write down a nought, to show there are no
units, and write the 3 at the top of the row of tens, to be
added in with the rest; and then, with these helps to
your memory, you cannot become confused, or forget
what you require to remember.   The adding in the
tens is usually called *carrying* the tens : thus, if our
units amount to 30, we are told to put down nought and
carry three : it is as well, perhaps, that you should use
the same expression, now you understand exactly what
it *means.*

[*Alfred.* But, mother, is not this a very silly mode of
expression—is it not much more rational to say, add the
tens to the tens, the hundreds to the hundreds, &c.; we
then know exactly what we are about?

*Mrs. D.* We might, perhaps, alter the phraseology for
the better ; but if we can by explanation affix clear ideas
to terms already in use, provided they be not palpably
absurd, or do not involve contradictions, it is as well not
to attempt to make any innovation.   The term is imma-

terial, provided the precise meaning be accurately defined; and it would, I fear, savour somewhat of pedantry or presumption to endeavour to introduce new though better terms : so, my dear boy, we will still carry our tens, though the greatest stretch of complaisance will not, I think, allow me, when we come to Subtraction, to borrow from one, and pay the debt to another.]

CHAPTER III.

SUBTRACTION.

*Mrs. D.* You already know how to take away or subtract any small number from a larger one less than ten, and this without the aid of counters. But suppose you have to take 6 from one ten and two units, or 12.

*Edmund.* There are only two units, and I have to take six from them. I cannot take six from two.

*Mrs. D.* But one ten and two are more than six, therefore you can take six from these.

*Edmund (after considering).* Yes, I must change the ten into units, and then I know that if six be taken from ten four will remain, and these four units added to the two units will be six : so if six be taken from one ten and two units, six will remain.

*Mrs. D.* In like manner you can take 6 from 14, 8 from 15, 9 from 11, and so on.

Now, if to this ten and two we put two more tens, and we wish from these three tens and two units to take two tens and six units, we should in the same way change one of the tens into units, take the six from the ten and add the remainder to the two units : these together we have already found would be 6; we should then have to take two tens from the two tens which remain after the one ten has been changed into units.

*Edmund.* But how can we take two from two?

*Mrs. D.* Why not? I have two counters in my hand, cannot you take two counters out of my hand?

*Edmund.* Yes; but then I shall take them all, I shall leave nothing.

*Mrs. D.* Precisely so. Therefore, when we have taken two tens and six units, or 26, from three tens and two units, or 32, we shall leave no tens and six units, exactly the same as before. Now let us put this down in the manner of a sum. Write down 32, and 26 exactly under it, then draw a line. Since we have to change one of the tens into units, and there will be only two tens left, we had better show this by drawing the pencil lightly across the 3 and writing 2 just above it. When you become very familiar with the work, you will readily do without this help to your memory; in the meantime you will find it of service.

$$
\begin{array}{r}
2 \\
\not{3}2 \\
26 \\
\hline
6
\end{array}
$$

*Edmund.* I have put down the answer under the line, a nought to show that there are no tens, and then 6 units.

*Mrs. D.* If there had been any figures of higher value than tens, you would have done quite right to denote the place of tens by this place-keeper; but since here are no figures to be stationed on the left of it, the nought is, in the present case, evidently unnecessary; 6 means exactly the same as no tens and six units (06), or as no hundreds, no tens, and six units (006). It is then useless, when there are only units, to express that there are no tens; or when there are only tens and units, to express that there are no hundreds; and in general to express that there are no figures of higher value than the actual number.

*Edmund.* I understand.

*Mrs. D.* In the same manner as you change one ten into units, you can change a hundred into tens, and so on, for any numbers of higher value whatever. Thus let us take 29389 from 37645:

$$\begin{array}{r} 2\ 53 \\ 3\dot{7}\dot{6}45 \\ 29389 \\ \hline 8256 \end{array}$$

9 are more than 5, so we must change one ten, and show this as we did in our last sum. Then 9 from 10 leave 1; 1 and 5 are 6, put down the 6 units.   Again, 8 are more than 3, 8 from 10 leave 2;  2 and 3 are 5, put down 5 tens; 3 from 5 leave 2, put down 2 hundreds; 9 are more than 7, 9 from 10 leave 1, 1 and 7 are 8, put down 8 thousands; 2 from 2 leave nothing.

Subtract $\left\{ \begin{array}{l} 7863478 \text{ from } 9526954 \\ 3762597 \text{ from } 7897645 \end{array} \right\}$ *

[*Alfred.* So your system is changing not borrowing? I am glad you have not used that word.

*Mrs. D.* When Edmund is expert in these matters he shall be told the usual method of subtraction; but I think that this is not only easier of comprehension, but likewise easier in execution, and I do not doubt he will always give it the preference.   Besides to have initiated

---

* More examples in addition and subtraction are not given, since these can be readily supplied by the instructors; but numerous examples and long practice are necessary, before it can be expected that the pupil will be very expert in the operations.

him into the borrowing system, I must have first proved, that if equals be added to two numbers, their difference will still be the same as before these were added. Now, no doubt, this would have been very easy, but still there is a simpler way of arriving at the same result; and I believe it to be my duty, as an instructor, in this and every case to select that explanation which is the simplest. The same motive influenced me in teaching the foregoing method of addition as well as that of subtraction. These may perhaps both appear, to persons who are accustomed to the ordinary way, more difficult than the latter. But let us take into consideration that it is only long practice which has made us so perfectly conversant with all the combinations of figures. For example, 8 added to 7 are identified in our own minds with 15; but though even you may not be able to recollect the time when this was not equally familiar to you, yet there was a time when you were in the same situation as our young pupil, and 8 added to 7 brought with them no corresponding 15 to your mind: you were then obliged to have recourse to strokes made on your slate, or to counters, before you could ascertain that the sum of these numbers was fifteen; and it was only from often-repeated trials, or from learning by rote, that you became assured of this truth, and associated the two ideas thus intimately together. Now it will be granted that a child can much more readily learn all the combinations under 10 than under 18, and this not only because there are fewer, but because these, taken singly, are less difficult to remember; the eye can readily embrace the lower numbers, and at once fix the group in the mind. You may perceive in how very short a time we have in the present case mastered these combinations. Assuming entire ignorance on the subject, is it not easier, in order to find out that 8 added to 9 are one ten and seven

units, or 17, to take one from the eight and add it to the
nine, than to count 9 and 8 together in the usual way?
A smaller effort of the mind is required, and this applies
equally to the manner of subtraction. Do you think our
Edmund's countenance would wear that bright smiling
aspect, while he was going over the common routine and
repeating words without affixing to them ideas, saying,
" take 8 from 3 I can't, borrow 10, take 8 from 13,
5 remain. I must pay the one I borrowed, 1 and 9 are
10, &c."]

<hr />

CHAPTER IV.

MULTIPLICATION.

*Mrs. D.* If you have two counters in one parcel and
two in another, how many will there be together?
*Edmund.* Four.
*Mrs. D.* And if you put two more to them?
*Edmund.* Six.
*Mrs. D.* And two more?
*Edmund.* Eight.
*Mrs. D.* And two more?
*Edmund.* Ten.
*Mrs. D.* How many parcels of twos have you now
added together?
*Edmund.* Five.
*Mrs. D.* Then you have found that five twos are 10?
*Edmund.* Yes.
*Mrs. D.* How did you know this?
*Edmund.* Because I have just added together the
five parcels, like an addition sum; let me put down the
five 2's, one under the other, on my slate, and write

their sum 10 at the bottom, just in the same manner as
in other additions.

$$
\begin{array}{r}
2 \\
2 \\
2 \\
2 \\
2 \\
\hline
10
\end{array}
$$

*Mrs. D.* If, however, you can recollect that five twos
are ten, you will then have no need to write the same
figure so many times, but simply write it thus,

$$
\begin{array}{r}
2 \\
5 \\
\hline
10
\end{array}
$$

which means that 2 taken 5 times are equal to or the
same as 10.    This is called multiplication, which is
simply addition, or adding together the same number,
any given number of times.

To make this easy for you to do, you must learn, and
store up in your memory, the multiplication of the nine
digits one into the other.   For example, I know that 3
multiplied by 8 are 24; but you, who do not know this,
must be content to go the long road, and find it out for
yourself, by adding the eight threes together.

*Edmund.* I do not like such a long way, and so I will
remember that eight threes are 24.

*Mrs. D.* Not quite so fast, my little man; you know
that eight threes are 24, merely because I have told you
so; you must likewise know it from the evidence of
your senses; therefore, take the counters and make
yourself certain of the fact.   In the same manner, you
must by degrees make for yourself a multiplication table.
As you tell me the additions I will write down the
figures in good order; and then, having convinced your-

self that the whole is correct, you can refer to the table when you do your sums, till you are so familiar with it as to have transferred it from the paper to your head. We may shorten our table, however, by a little previous explanation. Here are eight parcels, each containing three counters, if you collect in your hand one from each of these parcels, how many will you have in your hand?

*Ed.* Eight.

*Mrs. D.* Lay these down in a separate place, and now collect another from each parcel; these will likewise be eight, and how many will you have left on the table?

*Ed.* Eight.

*Mrs. D.* You have now three parcels, each containing eight, instead of eight parcels, each containing three, and you can, therefore, form the eight parcels, having three in each, into three parcels having eight in each; hence it follows, that three multiplied by eight are the same as eight multiplied by three.

*Alfred.* Which makes it sufficiently evident, that if two numbers are multiplied one by the other, it is exactly the same, whether the lesser number be multiplied by the greater, or the greater by the lesser.

*Mrs. D.* True; but generalizing will not do with a young child, the truth must be made apparent by more than one example.

We will place these three parcels of counters, each
containing four, in separate rows, thus
$$
\begin{array}{cccc}
0 & 0 & 0 & 0 \\
0 & 0 & 0 & 0 \\
0 & 0 & 0 & 0
\end{array}
$$
Now look at them, Edmund, and tell me if you feel quite sure that 3 multiplied by 4 is the same as 4 multiplied by 3?

*Ed.* Yes; for if I look at these counters one way, there are three rows of 4 each, and if I look at it another way, there are 4 rows of 3 each.

*Mrs. D.* Now, my child, that you are perfectly convinced of this, go and trundle your hoop four times multiplied by three, or three times multiplied by four, round your little grass plat.

*Ed.* Let me try one more before I go. 7 multiplied by 5, the same as 5 multiplied by 7.

```
0 0 0 0 0 0 0
0 0 0 0 0 0 0
0 0 0 0 0 0 0
0 0 0 0 0 0 0
0 0 0 0 0 0 0
```

| | | | | | | | |
|---|---|---|---|---|---|---|---|
| 2 multiplied by 2 are 4 | | | | 5 multiplied by 5 are 25 | | | |
| 2 | . . | 3 . . | 6 | 5 | . . | 6 . . | 30 |
| 2 | . . | 4 . . | 8 | 5 | . . | 7 . . | 35 |
| 2 | . . | 5 . . | 10 | 5 | . . | 8 . . | 40 |
| 2 | . . | 6 . . | 12 | 5 | . . | 9 . . | 45* |
| 2 | . . | 7 . . | 14 | | | | |
| 2 | . . | 8 . . | 16 | 6 | . . | 6 . . | 36 |
| 2 | . . | 9 . . | 18* | 6 | . . | 7 . . | 42 |
| | | | | 6 | . . | 8 . . | 48 |
| 3 | . . | 3 . . | 9 | 6 | . . | 9 . . | 54* |
| 3 | . . | 4 . . | 12 | | | | |
| 3 | . . | 5 . . | 15 | 7 | . . | 7 . . | 49 |
| 3 | . . | 6 . . | 18 | 7 | . . | 8 . . | 56 |
| 3 | . . | 7 . . | 21 | 7 | . . | 9 . . | 63* |
| 3 | . . | 8 . . | 24 | | | | |
| 3 | . . | 9 . . | 27* | 8 | . . | 8 . . | 64 |
| | | | | 8 | . . | 9 . . | 72* |
| 4 | . . | 4 . . | 16 | | | | |
| 4 | . . | 5 . . | 20 | 9 | . . | 9 . . | 81* |
| 4 | . . | 6 . . | 24 | | | | |
| 4 | . . | 7 . . | 28 | | | | |
| 4 | . . | 8 . . | 32 | | | | |
| 4 | . . | 9 . . | 36* | | | | |

* Let the pupil be made to observe, that the digits of each of the above numbers which is the product of nine, multiplied by some other number, are, if added together, equal to 9; and that of these, the one which represents the tens is always one less than the

*Mrs. D.* Now, you have completed your multiplication table, let us see how we can apply it to use, in
doing what is called a multiplication sum. We will, as
an example, multiply 748 by 3. Put 3 under the 8, to
show that the top line in this case 748 is to be multiplied
by 3, and draw a line under the 3.  3
$$\overline{\phantom{00}2244}$$
Here 8 units multiplied by 3 are 24, or 2 tens and 4
units; put down the 4 units, and recollect, or *carry* in
your head, that these 2 tens are to be added to the other
tens when multiplied; or you may write the figure 2 in
a vacant corner of your slate, to assist your memory.—
Again, 4 tens multiplied by 3 are 12 tens, add to these
the 2 tens left from the multiplication of the units, and
then there will be 14 tens, or 1 hundred and 4 tens;
put down the 4 tens next to the units, and recollect to
add this one hundred to the other multiplied hundreds;
7 hundreds multiplied by 3 are 21 hundreds, add the 1
hundred left from the multiplication of the tens, and
then there will be 22 hundreds, or 2 thousand and 2
hundred; put these down next to the tens. Now, I
think, you may quite understand, from this and from what
we have before done with the counters, that 2244 are 748
multiplied by 3, and that in the same manner any higher
numbers may be multiplied.

We need not, however, repeat the words units, tens,
hundreds, &c., the process will be exactly the same if
we say 8 multiplied by 3 are 24, put down 4 and carry
2; 4 multiplied by 3 are 12, 12 and 2 are 14, put down

number which is multiplied by 9 :—thus, 6 × 9 = 54, here 5 one
less than 6, and 5 and 4 are 9; 7 × 9 are 63, here 6 one less than
7, and 6 and 3 are 9. Hence, the multiplication by 9 is easily
known. If it be required to multiply 9 by 8, then the tens are one
less than 8 = 7; and 7 and 2 are 9, therefore, 7 tens and 2 units,
or 72, = the product of 9 × 8.

D 2

4, and carry 1, &c. You perceive, exactly the same thing is done, while needless repetitions are avoided, and, with a little practice, you will gradually of your own accord use still fewer words. Try another sum 92073 by 7

Multiplicand 92073
Multiplier          7
Product     644511

*Ed.* Here I have to multiply nought by 7; how can I multiply nothing?

*Mrs. D.* That is very true, you cannot multiply nothing: recollect the nought is only a place-keeper, and is in every other respect a nonentity; nothing cannot be multiplied to produce something. In this case, 0 is put to show that there are no hundreds, and, therefore, none can be multiplied: we, therefore, pass over the place of hundreds, and proceed to the thousands, recollecting, however, to put down the 5 which was carried from the tens, in the place of hundreds; if, instead of containing 7 tens the multiplicand had contained only one ten, there would have been no hundreds to carry, and we must have put down a nought as a place-keeper in the place of hundreds in the product. We will put down some more examples for exercise in multiplication, which you must practise very often before you learn anything new. I must not, however, omit to tell you, that, in a multiplication sum, the number to be multiplied is usually called the *multiplicand*, the number by which it is multiplied the *multiplier*, and the number produced by this multiplication the product. We will write these names to the last example, thus:

Multiply 374896 by 8; 8950863 by 9; 643706875 by 6; 3765240 by 4; 4037061 by 5; 7563209 by 7.

————

*Mrs. D.* You can now multiply very readily by any

number less than ten, but if the multiplier be more than 9, how shall we then proceed? Multiply 48 by 53 for example.

*Ed.* Shall I try this with the counters first?

*Mrs. D.* Yes; if you like.

*Ed.* But it will be a great deal of trouble to make 53 parcels; indeed I have not counters enough, I can never make 53 parcels.

*Mrs. D.* You can, however, tell me, without any trouble, how many there are in 3 parcels, each containing 48.

*Ed.* I can do that on my slate; 48 multiplied by 3 are 144.

*Mrs. D.* It now remains to be found to how much your 50 parcels will amount. Ten parcels, each containing 48, you already have proved (*see* p. 25) are the same as 48 parcels, each containing ten units, or one ten; and the ten parcels of 48 are, therefore, the same as 48 tens, or 480.

To multiply any number by 10, therefore, is and means the same as increasing its value ten times, (*see* p. 8,) and the product is shown by simply putting a 0 after the multiplicand. In like manner to multiply a number by 100, is shown by putting two noughts after it, or converting it into hundreds, and so on increasing in the number of noughts for higher numbers. It follows, that to multiply by any number of tens, hundreds, &c., is as easy as to multiply by the same number of units. Thus, 11 multiplied by 5 are 55; 11 multiplied by 50 are 550; 11 multiplied by 500 are 5500; and so on to any higher number. Let us now apply this to the sum before us,

$$
\begin{array}{cc}
48 & 48 \\
3 & 50 \\
\hline
144 & 2400
\end{array}
$$

If we add the product of 48 multiplied by 3, and the product of 48 multiplied by 50, we shall, it is clear, have
the product of 48 multiplied by 53.     144

                                         2400
                                         ————
              which will be              2544

Now, it will save trouble, and make our work look
neater, to do this altogether in one sum instead of three.

                  Thus, 48
                        53
                        ——
                       144
                      2400
                      ————
                      2544

Here you first multiply by the units, and then by the tens,
putting the latter product under the first, and then adding these together under the second line, performing the
three operations just as you did before, only arranging the
whole in a better manner.   If the multiplier contained
hundreds, or any higher number, you would understand
how, and be able, as it is called, to work the sum.

  *Ed.* Yes; but it would be more difficult.

  *Mrs. D.* Longer, but not more difficult, except, indeed,
that you would have to cast up three or more lines together, instead of only two.

      Thus, 507634                7857
             3702                  463
           ————————              ——————
           1015268               23571
          355343800              47142
         1522902000              31428
         ——————————             ——————
         1879261068             3637791

  In the first of these examples the multiplier has no
tens, therefore, after you have multiplied by the units,
you of course proceed directly to multiply by the hundreds, and put two noughts before the product.   In mul-

tiplying by the thousands, you in the same manner put three noughts before the product.

When the multiplier is a higher number than units, as in the present cases, the process is usually called long multiplication. After you have exercised yourself in a few sums of this kind, you will no doubt be able, without confusing yourself, to omit the noughts placed in the second and succeeding lines to show that there are no units, &c. Since the tens of the second line are put under the tens of the first line, and the hundreds of the third line under the hundreds of the second line—their relative situations are sufficiently indicated without the assistance of noughts—this is shown in the last example that we worked. But, as long as you find the putting down of the noughts of any use to you, do not discard them.

### EXAMPLES.

(1) 586745736 multiplied by 98.

(2) 34682090  multiplied by 583.

(3) 847305    multiplied by 47.

(4) 9036247   multiplied by 680.

(5) 25063408  multiplied by 5030.

----

### CHAPTER V.

### DIVISION.

*Mrs. D.* Here are 24 counters to divide equally between Emily, Alfred, and myself, that is, into three parts; how many shall we each have?

*Ed.* I must first give you each one a-piece; that will be three; and then I must give you each another, and another, till I have none left.

*Mrs. D.* And now you have divided them into three equal parts, how many are there in each part?

*Ed.* Eight.

*Mrs. D.* What you have just done is called division; you took away or subtracted three, and then three more, and so on. Division, therefore, is simply a number of subtractions, but in the same way as the manner of multiplication is addition shortened, so, division can be performed by a quicker method than that of continued subtractions. In fact, it is the reverse of multiplication, for, if you know that these three parcels, containing 8 each, are together equal to 24, or that 8 multiplied by 3 are 24, you will likewise know that in 24 there are just 3 eights; so your knowledge of multiplication teaches you division.

If I were to add to these 24 counters 6 hundred-counters, making the whole number 624, how would you divide these between us?

*Ed.* Here are just 2 for you, 2 for Alfred, and 2 for Emily, and so you have each got 2 hundred-counters and 8 unit-counters, or 208.

*Mrs. D.* You have then very readily found that 624 divided by 3 are equal to 208. But now, if I add another hundred, making the number 724, how many shall we each have then?

*Ed.* You will each have just the same, and this 1 hundred divided between you besides; but I do not know how to manage that.

*Mrs. D.* You will, no doubt, be able if you think a little about it.

*Ed.* Yes; if I change the hundred for ten tens. Now, if I divide these ten tens between you three, you will have three each, and again one over; what is to be done with that? I suppose I must change it into units, and of these you will each have three—now, what am I to do with this one? I cannot change it, can I?

*Mrs. D.* No; we must let that remain for the present, content with knowing that we have each an equal property in it.

*Ed.* Well, then, you will each have three tens and three units, or 33 to add to your 208; so your share will be together two hundreds, three tens, and eleven units, or 241.

*Mrs. D.* That is to say, 724 divided by 3 are equal to 241, and 1 remainder. Now we will divide the 724 between us at one operation instead of two. You have already seen that each of us will have two hundreds, and there will be one over from the hundreds, or ten tens: these added to the two tens, make 12, which, divided by 3, give exactly four tens. We have now to divide the four units by three, which will give us each 1 and 1 over.

*Ed.* Now let us do the sum on the slate.

*Mrs. D.* It is written down in this manner—

$$3)724$$
$$\overline{241} \text{ and 1 rem.}$$

The number to be divided (in this case 724) is called the dividend. The number of parts into which it is to be divided (in this case 3) is called the divisor, and the number contained in each part (in this case 241) is called the quotient. That number which is left after the division is called the remainder, which is written *rem.* for shortness. If we divide any number of counters into any number of equal parts, and there be some left which cannot be so divided, it is clear that whatever colour these counters may be, the same number will be over, whether these be called units, tens, or any number of higher value. In working a division sum, therefore, it is useless to repeat the words hundreds, tens, units: in the above example we should simply say, the threes in 7 are 2, and 1 over; the threes in 12 are 4: we know that we are speaking of hundreds and tens; we are perfectly certain of what is meant, and it would only serve to confuse if we made these repetitions at every step. You know that every place of figures is exactly of ten times more value than that immediately next to it on the right side, and therefore what I have said of hundreds and tens equally applies to all numbers, whether thousands, ten thousands, or any higher number. We will work one more sum, and then give you some examples for practice.

8)530572646

66321580 and 6 rem.

Divide 589706 by 7.   7463275 by 5.   43689067 by 9.

*Mrs. D.* When the divisor is a higher number than ten, or when you have to divide any number into a great many parts, you will of course be able, in the same manner, to find it out with your counters. Thus, instead of dividing 724 into 3 parts, divide them into 23 parts.

*Ed.* The twenty-threes in 700; this is very puzzling. I must change all the hundreds at once into tens, and now I have 72 ten-counters. If I take 23 from these, and 23 more, and 23 more, I shall leave 3; so there will be 3 twenty-threes in 72, and 3 over. These three ten-counters must now be changed into units; there will, therefore, be 34 units. I can only take one 23 from 34, and 11 will be over.

*Mrs. D.* You have, therefore, found that, if 724 be divided in 23 parts, there will be in each part 3 tens and 1 unit or 31, and 11 over. Now you have done this in exactly the same manner as you divided 724 by 3: it has only been more difficult because you could not readily discover, without trial, how many twenty-threes were contained in 72. In working the sum on your slate, you would find it very troublesome to multiply this high number in your head and subtract the product from 72, as you have been doing in simple division ; we therefore make another arrangement of our figures, by which the several operations are shown on the slate. Instead of writing the figures thus—

$$23)724$$

$$31 \text{ and } 11 \text{ rem.}$$

we write the quotient on the right hand of the dividend, thus—

$$23)724(31$$
$$69$$
$$\overline{\phantom{0}34}$$
$$23$$
$$\overline{\phantom{0}11 \text{ rem.}}$$

You see that what you have been doing with the counters is here expressed; we find by trial the number of times the divisor is contained in the first figures of the dividend; if it be not contained in the first and second figures of the dividend, try three figures, and so on, till you find a number in which it is contained: in this case we try how many times 23 is contained in 72, these will be three times; we therefore write 3 for the first figure of the quotient; we then subtract the product of the divisor multiplied by this figure from the figures of the dividend taken as above. Thus, 23 multiplied by 3 are 69, which we take from 72, just as you did with the counters, and find that 3 are left, or that 72 are 3 more than 3 times 23; to the number so left we bring down the next figure in value: thus to the 3 tens we bring down the 4 units; and so we have now to find how many times the divisor is contained in this second number: in this case we find that 23 is only contained once in 34, and we proceed as we did before, putting the 1 next the 3 in the quotient, and subtracting 23 from 34 we find that 11 will be left: in this manner we write down the operations which we have been doing with the counters, every step of which you perfectly understood.

*Ed.* Yes; but it is rather more puzzling when it is written down.

*Mrs. D.* Not at all. Let us work another sum on the slate, and a little practice will soon make you quite familiar with the method.

```
473)794506732(1679718
    473
    ───
    3215
    2838
    ────
     3770
     3311
     ────
      4596
      4257
      ────
       3397
       3311
       ────
        863
        473
        ───
        3902
        3784
        ────
        118 rem.
```

*Ed.* But, mother, it is very difficult; how am I to guess how many times this great great number is contained in the other number?

*Mrs. D.* You are certainly not to *guess*; you are to find out. I allow it requires some practice to be quite familiar with the subject; but, while you are at a loss, I would advise you to have recourse to your friends the counters. A little consideration of the two numbers will most generally enable us to discover the exact number of times the one number is contained in the other. But, even if you should make a trial of a wrong number, you will soon find out your mistake. For instance, if you suppose that 473 are contained 8 times in 3770, you will find that the product of 473 multiplied by 8 is 3784, which is more than 3770, and, therefore, 473 is not contained 8 times in 3770; again, try 6—the product of 473 multiplied by 6 is 2838; take this from

$$3770$$
$$2838$$

and 932 will remain; but 932 is more than 473, which is therefore contained more than 6 times in 3770.

*Ed.* But this trying and rubbing out, and then trying again, is very provoking work. I shall never like long division.

*Mrs. D.* By taking a little trouble at first beginning, you may avoid all uncertainty in this matter. Put down at the corner of your slate the divisor, and its amount when multiplied by each digit from 2 to 9, thus—

1— 473
2— 946
3—1419
4—1892
5—2365
6—2838
7—3311
8—3784
9—4257

This operation you will find very easy    To multiply

E

any number by 2 is not difficult, your third product may
be obtained by adding the two previous lines together;
the fourth by doubling the second; the fifth by adding
the second and third; and so on.   At the last you may
prove the correctness of your different multiples by adding the ninth product to the first, and this should give
you the divisor multiplied by 10; that is expressed by
the same numerals having a tenfold value given to them
by the 0 at their right hand.   This method has the further advantage of avoiding probable errors in putting
down the sum of the various multiplications required in
the progress of the division.   I think, however, that, in
a short time, you will not fall into these errors, but will
at once select the right number.   Try the following, you
will find it very easy :—

```
395)84544615(214037
    790
    ───
    554
    395
    ────
    1594
    1580
    ─────
     146*1
     1185
     ─────
      2765
      2765
      ─────
      . . . .
```

*Ed.* I have brought down the 6*, but 395 are not
contained in 146; what am I to do?

*Mrs. D.* How many times did you say 395 was contained in 146?

*Ed.* No times: 146 is less than 395, and so we cannot divide 146 counters into 395 parts.

*Mrs. D.* But suppose these were hundred-counters, could you not then divide them into 395 parts?

*Ed.* Yes; by changing them into tens, and then I suppose I must add the one ten to these, making 1461, to be divided into 395 parts.

*Mrs. D.* In dividing this number by 395, there are then no hundreds in each part, since you have been obliged to change these all into tens. How do you keep the place of the hundreds, or how do you show there are no hundreds in a number which has figures of a higher value?

*Ed.* By putting a nought. So I must write a 0 after the 4 in the quotient, and now I must find out how many times 395 is contained in 1461.

    (6) Divide 643905738 by 58.
    (7) Divide 85076039427 by 649.
    (8) Divide 49326874631 by 908.
    (9) Divide 7405325698 by 271.
    (10) Divide 364786239 by 999.

*Mrs. D.* Here are 8 hundred-counters, 5 ten-counters, and 3 unit-counters, divide them into 10 parts.

*Ed.* I shall not have to do that by long division, mother; it is very easy. If I change the hundreds into tens, their number will be 10 times 8 counters, or 80; and so, if we divide these into 10 parts, there will be 8 in each, or, 800 divided by 10 will be 8 tens, or 80.

*Mrs. D.* Exactly; and in the same way the 5 tens, or 50, divided by 10, will be 5 units, and, therefore, 853 divided by 10 will be 85 and 3 units over. It is then evident, that, in dividing by 10, we merely lower the value of the figures one step, the thousands will become hundreds, the hundreds tens, the tens units, and the units, being a number less than 10, will always be left as a remainder.   Divide 756 by 10.

*Ed.* Each part will be 75, and there will be 6 over.

*Mrs. D.* What is the quotient of 1940 divided by 10?

*Ed.* This will be exactly 194, because there are no units.

*Mrs. D.* To divide by 10 we then simply cut off the units, which is expressed thus, 75/6. In the same manner, to divide by 100, we lower the value of the figures two steps, or cut off the units and tens, thus 7/56. To divide by 1000, we lower the value of the figures three steps, thus 1/756, and so on.

*Ed.* Yes; I like this division better than any I have done yet.

*Mrs. D.* I shall begin to suspect that you are an idle boy. You found, that if 853 were divided into ten parts, each part would contain 85; now, if you divided 85 into any greater number of parts, say 5, then in each of these subdivisions there would be 17 ; and it is plain, that if each of the ten parts were so divided, there would be 5 times 10 or 50 parts; therefore, to divide any number by 50, is the same as dividing first by 10 and then by 5 ; and this is equally true if, instead of 5, there were any other number of tens. Thus, to divide 756 by 60, is the same as dividing 75 by 6, and we should express it

$$6/0)75/6$$
$$\overline{12 \text{ and } 36 \text{ rem.}}$$

In dividing each of the 10 parts by 6, we find there are 12 and 3 left; now, as this 3 is left in each of the 10 parts, it follows that there will be ten threes or three tens left; and if to these we add the 6 units left from the division by 10, there will be 36 remainder, after dividing 756 into 60 parts, each containing twelve. What has been said of tens it is evident equally applies to hundreds, or any higher number. Try the following examples :—

8/00)86437/56          9/000)7345/026

10804 and 556 rem.          816 and 1026 rem.
Divide 3745 by 700.  867530 by 90.  430768 by 4000.

---

CHAPTER VI.

## METHOD OF PROOF.

*Mrs. D.* I shall not now teach you any thing new for a long time till you are somewhat conversant in the practice of the foregoing rules; facility and quickness in performing the different operations can only be obtained by practice, and without these no person can be a really good accountant: but in working any arithmetical questions, correctness is of far more essential consequence than even facility and quickness; we must be *certain* that we are right, or otherwise our calculations are worse than useless.

*Ed.* Well, I can always be certain of this; for, if I count properly, I know I *must* be right.

*Mrs. D.* Very true, *if* you count correctly; but, in working long sums, is it not possible that you may commit some error? You may be confused and make a wrong statement, or indolent and trust to your memory, in cases where this is not sufficiently assured. You may be thoughtless and count incorrectly, or careless and put down a wrong figure. To prevent the possibility of mistake, it is therefore better, whenever we can, to prove our work, and if that cannot be done, to go carefully over the whole more than once.

*Ed.* What do you mean, mother, by " proving our work?"

E 3

*Mrs. D.* When we add two numbers together, and
then from their sum we take away either of these numbers, if we have counted correctly, the other number will
be left.  In like manner, if we take one number from
another, and then to their difference add the smaller
number, our correctness will be shown if the sum of
these be equal to the larger number.  For example, 17
and 13 are 30, and, if we take 13 from 30, 17 will remain; therefore, our second operation has verified or
proved the correctness of the first.  If we have to subtract 13 from 30, 17 will remain, or will be the difference of 30 and 13; 17 and 13 are 30, and this proves
that we have done the subtraction right.  If we had
made a mistake, and said that 16 was the difference of
13 and 30, then we should have found that 16 and 13
were 29 instead of 30, and, therefore, that we had done
our sum wrong.  Let us now add two higher numbers
together, and prove that we are right.

$$85768746 \text{ first number.}$$
$$94682395 \text{ second number.}$$
$$180151141 \text{ sum.}$$
$$85768746 \text{ first number.}$$
$$94682395 \text{ second number.}$$

From 97386453
subtract 84973596
difference 12412857
97386453

Here the bottom line is the sum of the lesser number and
of the difference, and should consequently be the same
as the top line; subtraction can therefore always be
proved in this manner; but, in addition, when more
than two numbers are to be added together, we cannot

well use the above method of proof, and then the best and simplest plan is to add the figures twice over—once beginning with the top figure and going downwards, and once beginning with the bottom figure and adding upwards: if you make the sum alike in both cases, you may reasonably suppose that you are correct. Now we have done with addition and subtraction, how are we to prove multiplication and division? I want you to find this out for yourself.

*Ed.* That is very easy, because division is just the contrary of multiplication; and, if I multiply a number by 3, and then divide this product by 3, it is plain that I shall have the number back again.

*Mrs. D.* Very true: so, to prove multiplication, we have only to divide the answer by the multiplier, and the quotient will be the multiplicand. To prove division, we multiply the quotient by the divisor, and their product will be the same as the dividend.

*Ed.* But what is to be done with the remainder?

*Mrs. D.* Well remembered. An example will make this sufficiently clear. We find that 37 contains 5 taken 7 times, and that there are then 2 remainder; so these 2 must be added to the product of 5 multiplied by 7, or 35, to make the number 37, or, in other words, the remainder must be added to the product of the quotient and divisor to produce a number the same as the dividend.

*Ed.* I understand; and now that I know how, I shall always prove that I am right.

*Mrs. D.* This is an excellent resolution, my dear child, and I hope you will never be disinclined to take a little extra trouble for so desirable an object. You need not then refer to a book, or ask the assistance of any person, to find whether your answer be correct, but you may say, without presumption or conceit, " I *know* that I am right."

[*Alfred*. What a pleasure it is to be able to say that little sentence!

*Mrs. D.* Yes; the peculiar beauty of this study is the certainty of its conclusions. You have not here to trust to the authority of books, or even to place your reliance on the testimony of your parents. You can, by your own unassisted efforts, be confident of your results, and thus a salutary habit of self-dependence is gradually acquired.

A knowledge of arithmetic does not, however, depend only upon mere practical skill. In the foregoing rules, we have our implements furnished to us for solving the most difficult problems. Do what we will in working the most intricate questions or laborious calculations, all is resolved into simple addition and subtraction. Many rules may be furnished to show how these operations can be lessened or facilitated; but however curiously and ingeniously these may be devised, the whole still continues a series of subtractions and additions.

Practical arithmetic, in a worldly point of view, is a useful, indeed a necessary acquirement; but mere expertness in reckoning does not teach us to think, compare, and reason: for this purpose it must be combined with the knowledge of the *rationale* of figures. An investigation of this subject powerfully tends to awaken and foster those habits of thought, and to develope and strengthen those powers of the mind, which I particularly wish should be yours in after life; and should your taste lead you to more abstruse inquiries in the further pursuit of mathematics, you will then be admirably prepared to continue the study with advantage.

Facility in performing the operations of arithmetic, you will perceive, is quite distinct from the power of arranging and combining these, in the solution of a numeral question. It is very possible to be what is called a good accountant, and yet to be wholly ignorant of the principles on which the different processes are founded. Some there are who continue nothing but mechanical labourers in arithmetic all their lives; they can do what they are told, but nothing more; they cannot think for themselves. I trust that you have a more laudable ambition, and will not be content merely to acquire dexterity in the handling of your instruments, but will likewise know how the edifice should be erected, and how and where the work should be applied. On the other hand, since we have not alone to direct the progress of the work, but to labour at it ourselves, it is necessary that we should combine the two, and not only be enlightened masters but skilful workmen. Your tools have not been put into your hands ready made; you have seen how they are fashioned, and are intimately acquainted with their structure: you know, you are certain that they will work true: you have yet to learn their more extended application. The acquiring of this knowledge developes and exercises the powers of the mind. Let me entreat one and all of you, my dear children, never to perform any process in arithmetic without perfectly understanding the reason on which it is founded. This is usually simple and easy to be discovered. There is no conjuration in figures; all can be made manifest; and those pupils in arithmetic who are willing to take for granted what is told them, without investigating for themselves, are mere labourers, and neglect the best opportunity their education affords for calling into action some of the finest faculties of the mind.]

## CHAPTER VII.

## QUESTIONS.

*Mrs. D.* QUESTION 1. I have just been reading of a traveller, who considered the whole delights of travelling to consist in going over much ground as rapidly as possible. He was out 7 days; the first day he travelled 113 miles; the second he only completed 99 more; the third, 57; the fourth, 115; fifth, 86; and, on the sixth and seventh together, he went 207 miles. How many miles did he travel in the whole week?

Q. 2. A farmer had many flocks of sheep in different stations:—the first flock consisted of 347 sheep; the second of 269; the third of 158; the fourth of 401; the fifth of 862; the sixth of 596; the seventh of 734; the eighth of 600. How many sheep had he altogether? Finding his stock too large, and wishing materially to reduce this, he sold at different times 573; then 291; then 643; and, lastly, 488. How many sheep had he left after these sales had been effected?

. Q. 3. The great philosopher Locke was born in the year 1632, and he died in the year 1704. What age was he when he died? and how long has he been dead?

Q. 4. The fire of London happened in the year 1666. How long is that ago?

Q. 5. I have read in a periodical work, that it is computed 32 lives were, on an average, annually lost in consequence of the dangerous cataracts caused by the bad construction of the old London Bridge. Now I by no means believe that this ancient structure is answerable for such a waste of human life; but assuming it to be a fact, how many lives have altogether been destroyed in this manner? The bridge was first built of stone in the year 1163, and it was pulled down in 1832?

Q. 6. There is a work in two volumes; the first volume contains 373 pages; the second, 436 pages; each page contains 28 lines, and each line 35 letters. There is another work in only one volume; it contains 278 pages, each page contains 38 lines, and each line 43 letters. What is the difference of the number of letters contained in these works? and how many pages would this difference of letters occupy in the first work? and also how many pages would it occupy in the second?

Q. 7. In the year 1830, 613,185 packages of cotton-wool were brought into this country from America; 192,267 packages from Brazil; from the West Indies, 12,648; from the East Indies, 35,212; and from Egypt, 13,596. What is the total amount of these quantities? Out of the whole quantity we sent to other places 35,450; how much did we retain for our own use?

Q. 8. If the wages of one man come to 13 shillings for one day, to how much will his wages amount for 267 days at the same price?

Q. 9. If a manufacturer pays 288 shillings weekly between 24 men, how much will each man have?

Q. 10. An engineer paid, during one year, 7644 pounds in wages—now reckoning 52 weeks in a year, how many men will he have kept in employ at the rate of 1 pound a week for each man?

Q. 11. If 1 yard of cloth cost 6 shillings, what will 8 cost?

Q. 12. If 3 yards cost 18 shillings, what will 1 yard cost?

Q. 13. 391,648 quarters of wheat were brought into this country in 1832, and 247,625 in 1833; what is the difference between the quantities?

Q. 14. A gentleman gave, on Christmas-day, to the poor of his parish 3708 pounds of bread; this was divided among 563 people: how much was each person's share?

# PART SECOND.

----

## CHAPTER I.

*Edmund.* MOTHER, why do not you teach me something new in arithmetic? I know the multiplication-table perfectly; I now do not find even long division difficult; and I can answer, without being confused, most of the questions you ask me.

*Mrs. D.* Since you are so far advanced, I think I may venture to explain to you some of the properties of numbers, by which many operations may be shortened and some steps entirely omitted. You are, likewise, at present, sufficiently familiarized with the use of figures to be able to understand them in conjunction with signs. You are, moreover, older and wiser than when we began our first lesson in arithmetic. Your exercises in reading have given you a knowledge of the meaning of words, and, therefore, I shall not any longer search out for easy expressions that you may the better comprehend me: if, however, I should use any words of which you do not understand the precise meaning, recollect that you always interrupt me, and ask for an explanation.

You have seen how beautifully simple is the contrivance which enables us to express every possible number by different arrangements of ten characters. To facilitate still further all complex calculations, and to avoid the useless repetition of words, mathematicians have invented some signs which represent words, and which are, with great advantage, used as their substitutes. The follow-- ing are some of these:—

The sign +, which is called *plus* or *more*, is used as the mark òf addition : thus, 4 + 3, means that 3 are to be added to 4.

—, called *minus* or *less*, is the sign for subtrac- tion : thus, 4 — 3, means that 3 are to be taken from 4 ; 8 — (3+2), means that both 3 and 2 are to be taken from 8 ; 8 — 3 + 2, means that 3 are to be taken from 8 and 2 are to be added.

× is the sign of multiplication : thus, 4 × 3, means that 4 are to be multiplied by 3, or taken 3 times ; 4 × $\overline{3 + 7}$, means that 4 are to be taken 3+7 or 10 times ; 4 × $\overline{7 - 3}$, means that 4 are to be taken 7 — 3 or 4 times; but, when there is no connecting line over the figures, or brackets enclosing them, then 4 × 3 + 7, means 4 taken 3 times and the product added to 7 ; and 4 × 7 — 3, means that 4 are to be taken 7 times and from their product 3 are to be subtracted. 4 × 7 × 5, means the continued product of 4, 7, and 5, that is, the product of 4 × 7, or 28, multiplied by 5.

÷ is the sign of division : thus, 8 ÷ 4 means that 8 are to be divided by 4 ; $\overline{12 + 8}$ ÷ 4, mean that 12 + 8 or 20 are to be divided by 4 ; $\overline{12 - 8}$ ÷ 4 that 12 — 8 or 4 are to be divided by 4. In the same manner the divisor may be two or more numbers connected by a line, but, if there be no line, the observations already made in re- gard to similar expressions having the sign of multiplica- tion, equally apply to division.

One number placed over and another under a line, thus, $\frac{8}{4}$, likewise denotes that the upper number is to be divided by the lower one, and this expression is more commodious and in more common use than the sign ÷ ;

$\dfrac{8-4}{4}$ means that 4 are to be taken from 8 and divided by 4.

$=$ is the sign of equality, thus $4+3=7$; $4-3=1$; $4 \times 3 = 12$; $\dfrac{8}{4}$ (or $8 \div 4$) $= 2$.

It is very necessary that you should have a perfect facility in the use of these signs, and become quite familiar with the different expressions; exercise yourself, therefore, in the following examples, and put down what they are equal to: thus $2 \times 3 + 7 \times 4 = 34$. Now find what

(11) $5 \times 6 + 8 \times 9 =$

(12) $3 + 4 - 5 - 8 + 12 + 7 =$

(13) $\overline{3 + 4} \times 5 + 8 \times \overline{12 - 7} =$

(14) $3 + 4 \times 5 + 8 \times 12 - 7 =$

(15) $\dfrac{40}{8} + \overline{7 - 5} \div 2 + 6 \times 9 =$

(16) $\overline{57 - 44} \times 3 + 8 + 9 \times 7 =$

(17) $\dfrac{29 - 5 - 7 + \overline{6 + 5} + 8 \times 4}{3} =$

*Mrs. D.* In explaining to you the four simple rules of arithmetic, I have studiously avoided confusing your mind with any properties of numbers, by the knowledge of which you might work the same sum in different ways. I have rather preferred showing you but one method for each rule, and that one has always been the simplest. You will now, I trust, understand, and even find out for yourself, different ways of producing the same result. For this purpose you must have a clear idea of the nature of numbers.

*Ed.* I shall like very much to work the sums I have been doing in another manner, and find the answers come out just the same.

*Mrs. D.* Suppose you have 27 counters in this heap, and 16 in another, what will be their difference?

*Ed.* Eleven.

*Mrs. D.* If I add 31 to this heap of 27, and 31 to this heap of 16, what will be the difference of the two numbers?

*Ed.* Eleven—just the same.

*Mrs. D.* Why so?

*Ed.* Because if I take one 31 from the other 31 nothing will remain; and so there will only be 16 to subtract from 27, the same as at first.

*Mrs. D.* Quite right; and it is evident that this applies equally to any other numbers whatever, provided the same number be added to the lesser as to the larger number, and therefore, in general terms, if to any two numbers any equal number be added to each, their difference will always be the same. On this principle the common method of subtraction is founded, in which, instead of changing the ten of the larger number, a ten is added to the bottom figure.

*Ed.* I do not exactly understand what you mean about the common method of subtraction; but I quite understand that, if I take 3 from 7, this difference is just the same as 7 from 11, 9 from 13, and so on.

*Mrs. D.* And that is all that is necessary for you to understand on the subject. We will now go to multiplication.

If you have 12 heaps, each containing eight counters, they amount to the same number as 6 heaps each containing 16, or $8 \times 12 = 8 \times 2 \times 6$; for make one heap of every 2 of the first heaps, then each heap will contain $8 \times 2$, or 16, and the number of heaps will be reduced to $\frac{12}{2}$ or 6 heaps. Again, if every two of these 6 heaps be put together, the number in each heap will then be

$8 \times 2 \times 2$, or 32, and the number of heaps will be 3; therefore, $8 \times 12 = 8 \times 2 \times 2 \times 3$: so, in the same way, if every 3 of the heaps containing 8 were put together, then the number of heaps would be reduced to $\frac{12}{3}$ or 4, and so $8 \times 3 \times 4 = 8 \times 12$. We therefore see that $8 \times 12 = 8 \times 2 \times 6 = 8 \times 2 \times 2 \times 3 = 8 \times 4 \times 3$. In like manner it may be shown of any other numbers. Therefore, if any number be multiplied by another number, the result will be the same if it be continually multiplied by other numbers, the product of which is equal to the first multiplier. Thus $3 \times 27 = 3 \times 3 \times 9 = 3 \times 3 \times 3 \times 3$.

Place any number of counters into any number of equal heaps; say, for example, 4 heaps, and 13 in each heap: then, if we separate each of these 13 into any number of equal or unequal parts, say 3, so that 5 shall be in one, 6 in another, and 2 in another, making together the 13, then the 4 fives, the 4 sixes, and the 4 twos, or $4 \times 5 + 4 \times 6 + 4 \times 2$, are the same as $13 \times 4$. For, if we take, first, $4 \times 5 = 20$

$$
\begin{array}{cc}
\text{then } 4 \times 6 = 24 & \text{or 13 at once} \\
\text{and then } 4 \times 2 = \underline{\phantom{0}8} & \underline{\phantom{0}4} \\
52 & 52
\end{array}
$$

we have only the same number of counters to put together, separate them in any number of heaps, or in any fashion our fancy may lead us; and it is plain that the same conclusion could be drawn if, instead of the above numbers, any others had been used. Therefore generally—if one number be divided into any number of equal or unequal parts, and each of these parts be multiplied by a certain number, and their products be added together, the sum of these will be equal to the product of the whole number multiplied by the same certain number. Now prove this for yourself in another example.

*Ed.* 19 × 6 = 10 × 6 + 9 × 6 = 7 × 6 + 8 × 6 + 4×6.

*Mrs. D.* If we have 4 heaps, each containing 20, and other 4 heaps, each containing 7, then if we take the 4×7 = 28 from the 20×4 = 80, their difference, or 80 − 28 = 52 will be the same as if we had first taken the 7 from the 20, and multiplied this difference by 4, or $\overline{20-7}$ × 4 = 13×4. For, in the first case, we take twenty 4 times, and then take from these seven 4 times, or from every 20 we take 7, leaving 4 times $\overline{20-7}$ or 4 × 13 = 52; therefore 20×4 − 7×4 = 13×4 = 52. The same may be shown of any other numbers, and therefore, generally, of any two numbers the difference of the two products obtained by the multiplication of each into any other number, is equal to the product obtained by multiplying their difference into that other number.

What has been said of multiplication is likewise equally true of division, and we can, by reversing our steps, show that $\frac{96}{12}$ is the same as 96 divided by 4, and this quotient divided by 3. For, divide 96 into 4 equal parts, and 24 will be in each parcel; again, subdivide each of these into 3 heaps, there will now be 4×3 or 12 heaps, and each will contain 8 units, since $\frac{24}{3}$=8 : therefore, if we divide 96 by 4, and this quotient by 3, it is the same as dividing 96 at once by 12. And in like manner, whatever number is to be divided, it is exactly the same, whether we first divide it into fewer equal parts, and then subdivide these into a number of equal parts, or whether we at once divide it by the product of all the divisors first used. It follows from the above, that the expressions $\frac{96}{12}, \frac{96}{4} \div 3, \frac{96}{4\times3}, \frac{96}{2\times2\times3}$, are

F 3

all equal to each other, and mean that 96 is to be divided by 3 and by 4, or by 2 by 2 and by 3, or by their product 12. Make yourself familiar with these expressions, not merely as regards these numbers alone, and have the certainty of the perfect identity of their results fully impressed on your mind, as you will find this knowledge, during our progress, of great practical benefit.

> Now divide 108 by 18 in two divisions.
> Divide 78432 by 24 in two divisions.
> Divide 24472 by 56 in two divisions.

*Ed.* I see this plan saves me from a long division sum—it is much easier to divide by 8 and then by 7 than by 56 at once.

*Mrs. D.* Yes, both in multiplication and division, it is sometimes a better and quicker way to perform the work by two short easy operations, than by one which is long and difficult. Here, however, the judgment of the arithmetician must be exercised to decide which, in any particular case, is the preferable method.

The result will be exactly the same whether we divide 52 (20+24+8) by 4, or whether we divide 20 by 4, then 24 by 4, and then 8 by 4, and add all these quotients together; or $\frac{52}{4} = \frac{20}{4} + \frac{24}{4} + \frac{8}{4}$. It is plain, that if we separate 52 counters into any number of parts, say 20+24+8 (together making 52), and divide each of these into 4 equal parts, the first of these containing 5 each, the second containing 6 each, and the third containing 2 each, since $\frac{20}{4} = 5, \frac{24}{4} = 6,$ and $\frac{8}{4} = 2$; the sum of these quotients will be the fourth part of the whole, or equal to the quotient of 52 divided by 4 = 13, which is made up of $\frac{20+24+8}{4}$. The same may be shown of any other numbers, and therefore generally, if any number is to be divided by any other number, whether the whole number be divided at once, or whether it be separated into any number of equal or unequal parts, and then divided by the same divisor—the first quotient will always be equal to the sum of the other quotients.

*Mrs. D.* If from 80 counters we take 28, and divide this difference by 4, or $\dfrac{80-28}{4} = \dfrac{52}{4} = 13$, the result is the same as if we first divide 80 by 4, and from this quotient take 28 divided by 4, or $\dfrac{80}{4} - \dfrac{28}{4} = 20 - 7 = 13$. For suppose the 80 to be divided into 4 parcels, containing $\dfrac{80}{4} = 20$ each, and the 28 to be divided into other 4 parcels, containing $\dfrac{28}{4} = 7$ each; then if we take each of these parcels of 7 from each of these parcels of 20, we take 4 times 7 or 28, from 4 times 20 or 80, and we shall leave in each parcel $\dfrac{80-28}{4}$, therefore $\dfrac{80}{4} - \dfrac{28}{4} = \dfrac{80-28}{4} = 13$. The same may be shown of any other numbers, and therefore, generally,

Of any two numbers, their difference divided by another number, is equal to the difference of the quotients obtained by the division of each number, by that same other number.

*Ed.* Will what you have shown me of division be of much use? It is easier to divide 52 by 4, than first 20, then 24, and then 8, and add these together. It is likewise better to divide 80 by 4, and——

*Mrs. D.* There may, however, both in multiplication

and division, be cases in which this manner of breaking numbers into parts may be of practical use; and even if it were not, it is necessary, to the perfect understanding of figures, to perceive clearly the identity of result produced by different operations. If many numbers were given to be multiplied or divided by the same number, it would often be better to add all the different numbers together before you otherwise operated upon them; and in multiplication it is sometimes attended with advantage to take two numbers, the difference of which is the real number to be operated upon. For example, multiply 99998 by 657. I will do the same, and then you shall judge which is the shortest process.

$$
\begin{array}{ll}
Ed. \quad 99998 & Mrs.\ D.\quad 65700000 \\
\phantom{Ed. \quad} 657 & \phantom{Mrs.\ D.\quad} 1314 \\
\hline
\phantom{Ed. \quad} 699986 & \phantom{Mrs.\ D.\quad} 65698686 \\
\phantom{Ed. \quad} 499990 & \\
\phantom{Ed. \quad} 599988 & \\
\hline
\phantom{Ed. \quad} 65698686 &
\end{array}
$$

Mrs. D. $99998 = 100000 - 2$; because $99998 + 2 = 100000$. So $100000 - 2 \times 657 = 65,700,000 - 1314 = 65,698,686$. So the whole of my process is to multiply 657 by 2, and take this from 65700000. I will put it down next to your sum.

———————

Mrs. D. If two numbers can be divided by any number without a remainder, their difference can likewise be divided without a remainder. For example, if 56 and 24 can be divided by 8 without a remainder, their difference 32 can likewise be divided by 8; for (see p. 55) $\frac{56}{8} - \frac{24}{8} = \frac{56 - 24}{8}$, and therefore, since 56 and 24 are both divisible by 8, their difference 32 is also divisible by 8. Shall I show you this with the counters?

*Ed.* Oh no: nothing is wanting to prove this; it is what Alfred calls "self-evident."

*Mrs. D.* There is another truth almost equally apparent. If, in division, the dividend and divisor be both multiplied by any equal number, the quotient will still be the same. Thus $\dfrac{28}{4} = \dfrac{28 \times 9}{4 \times 9} = \dfrac{252}{36}$. The value of any number multiplied by another number, and then divided by that same number, will, it is plain, still remain unaltered. This we have already seen in the method of proving multiplication by division, and the converse. Therefore, 28 is the same as $\dfrac{28 \times 9}{9}$ and $\dfrac{28}{4}$ is the same as $\dfrac{28 \times 9}{4 \times 9}$; and since, if we divide by 9 and then by 4, it is exactly the same as if we divide at once by $9 \times 4$, or 36; it follows that $\dfrac{28 \times 9}{4 \times 9}$ expresses the same as $\dfrac{256}{36}$, and this may be shown of any other numbers. In like manner, if the dividend and divisor be divided by the same number, the quotient will remain unaltered. Let 28 be the dividend and 4 the divisor, and divide each of these by 2, then $\dfrac{28}{4} = \dfrac{28 \div 2}{4 \div 2} = \dfrac{14}{2}$, because this expression is the same as $\dfrac{14 \times 2}{2 \times 2} = \dfrac{28}{4}$, and therefore $\dfrac{28}{4} = \dfrac{14}{2} = 7$. The same may be shown of any other numbers.

If any number, say 6, divided by any other number, say 3, be equal to another number, say 8, divided by a fourth number, say 4, then the first, multiplied by the fourth, will be equal to the third multiplied by the second. That is, if $\frac{6}{3} = \frac{8}{4}$, then $6 \times 4 = 3 \times 8$, and the converse, if $6 \times 4 = 3 \times 8$, then $\frac{6}{3} = \frac{8}{4}$ and $\frac{4}{3} = \frac{8}{6}$ and $\frac{4}{8} = \frac{3}{6}$.

The proof of this proposition rests on the following self-evident truths. If two equal quantities be multiplied the same number of times, the results will still remain equal; and if they each be divided into the same number of equal parts, the results will also be equal. That is to say, if these two sheets of paper be exactly equal to each other, any number, say 3, of the one kind, will be equal to the same number of the other; or if they each be divided into any number of parts, say 3, each part will be equal one to the other.

Now, if $\frac{6}{3} = \frac{8}{4}$, multiplying both equals by 4, they will still remain equal, or $\frac{6 \times 4}{3} = \frac{8 \times 4}{4}$; but 8, multiplied by 4, and then divided by 4, will still be simply 8: therefore, $\frac{6 \times 4}{3} = 8$, multiply both equals by 3, and $\frac{6 \times 4 \times 3}{3} = 8 \times 3 = 6 \times 4 = 8 \times 3$. Again, if $6 \times 4 = 8 \times 3$, then $\frac{6}{3} = \frac{8}{4}$. For, dividing both equals by 4, we have $6 = \frac{8 \times 3}{4}$, and dividing again by 3, we have $\frac{6}{3} = \frac{8}{4}$, or dividing by 6, and then by 3, we have $\frac{4}{3} = \frac{8}{6}$, or dividing by 8, and then by 6, we have $\dfrac{4}{8} = \dfrac{3}{6}$, and the same reasoning will apply to any other numbers whatever*.

---

## CHAPTER II.

*Mrs. D.* If we have 4 parcels containing 9 each to be divided into 3 parts, it is exactly the same whether we divide each of the parcels containing 9 by 3, and then multiply this quotient $\left(\dfrac{9}{3} = 3\right)$ by 4, or whether we put the 4 parcels together ($4 \times 9 = 36$) and divide the whole by 3; we shall, in either case, have 36 divided into 3 parts: in the first case, $3 \times 4 = 12$, and in the second, $\dfrac{36}{3} = 12$; therefore, the expressions $\dfrac{9 \times 4}{3}$ and $\dfrac{9}{3} \times 4$ mean the same; and it is immaterial whether we divide 9 by 3 and then multiply the quotient by 4, or whether we first multiply the 9 by 4 and then divide the product by 3: the same reasoning will equally apply to any other numbers, and therefore, generally, if any number is to be multiplied by one number, and divided by another, the result will be exactly the same whichever operation is first performed.

It is sometimes easier to do the one, and sometimes the other, and, therefore, when we have any question

---

* The properties of numbers treated of in this chapter should be very gradually developed to the pupil; a very *short* time at each lesson should be employed, and the counters should *always* be used. During the period of acquiring this knowledge, the pupil may, with advantage, be exercised in practical questions on the foregoing rules.

which involves multiplication and division, it is better to bring the expression at once to this form __×__ and then we can readily judge whether it will suit the particular question to divide or multiply first.

Now, let us apply the foregoing to practice.

You readily told me, some time back, that if one yard of cloth cost 6 shillings, 8 yards would cost 48 shillings (Q. 11); and if 3 yards cost 18 shillings, 1 yard would cost 6 shillings (Q. 12). Now, can you tell me, if 3 yards cost 18 shillings, what will 8 yards cost?

*Ed.* That is very easy; it is only the two questions put together. I must first, as I did before, divide 18 by 3 to find what 1 yard will cost, $\frac{18}{3} = 6$, and now I must multiply this 6 by 8, or $6 \times 8 = 48$, equal the cost of 8 yards.

*Mrs. D.* You have, therefore, divided 18 by 3, and multiplied the quotient by 8, or you have found $\frac{18 \times 8}{3} = 48$.

These questions are of very extensive practical use, and you must become very expert in their solution. Will you try another? I bought these 7 pencils for 9 pence; now, what should I give for 13?

*Ed.* 9 divided by 7 equal to $\frac{9}{7} = 1$, and 2 rem., so each pencil will cost 1 penny and 2 rem. What shall I do with this remainder? when I multiply by 13 it will be a very puzzling operation.

*Mrs. D.* Suppose, then, that you do nothing with the remainders at present; $\frac{9}{7}$ will express the price of each pencil, and this is to be multiplied by 13; then $\frac{9}{7} \times 13$

$$= \frac{9 \times 13}{7} = \frac{117}{7} = 16 \text{ and 5 remainder—so 13 would}$$

cost rather more than 16 pence: as we proceed, we shall show how to divide the 5 remainder into 13 parts, at present we must be satisfied with merely noting this excess.

You will observe, that in answering the two preceding questions, we found it more convenient in the first to divide before multiplying, and in the second to multiply before dividing. Why was this?

*Ed.* If we can divide the number without leaving any remainder, it is better to divide first; if not, it is better to multiply first.

*Mrs. D.* Exactly so. I will now give you one or two questions of a similar nature, that you may perfectly understand how they should be managed.

*Alfred.* Is not the rule for answering these questions, as given in the Tutor's Assistant, called the Golden Rule, or the Rule of Three?

*Mrs. D.* Yes; but I have preferred the above manner of statement, as being more simple in the explanation: when we come to geometrical proportion, the rationale of the rule of three will be fully shown, and those questions which more peculiarly belong to proportion can then be answered. In the meantime, we will, however, adopt the term in common use, and call the following

## QUESTIONS IN THE RULE OF THREE.

Q. 15. It is considered that 21 well-cultivated mulberry trees should yield in each season about 631 pounds of good leaves; now, what plantation of trees will be required to afford nourishment to the silk-worms proceeding from one ounce of eggs, supposing these consume during their short life 1182 pounds?

G

Q. 16. If 27 carrots weigh 117 pounds, how much will 568 weigh?

Q. 17. If 15 men can weave 405 yards of silk in 9 days, how many yards can 29 men weave in the same time?

---

*Emily.* Mother, our cousin Robert tells me he is in the rule of three inverse, and that he finds it very difficult. I wish you would teach it to me.

*Mrs. D.* Did he tell you why it was difficult?

*Emily.* He said something about more requiring less, and less requiring more, and that it was all guess work which of two ways was right.

*Mrs. D.* Ah, it is a sad mysterious affair, no doubt; but here comes our young pupil quite out of breath.

*Ed.* The gardener says that the piece of ground which is being dug up must be finished on Friday, in order that the potatoes may be planted on Saturday, and the four men who are at work cannot finish it before Friday evening week.

*Mrs. D.* We must then have more men to assist these, I suppose; will you find out for me how many more men we shall require?

*Ed.* There are now 3 days to Saturday, and 9 work-days from this time to Saturday week. What shall I do next?

*Mrs. D.* If 4 men can finish it in 9 days, how many days' labour of one man will it require to complete the whole?

*Ed.* Four times nine, to be sure, unless he works a great deal harder than these.

*Mrs. D.* But we suppose at present, that the men we employ are all equally strong and diligent; therefore, you have found that $4 \times 9$, or 36 days' labour of one man, is necessary for the completion of our work. Now, if we have this amount of actual labour, it matters not how we obtain it—whether in one day, two days, or any other number of days—the more men we employ the shorter time this amount of labour will be expended. Now, how many men will perform 36 days' labour of one man in three days?

*Ed.* Thirty-six divided by three. So $\frac{36}{3} = 12$ will be the number of men required.

*Mrs. D.* That is to say, 12 men will perform $12 \times 3$ or 36 days' labour of one man in 3 days.

*Ed.* So, I will go and tell the gardener to engage 8 men more.

*Mrs. D.* Stay, one moment.—Let us retrace our steps; we first multiplied 9 by 4, to know how long one man would take, and we then divided this by 3, to find how many men could complete the work in three days, and our whole sum is $\frac{9 \times 4}{3} = 12$.

*Ed.* We might in this case, then, have divided by 3 before we multiplied by 4.

*Mrs. D.* Now, Emily, will you try a sum of this kind? If a carrier charge 5 shillings for conveying a parcel, weighing 600 pounds, 36 miles, how many pounds will he carry 24 miles for the same money, charging for each pound according to the distance carried?

*Emily.* As the same money is to be paid in both cases, it is no matter to us at present what he charges, we have only to consider the pounds and miles. It would cost the same, likewise, to carry $600 \times 36$ one mile, since 600 pounds carried one mile would cost the same money divided by 36 ; and it would cost 24 times the money to convey $600 \times 36$ pounds 24 miles, and, therefore, for the same money, $\dfrac{600 \times 36}{24}$ pounds could

be carried 24 miles, and $\dfrac{600 \times 36}{24} = 900 =$ number

of pounds.

*Mrs. D.* Both you and Edmund have now solved, without any difficulty, questions which are usually called sums in the rule of three inverse.

*Emily.* Then, I have known this " puzzling rule," as Robert calls it, for a long time, without being aware that I was so wise!

*Mrs. D.* It frequently happens in practice that questions may arise involving more than one multiplication and division, but these, and indeed all questions in figures, will be much better answered after the consideration of some of the properties of figures, which will form the subject of the next few lessons. In the meantime, we will subjoin one or two simple questions for practice.

Q. 18. A wall that is to be built to the height of 21 feet, was raised 7 feet by 9 men in 6 days; how many men must be employed to finish the wall in 4 days, at the same rate of working? Here $21-7=14$, or twice the height of the first piece raised, is required to be done

in 4 days, therefore, $\dfrac{14}{2}=7$ must be accomplished in half

that time, or in two days ; but 7 feet can be raised by 9 men in 6 days, therefore, by $9 \times 6 = 54$ in one day, and

by $\dfrac{9 \times 6}{2}$ in 2 days, consequently, $\dfrac{9 \times 6}{2} =$ number of

men required.

Q. 19. If 50 men can perform a piece of work in 11 days, how long will 275 men take to accomplish a piece of work eight times as large?

Q. 20. If 2 horses can plough 3 acres of land in one

day, how many acres can be ploughed in 13 days with 9 horses? Here 9 horses can plough in one day $\dfrac{3 \times 9}{2}$ acres, and, therefore, in 13 days they can plough $\dfrac{3 \times 9 \times 13}{2}$ acres.

Q. 21. If 268 gallons of water can be evaporated or converted into steam in an hour, with 4 bushels of coals, how much can be evaporated in 7 hours, consuming 18 bushels of coals per hour?

----

## CHAPTER III.

*Mrs. D.* Any number into which another number can be divided, without leaving a remainder, is called a factor of the larger number—thus 3 and 4 are factors of 12; and any number which can be exactly divided into a certain number of parts is called a multiple of that certain number—thus 12 is a multiple of 2, of 3, of 4, and of 6: hence it follows, that a number is the product of two or more of its factors—thus $2 \times 6 = 3 \times 4 = 2 \times 2 \times 3 = 12$. Can you tell me what are the factors of 15?

*Ed.* 3 and 5; because $3 \times 5 = 15$.

*Mrs. D.* Has it any more factors?

*Ed.* No; those are the only two numbers which can divide 15 without leaving a remainder.

*Mrs. D.* Find the factors of 17.

*Ed.* I cannot find any number which will divide 17 without a remainder.

*Mrs. D.* It has, therefore, no factors, or it is not a multiple of any other number. Numbers of this de-

G 3

scription are called prime; 19, 23, 11, are likewise prime numbers.

*Ed.* How are we to find out when a number is prime?

*Mrs. D.* Persons who are at all conversant with figures soon become acquainted with the prime numbers, below thousands; and for any practical use, these are sufficient to be known. There is no certain rule for their discovery, but this operation may be much facilitated by an investigation into the nature and properties of numbers. We will, however, defer this discussion till you are a greater adept in arithmetic, and till your young mind, gaining strength by exercise, can enter into a train of reasoning, without being bewildered with any fancied intricacies.

In the meantime you can readily perceive that 2, 3, 5, 7, 11, 13, 17, 19, 23, 29, are prime numbers, since your knowledge of multiplication makes you certain that no two numbers multiplied together produce any of the above numbers; they therefore can have no factors.

*Ed.* Yes, I see that very plainly, and I should, of course, in the same way, know some of the numbers which have factors; are these called by any particular name?

*Mrs. D.* They are distinguished as composite numbers. Some of these must necessarily have many more factors than others. Those which can only be divided by a prime number into a prime number of parts, have, of course, only two prime factors—thus 14 has only 2 and 7 for factors, while 24 has 2, 3, 4, 6, 8, 12 for factors, some of which, you perceive, are prime, and some composite numbers.

*Ed.* I do not quite understand why the product of two prime numbers may not, therefore, sometimes be the product of two other prime numbers.

*Mrs. D.* Arrange these three parcels of counters,

each containing 5, into any other number of equal parcels.

*Ed.* If I take one from each, and make another parcel of these, then I shall have 3 parcels containing 4, and one parcel containing 3—that will not do; so I will take 2 from each parcel; I shall then have 3 parcels, each containing 3 and one containing 6. Ah! I can divide this into two parcels of 3 each, and then I shall have—5 parcels containing 3 each?—yes; I see now I can only divide them into 3 or into 5 equal parcels; but this is such a low number, and I knew very well beforehand that nothing else than 3 × 5 would produce 15; but might it not be different in very high numbers, mother?

*Mrs. D.* If you will consider a little, you will find that the same principle influences all primes alike, and that what is true of 3 × 5 equally applies to the product of any other two primes. Suppose you have 17 parcels containing 19 each, then it is clear that you can not arrange the 17 parcels into a fewer number of equal parcels, for the prime 17 cannot be divided without a remainder, nor can you divide them into a greater number of equal parcels except 19; for if, according to your plan, we take one from each parcel, there will be 17 parcels of 18 and one parcel of 17; if we take 2 away, then there will be 17 parcels of 17 and 2 of 17, or 19 parcels of 17; if we take 3 away from each, then there will be 17 × 16, and 3 × 17, and so on: as you diminish the number of seventeens on the one hand, you increase them on the other; their sum always making 19 seventeens; and it is evident that they could not be divided into any other equal parts; for 3 × 17, or 3 × 16 + 3, could not be divided in equal parcels containing 16 each; nor could 4 × 17, or 4 × 15 + 8, be divided in equal parcels containing 15 each, and so on; therefore there are no other factors of 323 but 17 and 19, and the same may be proved of any other prime factors whatever.

----

*Mrs. D.* Those numbers which have composite factors can, it is evident, have these subdivided into prime factors; thus $3 \times 8$ is the same as $3 \times 2 \times 4$, the same as $3 \times 2 \times 2 \times 2$; therefore when it is required to reduce a number (as 24) to its prime factors, it is thus expressed, $24 = 2 \times 2 \times 2 \times 3$. A little farther on, you will find the advantage of having obtained a facility in this work, and therefore we will consider a few numbers and trace our manner of proceeding. Name any number to be reduced to its prime factors.

*Ed.* 165.

*Mrs. D.* Since it is an odd number, we know that we cannot divide it by 2, the lowest prime, without leaving 1 as a remainder; so we proceed to 3, the next lowest prime, and find by trial that $\frac{165}{3} = 55 \times 3$; now we know that 55 is the same as $5 \times 11$, so $165 = 3 \times 5 \times 11$, and 3, 5, and 11 are the prime factors of 165.

With this number it would have been easier, perhaps, to have divided by 5 at first. We know immediately that any number which has no units can be divisible by 5, without a remainder, since $2 \times 5$ are ten, and therefore any even number of fives will be half that number of tens, and have no units, and one more five added to these will make an odd number of fives, and the whole will be a number having 5 units. Thus 6 times five are equal to 3 times ten, or $6 \times 5 = 30$, and $30 + 5 = 6 \times 5 + 5 = 7 \times 5$. Therefore all numbers having no units, or 5 units, are divisible by 5.

*Ed.* I wish there was as easy a way for knowing when other numbers are divisors.

*Mrs. D.* A knowledge of figures gives us a facility of very quickly discovering what description of numbers are divisible by all the digits, except 7. Every even number, you of course directly see, can be divided by 2.

Since one hundred can be divided into 4 parts without a remainder, it follows, that any number of hundreds are also divisible by 4; therefore, any number having no tens and no units, or having the tens and units together, divisible by 4, is always divisible by 4—thus, you know immediately that 17300, and that 6536 have 4 for a divisor. In like manner, 1000 being divisible by 8, or $\dfrac{1000}{8} = 125$, all numbers which have no hundreds, no tens, and no units, or which have these together divisible by 8, are always divisible by that number. Thus, I know without hesitation, that 27946783144 divided by 8 will leave no remainder, because I know that 8 is a factor of 144.

It is very easy to discover whether a number be divisible by 3 and by 9, but to understand the reason of this rather a longer explanation is necessary, and I would not, on any account, that you should be content to apply the rule, without having previously ascertained that it is unerring.

Since 10 is $9+1$, it follows that ten consists of one nine and one unit, that 2 tens, or 20, are 2 nines and 2 units; 3 tens, or 30, are 3 nines and 3 units, and, in like manner, any number of tens contains the same number of nines, and the same number of units, or any number of tens divided by nine will always have as a remainder the same number of units. In like manner, one hundred consists of nine tens and one ten, 2 hundred of 2 nine tens and 2 tens, or $100 = 90 +[10$; $200 = 2 \times 90 + 20$;

300 = 3 × 90 + 30, and so on.  But each of these tens consists of one nine and one unit, or 100 = 90 + 9 + 1; 200 = 2 × 90 + 2 × 9 + 2; 300 = 3 × 90 + 3 × 9 + 3; and, therefore, if any number of hundreds be divided by 9, there will always be a remainder of units equal to the same number of hundreds.  In the same manner we can prove that one thousand, or ten hundred, or nine hundred and one hundred, can be divided by 9, having one for a remainder, and that any number of thousands divided by 9 will always leave a remainder equal to the same number of units, or 1000 = 999 + 1; 2000 = 999 × 2 + 2; 3000 = 3 × 999 + 3, and so on of any other numbers of higher value.  To apply this, as well as to make it more apparent, let us suppose any number, for example 583767, which can be broken into 500000 + 80000 + 3000 + 700 + 60 + 7.  Divide each of these parts by 9.

$$
\begin{aligned}
500000 \div 9 &= 55555 \text{ and } 5 \text{ rem.} \\
80000 \div 9 &= \phantom{5}8888 \ldots 8 \ldots \\
3000 \div 9 &= \phantom{55}333 \ldots 3 \ldots \\
700 \div 9 &= \phantom{555}77 \ldots 7 \ldots \\
60 \div 9 &= \phantom{5555}6 \ldots 6 \ldots \\
7 \div 9 &= \phantom{5555}0 \ldots 7 \ldots \\
&\phantom{= 5555}\overline{\phantom{00}36}
\end{aligned}
$$

Now if the sum of these remainders can be exactly divided by 9, it follows, that since the other parts of the number are divisible by 9, the whole number must likewise be divisible by 9; for (*see* p. 54) if all its separate parts can be divided by any number, they can, taken together, be divided by the same number.  But the sum of these remainders is equal to the sum of the digits of the number.  Hence the rule, if the sum of the digits be divisible by 9, the whole number is divisible by 9.  In the present case, this sum of the digits equal 36 = 4 × 9;

and, therefore, the whole number, 583767, is likewise divisible by 9.

Since $9 = 3 \times 3$, it follows, that whatever can be divided by 9 can likewise be divided by 3, and $500000 - 5$, $80000 - 8$, can be divided by 3 as well as by 9, without a remainder; thus 6873, divided by 9, will have for remainders $6 + 8 + 7 + 3 = 24$; since

$$6000 \div 9 = 666 \text{ and } 6 \text{ rem.}$$
$$800 \div 9 = \quad 88 \ldots 8 \ldots$$
$$70 \div 9 = \quad 7 \ldots 7 \ldots$$
$$3 \div 9 = \quad 0 \ldots 3 \ldots$$
$$\overline{\phantom{00}24\phantom{00}}$$

and therefore it can be divided by 3, leaving the same remainders; the sum of these is found to be 24, which are divisible by 3 and not by 9; therefore 3 is a factor of 6873, but 9 is not.

Now as every even number can be divided by 2, it follows, that every number having the units even, and the sum of the digits, divisible by 3, will be divisible both by 2 and by 3; but $2 \times 3 = 6$, therefore it is divisible by 6. Thus we know at once that 6 is a factor of 8736, but not of 8746. In like manner, if the sum of the digits, of an even number, be divisible by 9, the whole number has 18 for a factor, as 479646.

Any number having the sum of the digits divisible by 3, and the tens and units together divisible by 4, has 12 for a factor, as 58272.

Any number having the sum of the digits divisible by 9, and the ten and units together divisible by 4, has 36 for a factor, as 786744. In like manner, finding that a number has 3 and 8 for factors, we know that $3 \times 8 = 24$ is likewise a factor, as 58742136; and any number having 9 and 8 for factors, has likewise 72 for a factor, as 84752136.

[*Alfred.* This property of the number nine certainly leads to very curious results. Thence it follows, that in any number, which has the sum of its digits divisible by 9, if we change the places of the figures at our pleasure, so as to form any other number, if it be composed of the same digits, no matter how transposed, it will likewise be divisible by 9: thus 583767, 853776, 785736, &c. &c., in almost endless variety, are all divisible by 9.

*Mrs. D.* Yes; and from this property of 9 many other interesting and remarkable properties of numbers arise. Thus the difference of any two numbers, formed of the same digits, but having these transposed at pleasure, will always be divisible by 9; for example, if

| from 9378 | from 9378 |
|---|---|
| we take 3789 | we take 8793 |
| 9)5589 | 9)585 |

the difference will always be divisible by 9.

If we break the numbers, the reason of this will be sufficiently evident.

$$9000 + 300 + 70 + 8 = 9378.$$
$$3000 + 700 + 80 + 9 = 3789.$$
$$8000 + 700 + 90 + 3 = 8793.$$

Now, since it has been shown that any number of tens, minus the same number of units, are always divisible by 9; thus any number of hundreds, minus the same number of tens or the same number of units, are always divisible by 9, and so on; it is readily seen that, in the difference, $(9000 - 9) - (3000 - 300) - (700 - 70) - (80 - 8)$, and in the difference, $(9000 - 90) + (300 - 3) - (700 - 70) - (8000 - 8)$; each of the circumflexed numbers $(9000 - 9)$, &c. must be divisible by 9; and that this result does not at all depend on the particular numbers here used.

This property of the number 9 is also applied in prov-

ing addition and multiplication, by what is called " casting out the nines." Addition is thus proved in the following manner:—Divide the sum of the digits of each
line by 9, and set down the remainder, if any, directly
even with the line on the right hand, as in the annexed
example—

$$
\begin{array}{ll}
538 & 7 \text{ rem.} \\
746 & 8 \;\; .. \\
\underline{892} & \underline{1} \;\; .. \\
2176 & 7
\end{array}
$$

Then if the excess of nines in the sum of the remainder
be equal to the excess of nines in the total sum, or in this
example, if $\dfrac{16}{9}$ leave the same remainder as $\dfrac{2176}{9}$, or as
$\dfrac{2 + 1 + 7 + 6}{9}$, then it is probable the work is right.
Since any number divided by 9 will leave the same remainder as the sum of its digits divided by 9, it follows,
that the sum of two or more numbers divided by 9 will
leave the same remainder as the aggregate remainders of
the sum of the digits of each number divided by 9.

Thus $\dfrac{538}{9}$ will have the same remainder as $\dfrac{5 + 3 + 8}{9}$

$\dfrac{746}{9}$ . . . . $\dfrac{7 + 4 + 6}{9}$

$\dfrac{892}{9}$ . . . $\dfrac{8 + 9 + 2}{9}$

and therefore $\dfrac{538 + 746 + 892}{9} = \dfrac{2176}{9}$ will have the

same remainder as $\dfrac{5 + 3 + 8 + 7 + 4 + 6 + 8 + 9 + 2}{9}$

This, however, is only a presumptive proof of the cor-

H

rectness of the work, and the sum may, by possibility, be wrong, although it may still answer this condition. For if, instead of the true result, any other number having the sum of its digits such as that, when divided by 9, 7 will be left as a remainder, had been put down, it is evident that this manner of proof could not have detected the error: thus, 6127, 9367, 5335, &c. &c. have 7 for the excess of nines; and although it is not perhaps probable that if there be mistakes in the addition, they should be such that the sum of the digits should be equal to the sum of the digits of the true result, yet the case is very possible, therefore this proof is by no means certain.

*Alfred.* Which is sufficient reason, I think, for not using this method.

*Mrs. D.* I am quite of your opinion, and therefore will not give any example of proving multiplication by casting out the nines, which is conducted on exactly the same principle; the excess of nines in the product of the remainders of the multiplicand and multiplier, being equal to the excess of nines in the whole product.]

Now take your slate and pencil, Edmund, and I will give you a number, say 364, to reduce to its prime factors.

*Ed.* I know that it can be divided by 2; $\frac{364}{2} = 182$, or $364 = 182 \times 2$; 182 can again be divided by 2, $\frac{182}{2} = 91$, or $182 = 91 \times 2$. I see directly that 91 cannot be divided by 3 without leaving 1 remainder; neither can it be divided by 5. Let me think—the next prime is seven; the sevens in 9 are one and two over; the sevens in 21 are three exactly: so 7 is a factor, and $91 = 13 \times 7$ both primes, mother.

*Mrs. D.* Very well; but let us finish our work. You

first divided by 2, then by 2, and then by 7, which last division left 13; so $364 = 2 \times 2 \times 7 \times 13$.

Now I will give you one more number; 53 for example.

*Ed.* I think I know what that is, but I will try it: 2 will not do, and if it be divided by 3, there will be 2 rem.; if by 5, 3 rem.; if by 7, 4 rem.; if by 11, 9 rem.

*Alfred.* Nay, Edmund, you need not try any higher primes than 7; for if the next prime 11 could divide 53, some of the lower primes could also divide it: for 11 × 5 are 55, and, therefore, 11 multiplied by any higher number than 5, must be more than 55, and consequently more than 53, and you have already found that the lower primes will not divide this number, and therefore 11, or any higher number, cannot.

*Ed.* And so I have proved what I thought it was at first, that 53 is a prime number.

*Mrs. D.* What Alfred has just said points out to you the limit to which our trials may be confined in the discovery of prime factors. If 7 be the lowest prime factor, for example, the parts in which it divides the number cannot be less than 7, for if it were, 7 would not be the lowest factor; therefore, any number less than $7 \times 7$, or 49, is a prime, unless it can be divided by 5, 3, or 2; any number less than $11 \times 11$, or 121, is a prime, unless it can be divided by 7, 5, 3, or 2, and so on with higher numbers.

Reduce to their prime factors the following numbers:—

(18) 1782
(19) 729
(20) 1001
(21) 343
(22) 3584

      (23)   1080
      (24)    851
      (25)    323
      (26)    273

*Mrs. D.* Do you think you are now quite familiar with the meaning of the words primes, factors, and multiples?

*Ed.* Yes; and I like finding out the factors; it is a great deal easier than doing long division, which I once complained of as being so difficult.

*Mrs. D.* You could now, perhaps, be able to discover if any two or more given numbers have a common factor, or divisor, that is, whether there be a number* which can divide either of these numbers without a remainder.

*Ed.* Give me an example, mother, if you please; I shall understand it so much better than by this manner of speaking; I am always sorry when you begin to talk of *any* number; I like to be told *some* number, and then it is all clear enough.

*Alfred.* That is what is called generalizing, and it is quite as easy to be understood as any particular case if a person will take the trouble to think about it.

*Mrs. D.* Not quite as easy to be understood, Alfred, but it is the preferable mode, because more mathematical. We will, however, give our little boy an example of what we mean. Write on your slate any two numbers, say 24 and 42, and now seek out some number which can divide them both without a remainder.

---

* This is usually called the common measure of two numbers; but, since the term factor has already been explained, and used in reference to single numbers, it has been thought better to continue this word rather than change it for another term.

*Ed.* I know 6 will divide them both, because 6 is the sum of the digits (see *p.* 71) of both 24 and 42.

*Mrs. D.* And 6 can be divided by 2 and by 3; therefore both the numbers can be divided by 6 and by 3, and by 2, without a remainder. Have they any other like factors?

*Ed.* No: for $6 \times 7 = 42$ and 7 is a prime number.

*Mrs. D.* Now try if 27 and 35 have any common factors.

*Ed.* I see directly that they have not, because 5 and 7 are the only two factors of 35, and 27 cannot be divided by either of these numbers.

*Mrs. D.* Two numbers, which have no common factor, are called prime to each other; therefore you have found that 35 and 27 are prime to each other. In the same manner that the common factors of two numbers may be found, so may those of 3 or more. Let it be required, for example, to find the common factors of 279, 496, 1085.

Find the prime factors of each or such composite factors as may readily be reduced into primes; then it is easily seen by inspection what factors the numbers have in common. Here

$$279 = 3 \times \quad 93 = 3 \times 3 \times 31$$
$$496 = 8 \times \quad 62 = 8 \times 2 \times 31$$
$$1085 = 5 \times 217 = 5 \times 7 \times 31$$

31 is, therefore, the only common factor of these three numbers.

It is evident that the same process could be pursued to find the common factors of more numbers than 3; it would only be longer according to the value of the numbers, and according to the number of these to be operated upon.

If it be required to find the least or the greatest common factor, these may likewise be readily discovered by the same method. For example, given 12, 36, 48, to find their greatest common factor ;

$$12 = 2 \times 2 \times 3$$
$$36 = 2 \times 2 \times 3 \times 3$$
$$48 = 2 \times 2 \times 3 \times 4$$

therefore 2 is the least common factor, and $2 \times 2 \times 3 = 12$ will be the greatest common factor, since they all have only the prime factors 2, 2, and 3, making up the composite factor 12 common to each other.

Q. 22. Find the greatest common factor of 108 and 729 ?

Q. 23. What are the common factors of 144 and 112?

Q. 24. Find the greatest common factor of 372, 657, and 216 ?

Q. 25. Find the common factors of 2704, 5088, and 3764.

————————

[*Alfred.* Is not another method generally given for finding the greatest common measure or factor of 2 numbers ?

*Mrs. D.* Yes; but I think the above is more convenient for practice; however, that you may judge for yourself, I will explain to you the reason of the following rule to find the greatest common measure of two numbers. Divide the greater by the less; then divide the divisor by the remainder, and so on, dividing always the last divisor by the last remainder, till nothing remains; so shall the last divisor of all be the greatest common measure sought. Let us find, by this method, the greatest common measure of 272 and 348.

```
272)348(1
272
   76)272(3
   228
      44)76(1
      44
        32)44(1
        32
          12)32(2
          24
             8)12(1
             8
              4)8(2
```

Therefore, 4 is the greatest common measure. If we retrace our steps, we shall clearly see that 4 must be a common factor or measure to the two numbers; for, since it measures 8, or 4 × 2, it also measures 8 × 4, or 12 (4 × 3) and 12 (4 × 3) × 2 + 8 (2 × 4) = 8 × 4 = 32, and 32 (8 × 4) + 12 (3 × 4) = 11 × 4 = 44 and 44 (11 × 4) + 32 (8 × 4) = 19 × 4 = 76 and 76 (19 × 4) × 3 + 44 (11 × 4) = 68 × 4 = 272 and 272 (68 × 4) + 76 (19 × 4) = 87 × 4 = 348.

It may also be proved that 4 is the greatest common measure; for, suppose there be a greater, then, since the greater measures 272 and 348, it will likewise measure the remainder 76; and since it measures 76 and 272, it also measures the remainder 44; and in the same manner it will be found to measure the remainder 4; that is the greater measure the less, which is absurd. Therefore 4 is the greatest common measure.]

*Mrs. D.* By finding the common factors, we can likewise obtain the least common multiple of any two or more numbers. Suppose it were required to find the least common multiple of 12, 36, and 48, then, since the greatest common factor is found to be 12,

$$12 \times 1 = 12$$
$$12 \times 3 = 36$$
$$12 \times 4 = 48$$

it follows that any number having 12, 4, and 3 as factors will be divisible by 12, 48, and 36; and that 12 × 4 × 3 is the least number which can be divided by these, and therefore it is their least common multiple, for it must have 1·2 and 3 as factors to be divisible by 36, and 12 and 4 to be divisible by 48; and since 3 and 4 are prime to each other, 12 × 3 × 4 is the least product divisible by those numbers.

Again, to find the least common multiple of 279, 496, and 1085.

$$\text{Here } 279 = 3 \times 3 \times 31 = 9 \times 31$$
$$496 = 8 \times 2 \times 31 = 16 \times 31$$
$$1085 = 5 \times 7 \times 31 = 35 \times 31$$

Now, if 9 were not a factor of the required number, it could not be divided by 279 (9 × 31); if 16 were not a factor, it could not be divided by 496 (16 × 31); and if 35 were not a factor, it could not be divided by 35 × 31 = 1085; and if 31 were not a factor it could not be divided by any of these numbers; therefore a number composed of the factors

$$9 \times 16 \times 35 \times 31 = \begin{cases} 279 \,(\, 9 \times 31) \times 35 \times 16 \\ 496 \,(16 \times 31) \times \, 9 \times 35 \\ 1085 \,(35 \times 31) \times \, 9 \times 16 \end{cases} = 156240$$

And since all these factors are prime to each other,

it follows that their product 156240 is their least common multiple, and therefore it is the least common multiple of 279, 496, 1085.

Now find the least common multiple of 28, 7, and 4.

*Ed.*
$$28 = 4 \times 7$$
$$7 = \quad 7$$
$$4 = \quad 4$$

Therefore any number divisible by 4 and 7 will be divisible by these 3 numbers, and $4 \times 7 = 28$ least common multiple of 28, 7, and 4.

(27) What is the least common multiple of 39, 54, and 63?

(28) Find the least common multiple of 127, 643, 587.

(29) Also of 144, 512, 316.    (30) And of 784, 656.

*Mrs. D.* You already know, that if any number be multiplied by another number, and then divided by that same number, the result is exactly the same as if it had not been multiplied or divided.

*Ed.* Oh yes; I learnt that ages ago, when you showed me how to prove my division sums.

*Emily.* Your ages are months, Edmund.

*Mrs. D.* Well, then, I am glad you have not forgotten this evident fact, although it is so many ages ago since you first had your attention drawn to it, and you feel certain that $\dfrac{8 \times 9}{9} = 8$, $\dfrac{59 \times 7}{7} = 59$, $\dfrac{8 \times 9 \times 5}{9}$

$= 8 \times 5$, $\dfrac{59 \times 7 \times 3}{7} = 59 \times 3$.

*Edmund.* Quite certain, without half a word of explanation.

*Mrs. D.* But $\dfrac{8 \times 9 \times 5}{9} = \dfrac{8 \times 45}{9}$ and $\dfrac{59 \times 7 \times 3}{7}$

$= \dfrac{59 \times 21}{7}$. Therefore, if I told you to multiply 8 by

45, and then divide by 9, the result would be exactly
the same if you merely multiplied 8 by 5.  Your work
in the one case would stand thus :  45

$$
\begin{array}{r}
45 \\
8 \\
\hline
9)360 \\
\hline
40
\end{array}
$$

Here, since 45 is the same as 9 $\times$ 5, you multiply
your 8 by 9, and then divide it by 9, which, you will
confess, is a very needless trouble : instead of this 5

$$
\begin{array}{r}
5 \\
8 \\
\hline
40
\end{array}
$$

is the only operation required.

Again, instead of multiplying 59 by 21, and then
dividing this by 7, we need only multiply by 3 to produce the same result.  The two workings would stand
thus :—

$$
\begin{array}{r}
59 \\
21 \\
\hline
59 \\
118 \\
\hline
7)1239 \\
\hline
177
\end{array}
\qquad
\begin{array}{r}
59 \\
3 \\
\hline
177
\end{array}
$$

*Ed.* And you may depend upon it, the second way will
always be my way.  I do not like to do that I may undo.

*Mrs. D.* This method of abridging labour is called
cancelling, and sometimes it happens, that, by having
recourse to it, many complicated calculations may be
reduced to extreme simplicity.  A facility in finding the
factors of numbers is, therefore, very useful in this as
well as in other respects to an arithmetician, since it
enables him at once to see how far cancelling may be
pursued, and this method cannot be applied to advantage
unless it can be readily practised.  Let us, then, dwell

somewhat on the subject, and reduce some expressions to their simplest forms.

*Ed.* What do you mean by their simplest forms?

*Mrs. D.* The putting of them in such a situation that their result may be produced with as little calculation as possible. Thus, $\dfrac{580 \times 7 \times 8}{112} = \dfrac{580 \times 7 \times 8}{2 \times 7 \times 8} = \dfrac{580}{2} = 290$. Or it saves the repetition of the figures to show the different steps thus: $\dfrac{\overset{290}{\cancel{580} \times \cancel{7} \times \cancel{8}}}{\underset{\underset{2}{16}}{\cancel{112}}} = 290.$

Here we have found by trial that 112 can be divided by 7 without a remainder, which we should express thus: $\dfrac{580 \times \cancel{7} \times 8}{\underset{16}{\cancel{112}}}$ drawing a line across or cancelling 7 and 112, putting 16 under 112 to show that $\dfrac{112}{7} = 16$; we have therefore, instead of multiplying by 7 and dividing by 7, cancelled this equal multiplier and divisor from the expression; again, $16 = 8 \times 2$; and, therefore, in like manner, we cancel the 8 thus: $\dfrac{580 \times \cancel{7} \times \cancel{8}}{\underset{\underset{2}{\cancel{16}}}{\cancel{112}}}$; lastly, we find that 2 is a factor of 580, and cancel the 2 thus:

$$\dfrac{\overset{290}{\cancel{580} \times \cancel{7} \times \cancel{8}}}{\underset{\underset{\cancel{2}}{\cancel{16}}}{\cancel{112}}} = 290$$

I have written down the expression at every different stage of the process, that you may the more readily trace its progress; but, of course, the whole may be done on the original expression. With a little practice the eye quickly catches the different factors, and the pencil is

rapidly drawn across the figures, thus:
$$\frac{348 \times 72}{96 \times 42} = \frac{87}{14}$$

the only numbers not cancelled. Now try if you cannot reduce $\dfrac{182 \times 216}{63 \times 24}$ to its simplest form.

*Ed.* There are one long multiplication and two long division sums: I hope we shall be able to do without them.

$$\frac{182 \times 216}{63 \times 24} = 26.$$

*Mrs. D.* Now see what you can do with $\dfrac{3456 \times 837}{243 \times 384}$.

*Ed.* $$\frac{3456 \times 837}{243 \times 384} = 31.$$

I will, just for this once, work the sum the long way, only that I may see what execution I have done with a few flourishes of my pencil.

$$3456$$
$$837$$
$$24192$$
$$10368$$
$$27648$$

243)2892672(384)11904(31

$$243 \qquad 1152$$

$$462 \qquad 384$$
$$243 \qquad 384$$

$$2196 \qquad \cdots$$
$$2187$$

$$972$$
$$972$$
$$\cdots$$

*Mrs. D.* In using the method of cancelling it is evident that we should defeat our purpose, which is the saving of time and trouble, if we try high factors, which we cannot work without an effort of the mind; it is not, therefore, recommended that recourse should be had to any factors higher than 12. Divisions with factors below that number can readily be mentally performed, and (*see* p. 71) it is at once found by inspection what of these factors any number contains. Now, reduce the following expressions to their simplest forms :—

(27) $\dfrac{576 \times 99}{1188 \times 48}$

(28) $\dfrac{484 \times 256}{704 \times 4 \times 11}$

(29) $\dfrac{144 \times 28 \times 63}{84 \times 36 \times 14}$

You will now, I think, be able to apply the cancelling system to practice, by means of the following examples :—

I

Q. 26. If 120 bushels of corn can serve 6 horses 56 days, how many days will 94 bushels serve 14 horses?

First $\dfrac{120 \times 14}{6}$ will serve 14 horses for 56 days, and

$\dfrac{120 \times 14}{6 \times 56}$ will serve 14 horses for 1 day; therefore, since they eat that quantity in 1 day, they will eat 94 bushels

in $94 \div \dfrac{120 \times 14}{6 \times 56}$ days, equal (*see* p. 57) $94 \times 6 \times 56$

$= \dfrac{94}{5} = 18$ days, and 4 remainder.

Q. 27. At a meeting held for the relief of the poor, 36 gentlemen agreed each to contribute 405 bushels of coals for sale at a cheap rate. This fuel was sent in equal quantities to 5 different stations, and at each station it was distributed equally among 486 poor families; how much fell to the share of each family?

Q. 28. If a family of 9 persons expend £120 in 4 months, how much will serve a family of 24 people during 8 months?

Q. 29. If a garrison of soldiers, consisting of 2268 men, consume 1296 cwt. of flour in 14 weeks, how much will 245 men consume in the same time?

Q. 30. If I spend £252 in 21 weeks, how much shall I spend at the same rate in 4 weeks?

---

## Chapter IV.

*Mrs. D.* You will think we are going many steps back when I now call your attention to the expression $\dfrac{8}{4}$, you are perfectly familiar with this manner of expressing that 8 is to be divided by 4, and that, in general terms, any two numbers so situated, show that the upper number is to be divided by the lower. When the upper number is less than the lower number, as $\frac{2}{3}$, the expression is called a fraction or *broken* number; when the upper number is more than the lower, but cannot be divided by the latter without a remainder, as $\frac{4}{3}$, the expression is called an improper fraction, but in every case the expression means exactly the same, and simply denotes that the upper number is to be divided by the lower. Thus, $\frac{1}{3}$ means that 1 is to be divided into three equal parts, or thirds, that $\frac{2}{3}$ are two of these thirds, that $\frac{3}{3}$ are three of these thirds, or one whole; that $\frac{4}{3}$ are 4 of these thirds, or one whole and one-third, which may likewise be expressed thus $1\frac{1}{3}$. In the same manner $\frac{1}{4}$ means 1 is to be divided into 4 equal parts, or that it is a fourth part of one; so $\frac{1}{5}$, or one divided into 5 equal parts, is called one-fifth; $\frac{1}{6}$, one-sixth, and so on. A whole number is called an integer, and a number composed of integers and fractions is called a mixed number.

*Ed.* Here is an unit-counter—now, how can I divide this into a number of equal parts—how can I divide it by 4, for example?

*Mrs. D.* *You* cannot divide it into 4 equal parts, because it is made of too hard a material, this might, however, be accomplished with proper instruments, and, in
the meantime, we can mark it out into four equal parts
with our pencil, thus—

or into six, or into any other number of equal parts, and
each portion would be correctly expressed by $\frac{1}{4}$ or by $\frac{1}{6}$,
or 1 divided by any number of parts into which the counter
is divided. If you would rather see the pieces separate,
let us take this wafer and cut it into six equal parts—

and now let us join them together again as a whole.
Well, here are $\frac{6}{6} = 1$.

*Ed.* Yes; now I understand that $\frac{1}{3}$ this fraction, as it
is called, only means one of these pieces, and that all of
them added together $\frac{1}{6} + \frac{1}{6} + \frac{1}{6} + \frac{1}{6} + \frac{1}{6} + \frac{1}{6} = 1$, or
the whole.

*Mrs. D.* Exactly so. Now let us cut another wafer
into the same number of equal parts, and, if from each
wafer you take one of these parts, what portion of each
will you have?

*Ed.* Each of these is a sixth, and therefore I have
got two-sixths in my hand.

*Mrs. D.* And what part of the two wafers are these
two-sixths?

*Ed.* I have taken a sixth from each of them, and so I have taken a sixth of the two.

*Mrs. D.* Therefore, two-sixths, or $\frac{2}{6}$, are the same as $\frac{1}{6}$ of 2, and in the same manner we may prove that $\frac{3}{6}$ is the same as $\frac{1}{6}$ of 3. In like manner, if you take 2 of these parts of each of the two wafers, then you will have $\frac{4}{6}$, or $\frac{2}{6}$ of 2; if you take 3 parts from each you will then have $\frac{6}{6}$, or $\frac{3}{6}$ of 2. Therefore, in general terms, a part or parts of any number, is that part or those parts of one multiplied by the number, thus, $\frac{1}{7}$ of 8, is $\frac{8}{7}$; $\frac{1}{9}$ of 7 is $\frac{7}{9}$; and so on; $\frac{2}{7}$ of 8 are $\frac{16}{7}$; $\frac{4}{9}$ of 7 are $\frac{28}{9}$; $\frac{5}{6}$ of 9 are $\frac{45}{6}$; and so on.

What are $\frac{3}{8}$ of 9; $\frac{6}{11}$ of 7; $\frac{9}{10}$ of 13; $\frac{11}{15}$ of 15?

———

From what has been said, you will readily perceive that in a fraction the lower number *denotes* the parts into which the whole is to be divided, and thence it is called the denominator; the upper number enumerates the number of these parts, and thence it is called the numerator. Thus, in $\frac{8}{9}$, 9 is called the denominator, and 8 is called the numerator, meaning that 1 is to be divided into 9 parts, and 8 of these parts are to be taken. But, although these terms are used, always keep in mind that a fraction merely expresses that the upper number is to be divided by the lower. Under this point of view fractions are as easily managed as whole numbers.

*Mrs. D.* If you cut this strip of paper into 5 equal parts, each of these parts will be—

*Ed.* One-fifth, or $\frac{1}{5}$.

*Mrs. D.* And if you again divide each of these equal parts into any other number of equal parts, say 9, how many pieces will you have altogether?

*Ed.* 5 × 9 or 45.

*Mrs. D.* Then, each of these pieces will be $\frac{1}{45}$ of the whole strip, and since each of the 5 equal parts contains 9 of these, it follows that $\frac{1}{5}$ is the same as $\frac{9}{45}$; that $\frac{2}{5}$ are the same as $\frac{18}{45}$; $\frac{3}{5}$, the same as $\frac{27}{45}$, and so on.

*Alfred.* This has been already proved more than once, for $\frac{5}{45}$ is the same as $\frac{1 \times 5}{9 \times 5}$, and therefore $\frac{5}{45}$ merely expresses $\frac{1}{9}$ multiplied by 5 and divided by 5.

*Mrs. D.* Very true; but when simple principles are made to apply very extensively to practice, it is as well to draw the attention of a young pupil to their new application, through the medium of his senses; and this method, more than any abstract reasoning, will, I believe, initiate Edmund in the true nature of fractions, and convince him that they are to be treated as whole numbers.

Now I do not doubt he feels quite certain that if, instead of dividing this piece of paper into 5 equal parts, he had divided them into any other number of equal parts, and again, instead of dividing each of these parts into other 9 equal parts, he had divided them into any other number of equal parts, the second number, divided by the whole number of parts, is the same as the whole, or one divided by the first number. Thus, $\dfrac{6}{18} = \dfrac{5}{15} =$

$\dfrac{4}{12} = \dfrac{3}{9} = \dfrac{2}{6} = \dfrac{1}{3}$; and $\dfrac{40}{45} = \dfrac{32}{36} = \dfrac{24}{27} = \dfrac{16}{18} = \dfrac{8}{9}$.

*Ed.* Yes, all this is very plain.

*Mrs. D.* Here $\dfrac{1}{3}$ and $\dfrac{8}{9}$ are fractions reduced to their lowest denomination, that is, the whole is divided into as few number of parts as the nature of the fraction will admit of, and the numerator and denominator are prime to each other. The method of cancelling at once shows how to reduce fractions to their lowest denomination. For example—

$$\frac{6}{18} = \frac{1}{3}; \quad \frac{40}{45} = \frac{\overset{8}{\cancel{40}}}{\underset{9}{\cancel{45}}} = \frac{8}{9};$$

$$\frac{96}{672} = \frac{\overset{\overset{\overset{1}{\cancel{3}}}{\cancel{12}}}{\cancel{96}}}{\underset{\underset{7}{\cancel{21}}}{\underset{\cancel{84}}{\cancel{672}}}} = \frac{1}{7}; \quad \frac{91}{119} = \frac{\overset{13}{\cancel{91}}}{\underset{17}{\cancel{119}}} = \frac{13}{17}.$$

Q. 31. Reduce $\dfrac{48}{272}$ to its lowest denomination.

Q. 32. Reduce $\dfrac{192}{576}$ to its lowest denomination .

Q. 33. Reduce $\frac{825}{960}$ to its lowest denomination.

Q. 34. Reduce $\frac{5184}{6912}$ to its lowest denomination.

Q. 35. Reduce $\frac{252}{364}$ to its lowest denomination.

———

*Mrs. D.* We have seen that $\frac{1}{5}$ of 8 is $\frac{8}{5}$, and that $\frac{2}{5}$ of 8 are $\frac{16}{5}$; now can you tell me what $\frac{2}{5}$ of $\frac{8}{4}$ are?

*Ed.* $\frac{8}{4} = 2$; so $\frac{2}{5}$ of $\frac{8}{4}$ is $\frac{2}{5}$ of 2, or $\frac{4}{5}$.

*Mrs. D.* If the 8, instead of being divided by 4, were divided by 9, what then would $\frac{2}{5}$ of $\frac{8}{9}$ be?

*Ed.* It would be much more puzzling to find this out, and I must think a great deal before I should know how to manage it.

$\frac{2}{5}$ of $\frac{8}{9}$

$\frac{40}{45} = \frac{8}{9}$

*Mrs. D.* At your last lesson you convinced yourself that $\frac{40}{45}$ are the same as $\frac{8}{9}$, that is to say, that $\frac{8}{9}$ of these 45 pieces of paper are 40; and $\frac{1}{5}$ of these 40 pieces is 8, since they can be divided into 5 equal parts, each containing 8, and therefore $\frac{2}{5}$ of $\frac{40}{45}$ $\left(\text{or } \frac{2}{5} \text{ of } \frac{8}{9}\right)$ will be $2 \times \frac{8}{45} = \frac{16}{45}$.

Now let us retrace our steps, that we may see what operations we have been performing to produce this result.

*Ed.* First just tell me why you brought the $\frac{8}{9}$ into $\frac{40}{45}$.

*Mrs. D.* In order that $\frac{8}{9}$ might be such a number of parts that these could be divided into 5 parts without a remainder.

*Ed.* But how did you know that 45 was that number?

*Mrs. D.* I knew it must be a number that could be divided by 9 and by 5, therefore I took their product; if it had not been divisible by 9 as well as by 5, the whole could not have been divided into 9 equal parts. To obtain a new denominator we therefore multiply the two denominators together. To find the numerator, or the number of parts of the new denominator, we first multiplied the 8 by 5 to make $\frac{8}{9} = \frac{40}{45}$; we then divided this product into 5 equal parts, and so we multiplied by 5 and then divided by 5, two unnecessary operations in practice, but which I did in the present case that you might clearly understand what we were about; we next multiplied the 8 (which had gone through these evolutions unchanged) by 2, because 8 was one-fifth and we wanted two-fifths; so we have simply to multiply the two numerators together for a new numerator, and the two denominators together for a new denominator, and $\frac{2}{5}$ of $\frac{8}{9} =$ $\frac{2 \times 8}{5 \times 9} = \frac{16}{45}$. I prefer that you should satisfy yourself of the truth of any rule by the evidence of your senses, otherwise the same might be more simply explained. Thus $\frac{2}{5}$ of $\frac{8}{9}$ are $\frac{2}{5}$ of $8 \div 9$; now $\frac{2}{5}$ of $8 = \frac{16}{5}$ and $\frac{16}{5}$

$$\div 9 = \frac{16}{5 \times 9} = \frac{16}{45}.$$ Hence the rule. So $\frac{4}{7}$ of $\frac{9}{10} = \frac{36}{70}$

$$\frac{\overset{18}{\cancel{36}}}{\underset{35}{\cancel{70}}} = \frac{18}{35}; \frac{5}{8} \text{ of } \frac{7}{9} = \frac{35}{72}.$$

Q. 36. What are $\frac{6}{11}$ of $\frac{12}{13}$?

Q. 37. What are $\frac{9}{10}$ of $\frac{7}{8}$?

Q. 38. Find $\frac{13}{17}$ of $\frac{19}{20}$.

———

*Ed.* I have promised Alfred $\frac{3}{8}$ of my cake, and Emily $\frac{2}{5}$; how can I manage to give them their exact shares?

*Mrs. D.* If you had to give away $\frac{3}{8}$ and $\frac{2}{5}$ of 40 nuts, you could accomplish that without much difficulty, I imagine?

*Ed.* Oh yes; for these divided into 8 parts would be 5 in each part, and therefore $\frac{1}{8}$ would be 5, and $\frac{3}{8}$ would be $5 \times 3 = 15$; so $\frac{1}{5}$ would be 8, and $\frac{2}{5}$ 16, and I should give Alfred 15, and Emily 16.

*Mrs. D.* Well, then, if I divide your cake into 40 equal parts, you will have no more difficulty with your cake than with your nuts; the one will have $\frac{15}{40}$, and the other $\frac{16}{40}$, of the whole cake.

*Ed.* Yes, if *I* have not the dividing of it, that will be easy enough. I know why you choose to divide the whole into 40, or 8 × 5, now, for the same reason that you gave me at my last lesson.

*Mrs. D.* Yes; the whole number of pieces must be divisible by 8 and by 5, in order that an eighth and a fifth may be certain numbers of these parts. Now since $\frac{1}{8}$ is the same as $\frac{5}{8 \times 5}$, $\frac{3}{8}$ will be equal to $\frac{3 \times 5}{8 \times 5} = \frac{15}{40}$, and $\frac{2}{5}$ will be equal $\frac{2 \times 8}{5 \times 8} = \frac{16}{40}$. This is called bringing the two fractions to a common denominator, and in the same way any two or more fractions may be brought to a common denominator, and hence the rule, multiply all the denominators together to obtain a new denominator, which will, therefore, be divisible by any of the denominators. To continue a fraction of its original value, it is evident, from what has gone before, that the numerator must be multiplied as many times as the denominator is multiplied, that is, in the present case, by the product of all the denominators except its own. Thus, to bring $\frac{2}{7}$ and $\frac{6}{11}$ to a common denominator.

$$\frac{2 \times 11}{7 \times 11} = \frac{22}{77} = \text{first fraction.}$$

$$\frac{6 \times 7}{11 \times 7} = \frac{42}{77} = \text{second fraction.}$$

*Ed.* This will be more troublesome when there are more than two fractions.

*Mrs. D.* Exactly the same, only rather more multiplication.

*Ed.* Suppose I were to give you $\frac{4}{7}$ of my cake, as well as Alfred $\frac{3}{8}$, and Emily $\frac{2}{5}$; now tell me how many pieces would you divide it in?

*Mrs. D.* I am afraid you will then have promised too much of your cake; but let us see. $\frac{3}{8}$, $\frac{2}{5}$, and $\frac{4}{7}$, are here to be brought to one common denominator. Then

$$\frac{3 \times 5 \times 7}{8 \times 5 \times 7} = \frac{105}{280} = \text{first fraction.}$$

$$\frac{2 \times 8 \times 7}{5 \times 8 \times 7} = \frac{112}{280} = \text{second fraction.}$$

$$\frac{4 \times 8 \times 5}{7 \times 8 \times 5} = \frac{160}{280} = \text{third fraction.}$$

Now try if you can bring some fractions to a common denominator; and to-morrow we will return to the cake.

Q. 39. Bring $\frac{5}{9}$, $\frac{3}{11}$, and $\frac{7}{8}$, to a common denominator.

Q. 40. Likewise $\frac{13}{16}$ and $\frac{9}{15}$. Q. 41. $\frac{8}{9}$ and $\frac{16}{31}$.

*Ed.* Must I multiply these high numbers in my head, mother?

*Mrs. D.* No; you may perform all the operations on your slate, only prepare your numbers in the manner I have done, as then you can never become confused, or hesitate for a moment what numbers are to be multiplied together

In some cases the process may, however, be much abridged. We multiply all the denominators together to obtain a common multiple of these denominators; but when they are not prime to each other, this, it is evident, will not be their least common multiple (*see* p. 80), and therefore we bring the fractions into a higher denomi-

nation than is necessary. For example, let us bring
$\frac{5}{12}, \frac{11}{36}$, and $\frac{13}{48}$, into fractions, having one common denominator; here $12 \times 3 \times 4 = 144 =$ least common
multiple of 12, 36, and 48; therefore

$$\frac{5}{12} = \frac{5 \times 3 \times 4}{12 \times 3 \times 4} = \frac{60}{144}.$$

$$\frac{11}{36} = \frac{11 \times 4}{36 \times 4} = \frac{44}{144}.$$

$$\frac{13}{48} = \frac{13 \times 3}{48 \times 3} = \frac{39}{144}.$$

*Mrs. D.* When we supposed your cake to be divided
into 40 equal parts, you assigned to Alfred 15 of these
parts, and 16 to Emily. How many would they then
have between them?

*Ed.* $15 + 16 = 31.$

*Mrs. D.* And how many more would Emily have
than Alfred?

*Ed.* $16 - 15 = 1.$

*Mrs. D.* And how many would you have left?

*Ed.* $40 - 31 = 9.$

*Mrs. D.* You see then we can, without any difficulty,
add and subtract fractions by first bringing them to a
common denominator. Thus you have found that $\frac{3}{8} +$
$\frac{2}{5} = \frac{31}{40}$; that $\frac{2}{5} - \frac{3}{8} = \frac{1}{40}$; and that $1 - \left(\frac{3}{2} + \frac{2}{5}\right)$, or
$1 - \frac{31}{40}$, or $\frac{40}{40} - \frac{31}{40} = \frac{9}{40}.$

*Ed.* Now let us see, when I have given you your
share of cake, what I shall have left for myself.

K

*Mrs. D.* We have supposed the cake, in that case, to be divided into 280 parts (*p.* 96), and of these Alfred's, or

The first share is 105
The second share 112
The third share 160
$$\overline{377}$$

So, to give us the proportions you promised us, you must give us 377 of those pieces.

*Ed.* But I have only got 280 pieces—how is that, mother?

*Mrs. D.* You have then promised more than your whole cake—that is a sad mistake.

*Ed.* I never thought that $\frac{3}{8}$, and $\frac{2}{5}$, and $\frac{4}{7}$, would have been together more than the whole, and now I find that they are a great deal more.

*Mrs. D.* Well, what is to be done that you may fulfil your engagements?

*Ed.* I believe that I must get another cake of exactly the same size, and divide it into exactly the same number of equal parts.

*Mrs. D.* And how much of this second cake will you be obliged to give us?

*Ed.* As many more pieces as 377 exceed 280; these I find are 97; so here are my first 280 pieces, or one whole, and here are 97 pieces more, which together will will make up your $\frac{377}{280} = \frac{3}{8} + \frac{2}{5} + \frac{4}{7}$.

*Mrs. D.* Thus, it is clear that a number of fractions added together may amount to more than one whole, and the result may be an improper fraction, which, in order to furnish the proper answer, we must change into a mixed number, thus, $\frac{377}{280} = 1\frac{97}{280}$: in the same manner we find $\dfrac{536}{6} = \dfrac{268}{3} = 89\,\dfrac{1}{3}$; because we find by division that there are 89 threes in 268, and one remainder, or 1 still left to be divided by 3. Therefore, in the addition and subtraction of fractions, we must bring them into others of the same value having a common denominator; then add or subtract them, and reduce the fraction thus obtained to its simplest form.

Add together $\dfrac{1}{7}$ and $\dfrac{1}{8}$; and likewise find their difference.

$Ed.$ $\left.\begin{array}{l}\dfrac{1\times 8}{7\times 8}=\dfrac{8}{56}\\[2mm]\dfrac{1\times 7}{7\times 8}=\dfrac{7}{56}\end{array}\right\} = \dfrac{8+7}{56} =$ their sum, and $\dfrac{8-7}{56}$ = their difference.

$Mrs.\ D.$ Here, since each of the numerators is only one unit, the numerator of the one multiplied by the denominator of the other, is simply the latter number, and therefore the sum or difference of two fractions which have only units for their numerator is simply the sum or difference of the denominators divided by their product. Thus $\dfrac{1}{2}+\dfrac{1}{3}=\dfrac{3+2}{2\times 3}=\dfrac{5}{6}$, and $\dfrac{1}{2}-\dfrac{1}{3}=\dfrac{3-2}{2\times 3}=\dfrac{1}{6}$. What are $\dfrac{1}{6}+\dfrac{1}{9}$? Find the difference of $\dfrac{1}{5}$ and $\dfrac{1}{11}$.

Now let us add together three fractions: $5\,\dfrac{7}{9}+8\,\dfrac{6}{11}+\dfrac{9}{10}=5+8+\dfrac{7}{9}+\dfrac{6}{11}+\dfrac{9}{10}$; $5+8=13$ we have no concern with at present.

K 2

$$\frac{7 \times 11 \times 10}{9 \times 11 \times 10} = \frac{770}{990}$$    770 1st numerator.

$$\frac{6 \times 9 \times 10}{11 \times 9 \times 10} = \frac{540}{990}$$    540 2nd.

$$\frac{9 \times 11 \times 9}{10 \times 11 \times 9} = \frac{891}{990}$$    891 3rd.
                                                        2201

So these fractions added together are $\frac{2201}{990}$, which we find by division to be $= 2\frac{221}{990}$; to this number the 13 we added together at first must be added, making the sum of the fractions and the two whole numbers equal to $15\frac{221}{990}$.

Shall we now find the difference of two mixed numbers?

*Ed.* Yes; $5\frac{2}{7}$ and $3\frac{8}{9}$.

*Mrs. D.* Here $\frac{2}{7} = \frac{2 \times 9}{7 \times 9} = \frac{18}{63}$.

$$\frac{8}{9} = \frac{8 \times 7}{9 \times 7} = \frac{56}{63}.$$

Therefore $5\frac{18}{63} - 3\frac{56}{63} = 2\frac{18}{63} - \frac{56}{63}$.

But $\frac{56}{63}$ are more than $\frac{18}{63}$; so we must take $\frac{56}{63}$ from one of the whole numbers, or change one of the whole numbers into 63 parts, thus: $1\frac{18}{63} + \frac{63}{63} - \frac{56}{63} = 1\frac{18}{63} + \frac{7}{63} = 1\frac{25}{63}$.

Q. 42. Add $\frac{2}{7} + \frac{3}{11} + \frac{6}{13}$.

Q. 43.   Likewise $3\frac{5}{16} + 7\frac{3}{10}$.

Q. 44.   Find the difference of $\frac{6}{7}$ and $\frac{4}{9}$.

Q. 45.   Take $2\frac{5}{9}$ from $6\frac{2}{7}$.

---

*Ed.* Emily tells me that two fractions multiplied together are less than either of those numbers, and that $\frac{1}{3} \times \frac{1}{2}$ is only $\frac{1}{6}$; now to make a number less by multiplying it, does seem an odd kind of multiplication.

*Mrs. D.* The fact as Emily states it is quite correct, although the term in general use makes it appear incongruous. To talk of multiplying one-third by one-half—of multiplying a number by less than unity, is, I quite agree with you, a palpable contradiction; but if we consider that $\frac{1}{2}$ truly represents 1 divided by 2; then $\frac{1}{3}$ taken one time or once still remains $\frac{1}{3}$, but this 1 time is to be divided by 2; therefore $\frac{1}{3}$ divided by two $= \frac{1}{3} \div 2 = \frac{1}{3 \times 2} = \frac{1}{6}$; that is to say, $\frac{1}{2}$ of $\frac{1}{3}$ is equal to $\frac{1}{6}$.

*Ed.* Then, instead of saying a third multiplied by a half, it would be better to say a third taken once and divided by two.

*Mrs. D.* Most certainly, if it be desirable to use accurate language through which only we can hope to obtain clear well-defined ideas. Now try $\frac{2}{7} \times \frac{4}{2}$.

K 3

*Ed.* This is $\frac{2}{7}$ taken 4 times, or multiplied by 4, which is to be divided by 2, so $\frac{2}{7} \times 4 \div 2 = \frac{2 \times 4}{7 \times 2} = \frac{8}{14} = \frac{4}{7}$, which is of course exactly the same as if I had divided the 4 first by 2, and then multiplied the other fraction by 2, or $\frac{2}{7} \times 2 = \frac{4}{7}$; in multiplying first by 4 and then by 2, I see I have been doing double work.

*Mrs. D.* I am glad that you have discovered this; but I was desirous that you should go the long road in this case, in order to convince your senses that there was nothing mysterious in what is called multiplication of fractions. If the 4 were divided by 9 instead of 2, then the expression would be $\frac{2}{7} \times \frac{4}{9}$, and you would proceed exactly as you did at first $\frac{2}{7} \times 4 \div 9 = \frac{2 \times 4}{7} \div 9 = \frac{2 \times 4}{7 \times 9} = \frac{8}{63}$. Hence the rule, multiply the numerators together for a new numerator, and the denominators together for a new denominator. Whether the expression be two fractions thus, $\frac{8}{7} \times \frac{4}{9} = \frac{8 \times 4}{7 \times 9}$, or three fractions thus, $\frac{2}{7} \times \frac{4}{9} \times \frac{3}{8} = \frac{2 \times 4 \times 3}{7 \times 9 \times 8}$, or any other number of fractions, it is plain that the result will in the same manner be truly obtained. Try

(35) $\frac{6}{11} \times \frac{5}{13}$; (36) $\frac{8}{15} \times \frac{9}{16} \times \frac{10}{17}$;

(37) $3\frac{7}{9} \times 8\frac{5}{6}$; (38) $5\frac{4}{7} \times \frac{3}{5}$.

*Ed.* How am I to multiply $3\frac{7}{9}$ by $8\frac{5}{6}$?

*Mrs. D.* By bringing the mixed numbers to impro-

per fractions thus: $3\frac{7}{9} = \frac{3 \times 9}{9} + \frac{7}{9} = \frac{34}{9}$, and $8\frac{5}{6}$

$= \frac{53}{6}$; therefore we have $\frac{34}{9} \times \frac{53}{6} = \frac{\overset{17}{\cancel{34}} \times 53}{9 \times \underset{3}{\cancel{6}}} = \frac{901}{27}$

$= 33\frac{10}{27}$.

---

*Ed.* I suppose, since division is the reverse of multi-plication, that a fraction divided by a fraction will make it a greater instead of a less number. What is $\frac{1}{2} \div \frac{1}{3}$, mother?

*Mrs. D.* $1\frac{1}{2}$, and I hope I shall be able to convince you that this is the true answer. As $1 \div 3$ expresses that 1 is to be divided into 3 parts, each of which will be $\frac{1}{3}$, so $1 \div \frac{1}{3}$ expresses the number of times into which it can be divided into thirds; but there are three of these in one, and therefore $1 \div \frac{1}{3}$ will be equal to 3, or, that is to say, there are 3 thirds in one: in like manner there are $1\frac{1}{2}$ thirds in $\frac{1}{2}$; and 6 thirds in 2, and so on. There-fore $\frac{1}{2} \div \frac{1}{3} = 1\frac{1}{2}$; and $2 \div \frac{1}{3} = 6$. The same may be proved otherwise by common division, if we divide 1 by $\frac{1}{3}$, 1 is the dividend, and $\frac{1}{3}$ the divisor, then (see *p.* ) if we multiply them both by the same number, the result will be the same as if we had not multiplied by that number—let us then multiply them in this case both by 3, and we shall have $1 \div \dfrac{1}{3} = 3 \div \dfrac{3}{3} = 3 \div 1 = 3$ and $\dfrac{1}{2} \div \dfrac{1}{3} = \dfrac{3}{2} \div \dfrac{3}{3} = \dfrac{3}{2} \div 1 = 1\dfrac{1}{2}$.  Now, try $1 \div \dfrac{15}{5}$, multiply by 5, then $5 \div \dfrac{15 \times 5}{5} = 5 \div 15 = \dfrac{5}{15} = \dfrac{1}{3}$.

*Ed.* Ah, here, and for the same reason as in multiplication, we have been doing double work again, and $1 \div \dfrac{15}{5}$, is the same as $1 \div 3 = \dfrac{1}{3}$.

*Mrs. D.* Now, try $\dfrac{3}{7} \div \dfrac{5}{8}$.

*Ed.* To get rid of the fraction in the divisor we must multiply both by 8, so $\dfrac{3}{7} \div \dfrac{5}{8} = \dfrac{3 \times 8}{7} \div \dfrac{5 \times 8}{8} = \dfrac{3 \times 8}{7} \div 5 = \dfrac{3 \times 8}{7 \times 5}$.

*Mrs. D.* Very well ; I perceive you understand clearly how to manage these fractional divisors and dividends; but let us examine into our different operations.—We first multiply both numerators by the denominator of the divisor, which, in this latter, only serves to cancel its denominator, and then we divide the dividend by the numerator of the divisor.  Or, simply, we multiply the numerator of the dividend by the denominator of the divisor for a new numerator, and multiply the denominator of the dividend by the numerator of the divisor for a new denominator.  Therefore, in working a sum in division, we should pass over the intermediate steps, which I have only used at present that you might the better understand the reasons for what we were doing. Thus, $\frac{3}{7} \div \frac{5}{8}$, we should at once write $\frac{3 \times 8}{7 \times 5} = \frac{24}{35}$.

(39) What are $\frac{6}{11} \div \frac{3}{4}$?

(40) Divide $\frac{9}{13}$ by $\frac{2}{5}$.

(41) Divide $3\frac{8}{15}$ by $\frac{4}{9}$.

---

## QUESTIONS IN FRACTIONS.

Q. 46. If one man can mow a piece of grass in 8 hours, and another man in 12 hours, how long will they take if they both work together? Here, since the first man can do the whole in 8 hours, it follows he can do $\frac{1}{8}$ in 1 hour, and the second man can do $\frac{1}{12}$ in 1 hour, therefore, both together they will do $\frac{1}{8} + \frac{1}{12}$ in 1 hour, equal to $\frac{8 + 12}{8 \times 12} = \frac{20}{96} = \frac{10}{48} = \frac{5}{24}$; therefore, they could both together do 5 pieces in 24 hours, and 1 piece of work in $\frac{1}{5}$ of that time, or 1 piece in $\frac{24}{5}$ hours $= 4\frac{4}{5}$ hours.

Q. 47. Divide 1 into 3 such parts that they may be in the proportion to each other of 5, 4, and 7; that is to say, that the 1st may have 5 equal portions, the 2nd 4, and the 3rd 7, all together making up one whole. If we divide the whole into $5 + 4 + 7 = 16$ equal parts, then it is evident that the conditions of the question can be readily answered, and that

the 1st will have $\dfrac{5}{16}$,

the 2nd . . $\dfrac{4}{16}$, and

the 3rd . . $\dfrac{7}{16}$,

and if instead of one whole we had any other number, say 27, to be thus divided, each would have that part of 27; the 1st $\dfrac{5}{16} \times 27$, the 2nd $\dfrac{4}{16} \times 27$, and the 3rd $\dfrac{7}{16} \times 27$.

---

Q. 48. A market gardener divided 5 acres of ground into 4 compartments—in the first he planted potatoes, in the second turnips, in the third cabbages, and the fourth carrots, the sizes of the different compartments were in the proportion of 6, 4, 3, and 2, how much space did he devote to each crop?

Q. 49. D., E., and F., join their stocks in trade; the amount of their stocks is £647, the respective contributions are in the proportion of 4, 6, and 8, and the amount of their gains is equal to D.'s stock; what is each man's stock and gain?

Q. 50. A farmer gave 19 bushels of corn to 13 of his labourers in part payment of their wages; this quantity was divided equally between them,—one of the men sold $\dfrac{2}{5}$ of his share, what part of the whole had he remaining, and what part of the whole did he sell?

Q. 51. If A. can do a piece of work in 9 days, and B. can do it in 7 days, how long will they take doing it together?

Q. 52. If A. can do a piece of work in 9 days, B. in 7, and C. in 8, how long will they take doing it all working together?

Q. 53. If A. and B. can do a piece of work in 4 days, and B. working alone takes 10 days, how long will A. take doing it by himself?

Q. 54. The following cause of dispute is found related in an Arabian manuscript :—Two Arabians sat down to dinner, one had 5 loaves, the other had 3 : a stranger passing by desired permission to eat with them, which they agreed to. The stranger dined, laid down 8 pieces of money, and departed. The proprietor of the 5 loaves took up 5 pieces and left 3 for the other, who objected, and insisted upon having half. The cause came on before Ali, the magistrate, who gave the following judgment :—" Let the owner of the 5 loaves have 7 pieces of money, and the owner of the 3 loaves 1." Prove the justice of the sentence.

---

## Chapter VII.

*Edmund.* FRACTIONS are easily managed when their denominators are low; but when these become high, I find, from the questions you have given me to do, that it is often a very troublesome and tedious process to bring them to a common denomination before I can add the fractions together; or to convert mixed numbers into improper fractions before multiplication.

*Mrs. D.* It would then be better if some fractions could be used which had not these inconveniences, and which could be operated upon with as much ease as whole numbers.

*Ed.* That would, indeed, be a fine invention; do you think it could be done?

*Mrs. D.* We have found the great advantages of the notation of whole numbers in facilitating calculations, could we not manage to make fractions equally easy? It is evident that $\frac{1}{10}$, or one-tenth, bears the same relation to one unit as one unit bears to one, that is to say, $\frac{1}{10}$ is contained as many times in 1 as 1 is contained in 10; and $\frac{1}{100}$, or one-hundredth part of one unit is contained as many times in 1 as 1 is contained in 100, and so on. If, then, we use fractional numbers, which according as they are placed *decrease* in value in the same regular manner as whole numbers *increase* in value, it is evident that we could operate upon them with as much ease as if they were integers. Fractions formed of tenths, hundredths, thousandths, &c., could be as readily added together as units, tens, hundreds, thousands, &c.

*Ed.* So they could, if we knew how to get rid of their denominators.

*Mrs. D.* Let us try.—Here are tens and units,—the placing the tens before the units expresses that the former are each ten times the value of one unit. Now, cannot you discover some method of denoting tenths without the use of a denominator?

*Ed.* I could place them after the units, and that

would show that each unit was of ten times greater value
than each tenth. Here are my units placed between
my tens and tenths, but see, how are you to know,
unless I tell you, that this number 372 means thirty-
seven and two-tenths? you would directly say that it
was three hundred and seventy-two: so my plan will not
do, and I cannot find out any other.

*Mrs. D.* Do not be in so much haste to reject this
arrangement; it only wants a very slight addition to
make it quite intelligible. Suppose we put a point after
the units, thus 37.2, then this number can readily be
distinguished from 372.

*Ed.* Oh, yes; and I should directly know that 37.2
means $37 \frac{2}{10}$; that is a most excellent contrivance.

*Mrs. D.* We cannot, however, lay claim to the discovery. Such fractions were invented a very long time
ago, and they are always used in long and difficult
calculations; their extensive application and importance
in the higher branches of mathematics can scarcely be
known and appreciated by the mere arithmetician; you
will one day, I trust, be acquainted with their full value.
These fractions are called decimals, from the Latin word
*decem*, ten, because their denominations are tenths, ten-
tenths, &c.

*Ed.* So, now I know what decimals are. I did not
expect that this would have meant such an easy matter,
for I always fancied they were very difficult—so difficult
that very few people knew anything about them.

*Mrs. D.* I hope you will soon be quite as familiar with
them as with whole numbers. Once clearly define the
place of the units, and it is then easy to remember that
the places of figures decrease in value as they recede
from the place of units on the right hand, exactly in the

L

same manner as they increase in value on the left of the units, thus—

> ᏸ Thousands
> ᴑ Hundreds
> ᴈ Tens
> ᴔ Units
> ᴀ Tenths
> ᴙ Hundredths
> ᴦ Thousandths, &c.

The number .5736 expresses five tenths, seven hundredths, three thousandths, and six ten-thousandths; 5.736 expresses five units, seven tenths, three hundredths, and six thousandths; 57.36 expresses five tens, seven units, three tenths, and six hundredths; 573.6 expresses five hundred, seven tens, three units, and six tenths; 5736 expresses five thousand, seven hundred, three tens, and six units. You perceive that this notation is exactly the same as that of whole numbers—the value of any number being increased ten times by the removal of this point one step on the right hand, in the same way as the value of a whole number is increased by putting a nought after it, and this altering of the situation of the point is, in fact, the same as multiplying by ten. Thus 5.736 = .5736 × 10; 57.36 = 5.736 × 10; 573.6 = 57.36 × 10; 5736 = 573.6 × 10; 57360 = 5736 × 10; and so on.

Now express in decimal notation—

4 hundredths and 7 thousandths.

3 units, 8 tenths, and 9 hundredths.

9 units, 7 tenths, and 5 thousandths.

*Ed.* In the first example, how am I to show that there are no tenths?

*Mrs. D.* Recollect that, in decimal notation, tenths,

hundredths, &c., have their places as well as tens, hundreds, &c. : how do you keep the places of the latter ?

*Ed.* Oh, I forgot; noughts are the place-keepers—so after putting a point to show that there are no units, I suppose we must put a nought to show the place of tenths, and the number will be written .047.

*Mrs. D.* Thus the notation of decimals is, in this respect, the reverse of whole numbers ; noughts placed on the left hand change the value of a decimal, while noughts being placed on the right hand do not in any way alter the number. For example, .35 is a thousand times more than .00035, while it is exactly the same as 35000, the noughts in this latter number merely expressing that there are no thousandths—no ten-thousandths—which is like expressing that there are no thousands, &c., in a number only amounting to hundreds.

In enumerating decimals instead of repeating so many tenths, so many hundredths, &c., the integer number is usually named, then the word decimal, and merely the name of each figure of the decimal is said. Thus we call 57.36 fifty-seven, decimal three-six, which is less troublesome than saying three-tenths, six-hundredths; but recollect, however, that the first is only an abbreviation of the latter.

----

*Mrs. D.* You are now quite familiar with the notation of decimals, and will have no difficulty in operating with them. Since units can be changed into tenths, or tenths into units—tenths into hundredths, or hundredths into tenths—in the same manner as tens can be changed into units, and units changed into tens, &c. &c. —it is evident that decimals can be operated upon like whole numbers ; the same reasoning which applies to

the one case being equally applicable to the other. In
adding and subtracting care must of course be taken to
place figures of the same value under each other; and
though quite as necessary in the addition and subtraction of whole numbers, a careless or inexperienced arithmetician may be more liable to make an error in placing
the decimals. If, however, in writing down a number,
you always begin with the units, placing them exactly
under those of the upper numbers, you cannot well
make a mistake.

Add together 305.786 + 57.03 + 890.0074 + 643.9 +
91.5001

$$
\begin{array}{r}
305.786 \\
57.03 \\
890.0074 \\
643.9 \\
\underline{91.5001} \\
1988.2235
\end{array}
$$

Q. 55. What are 58.0734 + .0034 + 7.506 + 385
equal to?

Q. 56. What is the sum of 4786.3 + 5.945 +
6.8745 + 100.001?

Subtract 37.5867 from 859.3.

Here one of the tenths must be changed into thousandths that the seven thousandths may be taken from it,
and one of the units must be changed into tenths, that
the five tenths may be taken from it. The sum will
then stand thus—

$$
\begin{array}{r}
8.299 \\
859.3000 \\
\underline{37.5867} \\
821.7133
\end{array}
$$

Q. 57. Subtract 427.56347 from 9583.436725.

Q. 58. What is the difference between 375.6402 and
638.495089?

In multiplying a decimal any certain number of times, or in dividing it into any certain number of parts, exactly the same process must of course be pursued as in multiplying and dividing whole numbers, since, in like manner, the excess of any denomination may be changed into the next. When the multiplier or divisor is a mixed number, or only a decimal, the operations are the same, but we must then take into consideration the value of the respective places of the figures. First, in multiplication. If we multiply any number, 98.67 for example, by any other number, say 30, we see immediately that it can be readily found by taking 98·67 thirty times, or

$$98.67 \times 30 = 2960.1, \quad \begin{array}{r} 98.67 \\ 30 \\ \hline 2960.10 \end{array} \quad ; \text{ and } 98.67 \times 3, \text{ or } 98.67,$$

taken three times will be only one-tenth of 98.67 × 3 × 10, or 2960.1 ÷ 10 = 295.01. In the same manner 98.67 × .3 will be one-tenth of 98.67 × 3, or 296.01 ÷ 10 = 29.601. Hence it is evident that any number is in fact diminished in value in the same manner as in common fractions, by being what is called multiplied by a decimal.

*Ed.* Then it is clear that multiplication is a wrong term.

*Mrs. D.* True ; but we must, I believe, in this case, still continue to make use of the same expression, since our multiplier is often a mixed number, and this extreme exactness of language would here rather confuse than simplify the subject.

It is evident, from the above examples, that multiplying by any number of tenths is the same as multiplying by the same number of units, and then dividing the product by 10 ; multiplying by any number of hundredths is the same as multiplying by the same number of units, and dividing the product by 100, and so on. To apply

L 3

this to practice, let us multiply 37.6 by .46. First, 4 tenths are the same as 40 hundredths; so .46 are 46 hundredths; .46 therefore means the same as $\frac{46}{100}$ and 37.6 × .46 = $\frac{37.6 \times 46}{100}$. Now work this sum, and likewise multiply 53.67 by 5. 9.

*Ed.*     37.6
      46
             
   225.6
  1504
            
  1729.6 ÷ 100 = 17.296.

$$53.67 \times 5.9 = 53.67 \times \frac{5.9 \times 10}{10} = \frac{53.67 \times 59}{10}$$

     53.67
       59
          
    48303
   6835
          
   3166.53 ÷ 10 = 316.653.

*Mrs. D.* Now since any decimal number multiplied by a whole number must always retain the same number of decimal places in the product, we have no more doubt as to the point where the decimal should begin than we have as to the place of units in the multiplication of whole numbers. When the multiplier is, instead of being an integer, a decimal number, the product is decreased in value according to the denomination of the decimal: thus, if this be tenths, the product is decreased ten times; if hundredths, a hundred times; and this is shown by removing the decimal point a step or steps to the left, which has been before explained. For example, 53.67 × 59 = 3166.53, and 53.67 × 5.9 = 316.653; 37.6 × 46 = 1729.6, and 37.6 × .46 =

17.296. The number of decimal places in the product of two decimal numbers is, therefore, always equal to the sum of the decimal places in the multiplicand and multiplier. Hence is deduced a general and simple rule.

When two decimal numbers are to be multiplied together, proceed exactly as in whole numbers, without regard to the decimal places until the process is finished, and then point off as many places in the product as there are decimal places in both multiplicand and multiplier.

Now multiply .257 by .13.

*Ed.*    .257
     .13
     ———
     771
    257
    ———
   3341

Ansr. .03341.

But here are only four places in the product, and, according to the rule, there should be five places of decimals, since the sum of those in the multiplier and divisor is five. What is to be done?

*Mrs. D.* Recollect that the product of .257 × 13 = 3. 341 is a hundred times more than if the multiplier were .13, or a hundredth part of 13; therefore the hundredth part of 3. 341 = $\dfrac{3.341}{100}$ = 257 × .13.

*Ed.* If I divide by 10, I change the units into tenths; and if I divide by 100, I change the units into hundredths; and therefore $\dfrac{3.341}{100}$ = .03341 = .257 × .13.

*Mrs. D.* Hence the rule, that when the number of figures in the product is less than the sum of the decimal places in the multiplicand and multiplier, the deficiency is supplied by adding a nought or noughts to the left of the number.

Q. 59. Multiply 37486 by .458.

Q. 60. What is the product of 2.37 × .0035?

Q. 61. What is the product of 1034.0007 × 58.67?

---

*Mrs. D.* In dividing by a decimal, the same reasoning which is used in multiplication is equally applicable.
The most simple practical rule is to clear the divisor of
decimals by multiplication, and then proceed exactly as
in whole numbers. For example, given 45.678 to be

divided by 23.74 $= \dfrac{\cdot 45.678}{23.74} = \dfrac{45.678 \times 100}{23.74 \times 100} = \dfrac{4567.8}{3474}$

Now let us work this sum.

$$
\begin{array}{r}
2374)4567.8(1.92 \\
2374 \\
\hline
2193.8 \\
2136.6 \\
\hline
57.20 \\
47.48 \\
\hline
9.72
\end{array}
$$

We have here found that 4567.8 being divided into
2374 parts, there is for each part, first, 1 integer and
2193.8, or 21938 tenths remainder; these now divided
by 2374, we find there are 9 for each part, and 572
tenths remainder; if we change these into hundredths,
we shall be able to make a still further division, 572
tenths = 5720 hundredths, we find 2 .of these will belong to each part, and there will be 972 remainder;
these in like manner, by putting a nought after them,
can be changed into thousandths; these again can be
divided, and so we proceed exactly the same as in common division, continuing our decimal number to any
degree of exactness required, by changing our number
into the denomination next in value.

*Ed.* But, mother, what do you mean by " to any degree of exactness required ;" why not continue dividing and dividing till at last we have no remainder?

*Mrs. D.* In many cases we may do this, but there are some divisors which can never exactly divide a number into tenths, hundredths, &c.; divide it as long as you will, there will always be a remainder.

*Ed.* I do not quite understand you—pray give me an example.

*Mrs. D.* Let us then divide this strip of paper, marked out into tenths, hundredths, &c., into 8 parts. How many tenths will there be in each part?

*Ed.* One tenth, and two tenths over.

*Mrs. D.* Change these tenths into hundredths.

*Ed.* Then 2 tenths or 20 hundredths divided by 8 are 2 and 4 over; 4 hundredths or 40 thousandths divided by 8 = 5, and no remainder.

*Mrs. D.* Therefore .125 is exactly 1 divided by 8, or $\frac{1}{8} = .125$. Now divide this same strip of paper into 3 parts.

*Ed.* Each part will be 3 tenths and 1 over; this 1 tenth changed into 10 hundredths, there will be three of these for each and one over; this one hun——

*Mrs. D.* How long must you continue changing this 1 into 10 and dividing by 3, before, as in the last example, we shall be able to make a division without leaving a remainder.

*Ed.* For ever, I believe; this 1 would always be left after every division.

*Mrs. D.* Then 1 divided by 3, or $\frac{1}{3} = .33333$,

&c., having three for every denomination as far as, and still farther than our patience will carry us.

*Ed.* Yes, I see now if I were to fill this slate with figures 3 I should still have a remainder; but I could not, in reality, cut the paper into all these very little parts.

*Mrs. D.* No; but the last division you were able to make would still leave you a remainder, which, however minute, would belong in equal portions to each of the three parts, although this remainder might be so very very small as to be laid aside, and the division would be sufficiently correct for all practical purposes. Thus 3333333 is $\frac{1}{3}$ all but a ten millionth part of an unit, divided by 3, or $\frac{1}{30,000,000}$; and this remainder, so minute, may in most calculations be safely rejected, without causing any error which can invalidate the result.

Q. 62. Divide 586.47 by 6.58.

Q. 63. Divide .007689 by .093.

Q. 64. Divide 3476.83 by 5.007.

---

*Mrs. D.* From the explanations and examples given in division, you can now, without doubt, readily see how a fraction can be changed into a decimal having the same or nearly the same value.

*Ed.* Yes, we have already found that $\frac{1}{8} = .125$ and $\frac{1}{3}$ $= .333$, &c. I suppose we can, in the same manner, find the value of other fractions, but I do not know the best way of doing this on my slate.

*Mrs. D.* Since 1 is equal to one, and no tenths, no

hundredths, &c. $1 = 1.000$; therefore $\dfrac{1}{8}$ the same as

$\dfrac{1.000}{8}$, which is a common division sum thus, $\begin{array}{r} 8)\overline{1.000} \\ \hline .125 \end{array}$.

In like manner $\dfrac{1}{3}$ is converted into a decimal $\begin{array}{r} 3)\overline{1.00000} \\ \hline .33333 \end{array}$,

&c., where, as these noughts give no value to the number, we may add them at pleasure, that is to say, we may change our remainder to the next denomination as long as we may consider requisite. If the numerator be not merely unity, but any other number whatever, it is clear that the process would be exactly the same; dividing the numerator by the denominator, changing as we proceed the units into tenths, hundredths, &c., we obtain a fractional number broken into decimal parts. Let us express $\dfrac{57}{83}$, $\dfrac{5}{164}$, and $\dfrac{8}{9}$, in decimal parts :—

```
83)57.0(.6867469879518072, &c.
   49 8
   ————
    7.20
    6 64
    ————
     560
     498
     ————
      620
      581
      ————
       390
       332
       ————
        580
        498
        ————
         820
         747
         ————
          730
          664
          ————
           660
           581
           ————
            790
            747
            ————
             430
             415
             ————
              150
               83
              ————
               670
               664
               ————
                600
                581
                ————
                 190
                 166
                 ————
                  24
```

Having seen the first example thus worked at length, you will no doubt readily be able, without assistance, to bring the other two fractions into decimal parts (42) (43).

In many cases when we cannot divide tenths, hundredths, &c., into exactly the number of parts required, we can, generally, after a few divisions, find what the decimal will be to any number of places whatever. Thus, we have found that 1 divided by 3 is 3 tenths 3 hundredths, &c., the 3 always being repeated through every denomination, the decimal is in such case more simply expressed by writing only one 3, and placing a point over it; thus, $\dot{3}$, expresses the same as .33333, &c. In like manner, if two or more figures are repeated in regular order, points placed over the first and last of these figures denote their constant and unvarying repetition; —thus, $.\dot{0}\dot{9}$ expresses the same as .09090909, &c.; $.\dot{8}1\dot{4}$ the same as .814814814814814, &c. Such decimals are called recurring or circulating, and the repeating figure or figures the repetend.

*Ed.* But when you see a decimal which has the figures thus repeated, how do you know that they are not decimals which may at last terminate?

*Mrs. D.* There certainly may be decimals having the same figure or figures repeated for only a certain number of times, for example, $\frac{1}{3} - \frac{1}{3000} = .333$. Since $\frac{1}{3} =$ ·3333333, &c., and $\frac{1}{3000} = .0003333$, &c.; therefore $.\dot{3} - .0003 = .333$.

But we should improperly express this .333 as a *constantly* recurring decimal, which means that the same figures after a certain number of divisions will always

M

recur, however long the division may be continued. Let
us trace the formation of another recurring decimal.—
Let us divide the strip of paper marked out into tenths,
&c. as before, into 7 equal parts,

$$7)1.000000000000$$

$$.142857142857$$

we shall find after six divisions, that the remainder is 1,
and therefore, if we continue our divisions to six places
more, we shall repeat the same six figures because the
remainders will be respectively the same as in the first
six divisions, until we come again to the remainder 1,
and then we go on with our repetitions—thus, 142857
142857 142857, &c. &c.—the decimal of $\frac{1}{7}$ is a recurring decimal of six places, and is expressed $.\dot{1}4285\dot{7}$.

It is evident when unity, or 1, is divided by any number into decimal parts, the same figures will recur when
the remainder becomes 1 ; and in like manner, if, instead
of unity, any number be so divided, the same figure or
figures will recur when the remainder becomes the same
as the first number or dividend, or the same as some
former remainder. Now, every recurring decimal is obtained by the division of one or a greater number of units
into a certain number of tenths, hundredths, &c.; and
in dividing any number into a certain number of parts,
the result will be exactly the same, whether we first
divide each one into these parts and then add one part
taken from each together, or whether we divide the
whole number at once into these parts. Thus, $\frac{2}{3} = \frac{1}{3}$
$\times 2; \frac{5}{7} = \frac{1}{7} \times 5$. Every recurring decimal may, therefore, be produced by the decimal division of one whole
into a certain number of parts, and is either the quo-

tient thus obtained, or this quotient multiplied by any other number. For example, $.\dot{6} = .\dot{3} \times 2$; $.\dot{5}\dot{4} = .\dot{0}\dot{9} \times 6$.

When recurring decimals occur in practice, it is sometimes much less troublesome to convert them into common fractions, in order to operate upon them; thus, you would find it easier to multiply $\dfrac{1}{3}$ by $\dfrac{1}{7}$ than to multiply .3333, &c., by $.\dot{1}4285\dot{7}$;—it is, therefore, useful to know how to change readily a recurring decimal into a common fraction of the same value.

If, instead of marking the strip of paper into tenths, I had marked it into ninths, we should then have had no difficulty in dividing the whole into 3 equal parts, since the ten tenths could be divided into 3 parts, having one over, it follows that $10 - 1$ could be divided into 3 parts without leaving any remainder. In like manner, if the paper had been marked into 999999 parts, these could have been divided by 7 without a remainder, since we have found that $1000000 \div$ by $7 = 142857$, and one over, it follows that $1000000 - 1 = 999999$ can be divided by 7 without a remainder, each part being 142857. Therefore $\dfrac{3}{9}$ is the same as decimal $.\dot{3} = \dfrac{1}{3}$, and $\dfrac{142857}{999999}$ the same as $.\dot{1}4285\dot{7} = \dfrac{1}{7}$. What has been said above, shows that the same reasoning will equally apply to any other recurring decimal. Therefore, speaking generally, any recurring decimal is truly represented by a fraction, the numerator of which is the repetend, and the denominator 9, repeated to as many places as there are figures in the repetend.

When it is a mixed decimal—that is, when the recurring part does not commence immediately, such as

$.79\dot{5}\dot{4}$; $.86\dot{7}\dot{3}$; then, by breaking the numbers into frac-

tions, we have $.79\dot{5}\dot{4} = \dfrac{79.\,\dot{5}\dot{4}}{100} = \dfrac{79}{100}$ and $\dfrac{.\dot{5}\dot{4}}{100}$; but $\dfrac{.\dot{5}\dot{4}}{100}$

$= .\dot{5}\dot{4} \times \dfrac{1}{100} = \dfrac{54}{99} \times \dfrac{1}{100} = \dfrac{6}{1100}$; therefore $\dfrac{79}{100} +$

$\dfrac{6}{1100} = \dfrac{875}{1100} = .79\dot{5}\dot{4}$, and $.86\dot{7}\dot{3} = \dfrac{867}{1000} + \dfrac{.\dot{3}}{1000}$; but

$\dfrac{.\dot{3}}{1000} = .\dot{3} \times \dfrac{1}{1000} = \dfrac{3}{9} \times \dfrac{1}{1000} = \dfrac{1}{3000}$; therefore $\dfrac{867}{1000}$

$+ \dfrac{1}{3000} = \dfrac{2602}{3000} = .86\dot{7}\dot{3}$.

(44) Bring $.85\dot{6}\dot{3}$ into a fraction.

(45) Also $.76\dot{1}1\dot{7}$.

# PART THIRD.

## COMMERCIAL ARITHMETIC.

### Chapter I.

*Mrs. D.* Besides common and decimal fractions there are other fractions which we must now take into consideration.

Every people who have become sufficiently civilized to understand the advantage arising from mutual exchanges, have found the necessity of using different denominations in their measures of weight and capacity : in a further stage of civilization, when exchanges become more complicated, a medium of value or money is adopted. This would, however, ill answer its purpose if it were confined to coins of only one value : if you had no smaller coins than sovereigns or 20 shilling pieces, you would find it inconvenient to make your various purchases at the shop ; and if there were no lower weight than a pound, or no lower measure of capacity than a gallon, the shopman would be equally at a loss to serve you with your ounces of sweets, and pints of nuts.

*Ed.* Yes ; I know very well how convenient shillings and pence are ; and I knew long ago how many pence are equal to one shilling—how many ounces are equal to one pound—and how many pints are equal to one gallon.

*Mrs. D.* You know, also, that days are divided into hours, and yards into feet.

*Ed.* Yes ; but have these anything to do with fractions ?

M 3

*Mrs. D.* Certainly: for example, are not one penny $\frac{1}{12}$ of a shilling, and one foot $\frac{1}{3}$ of a yard; and so we must consider them in all calculations of which they form a part.

*Ed.* If this $\frac{1}{12}$ and this $\frac{1}{3}$ were tenths, or any number of tenths, how much easier we should be able to manage them.

*Mrs. D.* True: the most simple as well as the most scientific arrangement would have been to make the lower denominations, decimal parts of the highest denomination; but, unfortunately for accountants, these commercial fractions were not originally formed by philosophers. The Portuguese, indeed, for a very long period, have made, and the Americans and French now make, their calculations in different coins, the values of which are decimal parts of a higher coin; so that it is as easy to calculate their money of different denominations, as it is to calculate ours when reduced to one denomination.

But these subdivisions, depending on the customs of different nations, are, for the most part, various and arbitrary. Thus, in England, we divide our money into twentieth, twelfths, and fourths—our weights, sometimes into some fractional parts, sometimes into others; our measures of length into numerous incongruous subdivisions;—in short, it seems as if all these denominations were capricious inventions to perplex and lengthen calculations.

Since, however, this is the case, it is necessary that we should make ourselves acquainted with the different fractional parts in use, at least in our own country. I have therefore transcribed for your benefit the following tables, which comprise nearly all the information you

will find requisite in applying your previous knowledge
to domestic and commercial calculations.

### Table of Money.

4*Farthings are 1 Penny ........ written 1*d.*
12 Pence ...... 1 Shilling ............ 1*s.*
20 Shillings.... 1 Pound or Sovereign.... £1.

farthings.   d.
4 =   1
s.
48 =  12 =  1
£.
960 =. 240 = 20 = 1

### 2. Table of Avoirdupois Weight.

16 Drachms .. are 1 Ounce ...... written 1 oz.
16 Ounces ...... 1 Pound ............ 1 lb.
28 Pounds ...... 1 Quarter .......... 1 qr.
4 Quarters  .... 1 Hundredweight .... 1 cwt.
20 Hundredweight 1 Ton ............ 1 ton.

drs.        oz.
16 =        1
lbs.
256 =       16 =      1
qrs.
7168 =      448 =     28 =  1
cwt.
28672 =    1792 =    112 =   4 =   1
ton.
573440 = 35840 = 2240 = 80 = 20 = 1

There are several other denominations in this weight

---

* Farthings are written as the fractional parts of a penny.
1 = ¼
2 = ½
3 = ¾

which are used in weighing some particular goods, but it is scarcely necessary to enumerate these at present.

---

### 3. *Table of Troy Weight.*

24 Grains .... are 1 Pennyweight .... written 1 dwt.
20 Pennyweights. . 1 Ounce................ 1 oz.
12 Ounces  ...... 1 Pound........, ....... 1 lb.

$$
\begin{array}{l}
\text{grs.} \quad \text{dwt.} \\
24 = 1 \\
\qquad\qquad\quad \text{oz.} \\
480 = 20 = 1 \\
\qquad\qquad\qquad\qquad \text{lb.} \\
5760 = 240 = 12 :\: : 1
\end{array}
$$

Gold, silver, and jewels, are wei$_i$ ied by this weight ; 7000 grains troy are equal to 1 lb.  voirdupois ; and as the pound troy contains 5760 grains it follows that

| troy. | avoirdupois. |
|---|---|
| 175 lb. | = 144 lb. |
| 1 lb. | = 13 oz. 2$\frac{1}{2}$ drs. |
| 1 lb. 2 oz. 11 dwt. 16 gr. | = 1 lb. |

---

### 4. *Table of Apothecaries' Weight.*

20 Grains ....... are 1 Scruple ........ marked Э
3 Scruples.......... 1 Drachm ............. З
8 Drachms ........ 1 Ounce............... ҙ
12 Ounces.......... 1 Pound ............. ℔

$$
\begin{array}{l}
\text{grs.} \quad \text{Э} \\
20 = 1 \\
\qquad\qquad\quad \text{З} \\
60 = 3 = 1 \\
\qquad\qquad\qquad\qquad \text{ҙ} \\
480 = 24 = 8 = 1 \\
\qquad\qquad\qquad\qquad\qquad\quad \text{℔} \\
5760 = 288 = 96 = 12 = 1
\end{array}
$$

These grains are the same as troy grains, so that the pound and ounce apothecaries' weight weigh the same as the pound and ounce troy.

_____

### 5. *Table of Imperial Measure.*

| | | |
|---|---|---|
| 4 Gills .......... are | 1 Pint ....... written | 1 pt. |
| 2 Pints ........... | 1 Quart ........... | 1 qt. |
| 4 Quarts........... | 1 Gallon........... | 1 gall. |
| 2 Gallons .......... | 1 Peck ............ | 1 pk. |
| 4 Pecks............ | 1 Bushel.......... | 1 bu. |
| 8 Bushels.......... | 1 Quarter.......... | 1 qr. |
| 5 Quarters.......... | 1 Load ........... | 1 ld. |

$$\begin{array}{l} \overset{\text{g.}}{4} = \overset{\text{pt.}}{1} \\ 8 = 2 = \overset{\text{qt.}}{1} \\ 32 = 8 = 4 = \overset{\text{gal.}}{1} \\ 64 = 16 = 8 = 2 = \overset{\text{pk.}}{1} \\ 256 = 64 = 32 = 8 = 4 = \overset{\text{bu.}}{1} \end{array}$$

By this measure both liquids and dry goods are measured. For the former only the four first measures are used. This gallon contains 277.274 cubic inches, and the distilled water,* which it is capable of holding, should weigh 10 lbs.

Custom had long established that some articles should be sold by the quantity which the measure will exactly hold, without rising in any part above its brim, and which, from the circumstance of a staff being used to strike off evenly the upper surface, is called strike measure; while other articles were sold by the quantity which the measure can be made to carry when heaped up six inches above the brim in a conical form towards the centre, and

_____

* At the temperature of 62° Faht.

this is characteristically called heaped measure.  But it is evident short quantities measured in this manner might vary from many causes, either from design or from the degree of expertness of the seller; therefore, by an Act of Parliament, which came into operation in January 1835, this mode of measuring is now declared illegal.

---

### 6. *Table of Cloth Measure.*

| | | |
|---|---|---|
| 2¼ Inches ......... are 1 Nail .... | written 1 n. |
| 4  Nails ............. 1 Quarter ........ | 1 qr. |
| 3  Quarters .......... 1 Flemish Ell..... | 1 F. E. |
| 4  Quarters .......... 1 Yard .......... | 1 yd. |
| 5″ Quarters .......... 1 English Ell ..... | 1 E. E. |
| 6  Quarters .......... 1 French Ell...... | 1 Fr. E. |

$$2\tfrac{1}{4} = \overset{\text{n.}}{1}$$
$$9 = 4 = \overset{\text{qr.}}{1}$$
$$27 = 12 = 3 = \overset{\text{F.E.}}{1}$$
$$36 = 16 = 4 = \overset{\text{yd.}}{1}$$
$$45 = 20 = 5 = \overset{\text{E.E.}}{1}$$
$$54 = 24 = 6 = \overset{\text{Fr. E.}}{1}$$

---

### 7. *Table of Long Measure.*

| | | |
|---|---|---|
| 3  Barley-corns are 1 Inch ........ | written 1 in. |
| 12 Inches........ 1 Foot............... | 1 ft. |
| 3  Feet ......... 1 Yard ............. | 1 yd. |
| 6  Feet ......... 1 Fathom........... | 1 fth. |
| 5½ Yards........ 1 Rod, Pole, or Perch .. | 1 rod. p. |
| 40 Poles ........ 1 Furlong ......... ... | 1 fur. |
| 8  Furlongs...... 1 Mile............... | 1 mile. |
| 3  Miles ........ 1 League............. | 1 leag. |

| bar. | in. | | | | | | |
|------|-----|------|------|------|------|------|------|
| 3= | 1 | | | | | | |
| | | ft. | | | | | |
| 36= | 12= | 1 | | | | | |
| | | | yd. | | | | |
| 108= | 36= | 3= | 1 | | | | |
| | | | | fth. | | | |
| 216= | 72= | 6= | 2 = 1 | | | | |
| | | | | | p. | | |
| 594= | 198= | 16½= | 5½ =.. | 1 | | | |
| | | | | | | fur. | |
| 23760= | 7920= | 660= | 220 =.. | 40= 1 | | | |
| | | | | | | | miles. |
| 190080= | 63360= | 5280=1760 = | ..320= | 8=1 | | | |
| | | | | | | | leag. |
| 570240=190080=15840=5280 = | | | ..960=24=3=1 | | | | |

---

## 8. *Table of the Measure of Surface.*

| 144 | Square Inches are 1 Square Foot written 1 sq. ft. |
|-----|---------------------------------------------------|
| 9 | Feet..... 1      Yard ..... 1 sq. yd. |
| 272¼ | Feet..... 1      Pole ...... 1 sq..p. |
| 40 | Poles.... 1 Rood........... 1 rd. |
| 4 | Roods ........ 1 Acre ........... 1 ac. |
| 640 | Acres ........ 1 Square Mile...... 1 sq. m. |

| in. | ft. | | | | |
|-----|-----|------|------|------|------|
| 144= | 1 | | | | |
| | | yd. | | | |
| 1296= | 9= | 1 | | | |
| | | | p. | | |
| 39204= | 272½= | 30¼= | 1 | | |
| | | | | rd. | |
| 1568160= | 10890= | 1210 = | 40= | 1 | |
| | | | | | ac. |
| 6272640= | 43560= | 4840= | 160= | 4= | 1 |
| | | | | | m |
| 4014489600=27878400=3097600=102400=2560=640= 1 | | | | | |

---

### 9. *Table of the Measure of Time.*

60 Seconds ..... are 1 Minute ...... written 1
60 Minutes........ 1 Hour .............. 1 h.
24 Hours......... 1 Day .............. 1 d.
7 Days.......... 1 Week.............. 1 wk.
365 Days.......... 1 Year*.............. 1 yr.

$$\begin{array}{l} \text{seconds.} \quad \text{'} \\ 60 = \quad 1 \\ \quad\quad\quad\quad\quad \text{h.} \\ 3600 = \quad 60 = \quad 1 \\ \quad\quad\quad\quad\quad\quad\quad\quad \text{d.} \\ 86400 = 1440 = 24 = 1 \\ \quad\quad\quad\quad\quad\quad\quad\quad\quad\quad \text{wk.} \\ 604800 = 10080 = 168 = 7 = 1 \end{array}$$

*Mrs. D.* It is almost needless to point out to you the impossibility of answering any question involving numbers of more than one denomination without bringing these into one common denomination. For example, suppose you are asked the following question :—If 1 ounce of tea cost 5*d.* what will 1 lb. cost?.. It is evident that, unless you know how many times 1 oz. is contained in 1 lb., you could not furnish an answer; but you have no difficulty in discovering immediately that, if 1 oz. cost 5*d.*, 16 oz. will cost 5 × 16 = 80*d.*

*Ed.* But we never say 80*d.*, mother; that sounds very awkward.

*Mrs. D.* And it would be still more awkward to count out eighty pence to pay for our pound of tea; something more is still wanting to complete our answer to this question.

---

* Every fourth year has an additional day in the month of February, and is called leap year. This leap year may always be known by its being divisible by 4 without any remainder.

*Ed.* Yes; we must know how many pennies or pence there arc in a shilling, and then find out how many shillings arc contained in 80 pence. Since there are 12 pence in one shilling, $\frac{80}{12}$ will give the number of shillings contained in 80 pence ; $\frac{80}{12} = 6\,\frac{8}{12}$, or 6 shillings and 8 over ; so $80 = \overset{d.}{6} : \overset{s.\quad d.}{8}$.

*Mrs. D.* If you have any number in a low denomination which you wish to bring into a number of a higher denomination, you can readily pursue the same method. Divide the given number into as many parts as the low denomination is contained in the higher; the remainder will be that number left in the low denomination, which is too small to be changed into the higher; this higher denomination may then be changed into one still higher, and so on. For example, 8357 farthings are $= \frac{8357}{4}$ pence $= \frac{8357}{4 \times 12}$ shillings $= \frac{8357}{4 \times 12 \times 20}$ pounds, the sum being worked as under :—

$$4)8357$$
$$12)2089\tfrac{1}{4}\ \text{pence.}$$
$$2.0)\ \overset{s.\quad d.}{17.4 : 1\tfrac{1}{4}}$$
$$£\,\overset{s.\quad d.}{8 : 14 : 1\tfrac{1}{4}}$$

Now bring 28690 avoirdupois ounces into pounds, quarters, and hundredweights.

*Ed.* Here we must divide by 16 to bring into pounds; these pounds by 28 to bring them into quarters; and these quarters by 4 to bring them into hundredweights.

16)28690(28)1793(4)64  
   16       168    $\overline{16}$ cwt. no qrs. 1lb. 2oz.  
  $\overline{126}$     $\overline{113}$  
  112      112  
  $\overline{149}$     $\overline{1lb.}$  
  144  
   $\overline{50}$  
   42  
   $\overline{2oz.}$

*Mrs. D.* You will perceive that it is very easy to do the reverse of what we have been doing, and bring numbers consisting of several denominations into a lower or the lowest denomination. Thus, let us reduce $\overset{\text{£. s. d.}}{8:14:1\frac{1}{4}}$. Here $\overset{\text{£.}}{8} = 8 \times 20 = 160$ shillings; and, therefore, $\overset{\text{£. s.}}{8:14} = 160 + 14 = 174$ shillings; and $\overset{\text{s.}}{174} \times 12 = 2088$ pence; therefore, $\overset{\text{s. d.}}{174:1} = 2088 + 1 = 2089$ pence; and $\overset{\text{d.}}{2089} \times 4 = 8356$ farthings; therefore, $\overset{\text{d.}}{2089\frac{1}{4}} = 8356 + 1 = 8357$ farthings $= \overset{\text{£. s. d.}}{8:14:1\frac{1}{4}}$. All that we have been doing being worked as under

$$\overset{\text{£. s. d.}}{8:14:1\frac{1}{4}}$$
$$20$$
$$\overline{174}$$
$$12$$
$$\overline{2089}$$
$$4$$
$$\overline{8357}$$

Hence, to bring any mixed number consisting of different denominations into a number of equal value in the

lowest denomination—we first multiply the highest denomination by a number equal to the number of times
that one in this denomination contains one in the next
highest denomination; to this product add the number,
if any, which is in the next denomination, and proceed
exactly as before  It is usual to add these numbers as
we multiply, in the same manner as we add in the tens
in common multiplication, instead of first multiplying
and then adding.  Thus, in the above example I have
not first multiplied by 20 and then added 14, but I have
brought down the 4 units at once and added the 1 ten to
the 16 tens, and then I have written them down.  But
this is mere arrangement, and whether the 14 be added
at first or afterwards, can, it is plain, make no difference
in the result.  In the same way 2089 is $174 \times 12 + 1$,
and 8357 is $2089 \times 4 + 1$.

A few examples for practice will, I think, be now all
that is necessary to perfect you in this rule, which is
called reduction

Q. 65. Bring 58675 farthings into pounds, shillings,
and pence.

Q. 66. How many seconds are there in a solar year,
or 365 days, 5 hours, 48 minutes, and 48 seconds ?

Q. 67. It has been ascertained by various experiments
that sound travels uniformly at the rate of about 1142
feet in a second of time.  The interval between seeing a
flash of lightning and hearing the report is the time the
sound takes travelling to us, and, therefore, if we notice
the length of this period we shall be enabled to calculate
how far distant the electric cloud is from us.  In the
last thunderstorm $\frac{2}{3}$ min. elapsed between seeing the
lightning and hearing the thunder, how many miles was
the thunder cloud from us ?

Q. 68. Agriculturists have found that nipping off the

N 2

blossoms of the potato plants causes, on an average, an increase of $\frac{1}{2}$ oz. in weight per root, and if this be reckoned an increase of a ton per acre, how many plants are there in that space of ground?

Q. 69. If an acre of ground produces 539 bushels of potatoes, each bushel weighing 82 lbs., and another acre produces 665 bushels, each weighing 82 lbs., what is the difference of the produce of the two acres, reckoned in tons, cwts., qrs., and lbs.?

Q. 70. Count Dandolo, an Italian nobleman, who devoted much of his attention to the rearing of silk-worms, found that 39,168 silk-worms' eggs weigh one French ounce, which is about $1\frac{1}{12}$ oz. avoirdupois; now, what is the weight of each egg? In a few weeks, the silk-worms produced from these eggs attain to their full growth, and then six of them weigh one French ounce, what is the weight of each silk-worm in avoirdupois weight?

There are many ways by which the working of sums in reduction may be facilitated. Persons who are much in the habit of calculating, generally erect some standard or landmark for themselves, by which they are enabled to obtain their result with more rapidity; and in almost every trade or business in the details of which arithmetic is in constant requisition, methods of shortening processes peculiar to each are adopted. I do not profess to give these, as I would rather your own ingenuity should be exercised in discovering them, and I hope you will one day be able to find out for yourself the best means of arriving at a required result.

I will merely give you one example to show you how to conduct your inquiries. Thus, 100 farthings are 25 pence, or 2 : 1; and 1000 farthings are 1 : 0 : 10; therefore, if a number of farthings be given to be brought into pounds, shillings, and pence, for example, 7863, we know directly there are

$$
\begin{array}{rcl}
\text{£.} & \text{s.} & \text{d.} \\
7 : & 0 : & 70 \quad \text{in} \quad 7000 \\
16 : & 8 & \text{.. } \quad 800 \\
& 15\frac{3}{4} & \text{.. } \quad 63 \\
\hline
\text{£7} : 16 : & 93\frac{3}{4} \\
7 : & 9\frac{3}{4} = 93\frac{3}{4} \\
\hline
\text{£8} : 3 : & 9\frac{3}{4}
\end{array}
$$

All this may appear formidable on paper, and perhaps more difficult than the regular way, but after a little practice it is astonishing with what celerity these calculations may be made mentally, without having recourse to writing down any of the figures—thus, 547 farthings, I see at once are $10 : 5 + 11\frac{3}{4} = 11 : 4\frac{3}{4}$.

You would fancy I was departing from the sober language befitting arithmetical subjects were I to tell you how many sums of a similar nature were answered in a very short space of time by some pupils, at a school in which extraordinary facility had been gained, by constant practice in such questions.

---

## CHAPTER II.

*Mrs. D.* A mixed number, consisting of several denominations, as $2 : 7 : 5 : 6$, is called a compound quantity. The adding together or subtracting compound quantities of the same sort is of course conducted on the same principle as in common addition and subtraction, and it may be very simply shown how to apply this principle to practice. If these red counters, instead of each repre-senting ten white counters, represented 12 or any other number, and these three counters, instead of each re-presenting ten red counters, represented 3 or any other number, it is clear we could add, subtract, multiply, and divide them exactly in the same manner as we can perform these operations on units, tens, and hundreds, only the different processes would be more troublesome because the values of the differently-coloured counters have no uniform rate of increase.

*Ed.* Yes; in addition I should add all the white counters together, change as many of them as I could into red, and add these to the other red counters, and then add together all the red counters; change as many of them as I could into blue, and add up all the blue counters exactly the same as if they were units, tens, and hundreds.

*Mrs. D.* Now reduce this to practice, and add together $7 : 2 : 9 + 6 : 1 : 7 + 5 : 2 : 8 + 3 : 0 : 5$.

*Ed.* I suppose I must place them in rows, being careful to put the inches under the inches, the feet under the feet, and the yards under the yards, thus:

| yds. | ft. | in. |
|------|-----|-----|
| 7 .. | 2 .. | 9 |
| 6 .. | 1 .. | 7 |
| 5 .. | 2 .. | 8 |
| 3 .. | 0 .. | 5 |
| 23 :. | 1 .. | 5 |

Here are 29 inches which are equal to $\frac{29}{12}$ feet $= 2$ feet and five inches. I then put the five under the inches and add the 2 feet to the others; these together are 7, which are equal to $\dfrac{7}{3}$ yards = 2 yards and 1 foot; put down the 1 under the feet and add the 2 yards to the others, making together 23 yards.

*Mrs. D.* Very well: now you can as readily add together any other similar compound quantities.

Q. 71. Add together 56 : 5 : 8 $+$ 91 : 7 : 3½ $+$ 18 : 6 $+$ 107 : 13 : 5¾.

Q. 72. What is the amount of weight of 6 casks of sugar, each cask weighing as under:

| | cwt. | qrs. | lb. | oz. |
|------|------|------|-----|-----|
| 1st. | 15 | 1 | 9 | 6 |
| 2nd. | 17 | 3 | 17 | 0 |
| 3d. | 16 | 0 | 25 | 7 |
| 4th. | 19 | 2 | 3 | 5 |
| 5th. | 18 | 3 | 19 | 14 |
| 6th. | 14 | 1 | 20 | 13 |

Q. 73. Add together

| acres. | rds. | poles. |
|--------|------|--------|
| 225 | 7 | 7 |
| 16 | 1 | 25 |
| 7 | 2 | 13 |
| 4 | 2 | 9 |
| 42 | 1 | 19 |
| 7 | 0 | 6 |

---

*Mrs. D.* The manner of subtracting compound quantities scarcely requires explanation. You can no doubt, without hesitation, subtract 2 : 15 : 9 from 7 : 16 : 10, where the number to be subtracted in each denomination is less than the number from which it is to be taken. When this is not the case, and in any of the denominations we have to subtract a higher number from a less, we change one from the next highest deno-

mination into this denomination, and then we have no
difficulty in proceeding.

I have here $\overset{£}{7} : \overset{s.}{6} : \overset{d.}{8}$, and I have to pay out of it
$\overset{£}{2} : \overset{s.}{15} : \overset{d.}{9}$; how much shall I have left when the debt is
discharged?

*Ed.* Since we cannot take 9 from 8, we must change
$\overset{s.}{1}$ into 12 pence; then 9 from 12 are 3; 3 and 8
are 11.

*Mrs. D.* Therefore, if we take $\overset{d.}{9}$ from $\overset{s.\ d.}{1:8}$, $\overset{d.}{11}$ will
remain.

*Ed.* Now I cannot take these 15 shillings from the
remaining 5 shillings, so I must change one of the
pounds into $\overset{s.}{20}$; take 15 from 20, 5 remains; 5 and 5
are 10, or $\overset{s.}{15}$ taken from $\overset{£\ s.}{1:5}$ leave $\overset{s.}{10}$; and lastly, the
$\overset{£}{2}$ taken from the $\overset{£}{6}$, leave $\overset{£}{4}$.

$$
\begin{array}{r}
£\ \ \ s.\ \ \ \ d. \\
7:\ 6:\ 8 \\
2:15:\ 9 \\
\hline
4:10:11
\end{array}
$$

Q. 74. Subtract $\overset{\text{cwt. qrs. lb. oz. dr.}}{8:2:23:12:13}$ from $\overset{\text{cwt. qrs. lb. oz. dr.}}{17:1:0:9:12}$.

Q. 75. Take $\overset{\text{wk. d. h. m.}}{2:3:7:10}$ from $\overset{\text{wk. d. h. m.}}{3:2:9:7}$.

———

*Mrs. D.* The methods of multiplying and dividing
compound quantities will scarcely require any explanation; a few examples will make these sufficiently appa-
rent. Try if you can multiply $\overset{£}{3} : \overset{s.}{7} : \overset{d.}{8}$ by 7.

*Ed.* I first multiply the 8 by 7 and find there are 56.$^{d.}$
I change these into shillings, $\dfrac{56}{12} = 4\dfrac{8}{12}$, or 4$^{s.}$ and 8$^{d.}$ I

put down the 8,$^{d.}$ and keep in mind that the 4$^{s.}$ are to be
added to the other shillings; $7 \times 7$ are 49; $49 + 4 =$

53; $53 = \dfrac{53}{20} = 2\dfrac{13}{20}$, or 2$^{£}$ : 13$^{s.}$; I put down the 13

shillings, and reserve the 2$^{£}$ to be added to the others;
$3 \times 7 = 21$; $21 + 2 = 23$; therefore the whole product is 23 : 13 : 8.
$$\begin{array}{ccc} £. & s. & d. \\ 3 : & 7 : & 8 \\ & & 7 \\ \hline 23 : & 13 : & 8 \end{array}$$

*Mrs. D.* In like manner any other compound quantity may be multiplied by a whole number. When the
multiplier is more than 12, we must have recourse to
the method already shown (p. 52). Thus, if it be re-
quired to multiply 9 : 3 : 2$^{\text{yds. qr. n.}}$ by 367, this is the same as
multiplying it by $360 + 7$, and $360 = 6 \times 6 \times 10$;
the same result is obtained whether we multiply by a
number or by the factors which, multiplied together,
will produce that number; therefore, $9 : 3 : 2^{\text{yds.qrs.n.}} \times 6 \times$
$6 \times 10 + 9 : 3 : 2^{\text{yds.qrs.n.}} \times 7 = 9 : 3 : 2 \times 367$. Now work
this sum.

```
                              yds.  qrs.  n.
   9..3..2                     9 ..3..2
          7                           6
   ─────────                   ─────────
  69..0..2                    59 ..1..0
                                      6
                              ─────────
                             355 ..2..0
                                     10
                              ─────────
                            3555 ..0..0
                              69 ..0..2
                         ─────────────────
                  yds. 3624 ..0..2
```

£.   s.   d.

Q. 76. A person's weekly expenses are 5 : 7 : 6, how much does he spend in the year?

Q. 77. A merchant received from abroad 96 bags of rice, each weighing <sup>cwt. qr. lbs.</sup> 1 : 1 : 7, what is their aggregate weight?

cwt. qr. lbs.

*Mrs. D.* In the division of a compound quantity we first divide the number in the highest denomination, then bring the remainder, if any, to the next denomination, and add these to the number, if any, in this denomination, then divide and proceed as before. Now divide 23 : 13 : 8 into 7 parts.

£.   s.   d.

*Ed.* First, the sevens in 23 are 3, and 2 remainder.

£.   s.   d.

$$7)23 : 13 : 8$$
$$\overline{\quad 3 : \ 7 : 8 \quad}$$

I put down the 3 under the pounds, and change the remaining 2 pounds into shillings, and add these to the other shillings, $2 \times 20 + 13 = 53$; 7 in 53 are 7, and 4 over. I put down the 7, and bring the remaining 4 into pence; $4 \times 12 + 8 = 56$; 7 in 56 are 8, and no remainder.

*Mrs. D.* And if there had been a remainder?

*Ed.* I should have brought it into farthings, and divided those by 7.

*Mrs. D.* You would likewise have no difficulty in dividing by a number higher than 12. Let us divide

yds.   qrs.   n.
3624 . . 0 . . 2 by 367.

$$\begin{array}{r} \text{yds.} \quad \text{qrs.} \quad \text{n.} \\ 367)3624 . . 0 . . 2(9 . . 3 . . 2 \\ \underline{3303} \\ 321 \\ \underline{4} \\ 1284 \text{ qrs.} \\ 1101 \\ \underline{\phantom{00}183\phantom{0}} \\ 4 \\ \underline{\phantom{0}734 \text{ n.}} \\ 734 \\ \overline{\phantom{00}. . .} \end{array}$$

cwts.   qrs.   lbs.   oz.   dr.
Q. 78.. Divide 53 . . 0 . . 7 . . 4 . . 8 into 6 parts.

£.
Q. 79. A gentleman left in his will 1397 to be equally divided among the poor of his parish.—There appeared 763 claimants to participate in this donation. If so divided, what would be each person's share?

Q. 80. If you had a work to accomplish in the course of the year, which would take you 57 whole days, or 57 × 12 hours, and if you worked at it uniformly, how much of each day would it occupy you?

## CHAPTER III.

*Mrs. D.* We have seen how a compound quantity may be reduced to a simple quantity in its lowest denomination; it may likewise, by the use of decimal notation, be brought into a simple quantity in its highest denomination. Let us bring $6\overset{\text{d.}}{}$ into the denomination of $1\overset{\text{s.}}{}$; now, what step do we take to bring pence into shillings?

*Ed.* Divide by 12, because there are 12 pence in 1 shilling.

*Mrs. D.* How many shillings are there in 60 pence?

*Ed.* $\dfrac{60}{12} = 5.$

*Mrs. D.* And how many decimal parts of a shilling are there in 6.0 pence?

*Ed.* $\dfrac{6.0}{12} = .5.$

*Mrs. D.* Therefore, to reduce a number of one denomination into decimal parts of a higher denomination, you pursue exactly the same method as in whole numbers. Can you tell me what decimal parts of a pound are $14\overset{\text{s.}}{} : 8\tfrac{1}{2}\overset{\text{d.}}{}$?

*Ed.* First, $\dfrac{1}{2} = \dfrac{1.0}{2} = .5$; 8.5 pence to be brought into decimal parts of a shilling, must be divided by 12; $8.5\overset{\text{d.}}{} = \dfrac{8.5}{12}$ shillings $= .708\dot{3}$; so here are 14.708$\dot{3}$ shillings to bring into decimal parts of $1\overset{\text{£.}}{}$; $14.708\dot{3} = \dfrac{14.7083}{20}$ pounds $= .73541\dot{6}$ of a pound.

To express this with clearness on your slate, it is better to write the given numbers of each denomination perpendicularly under each other, beginning from the lowest denomination to the highest.   Thus,

$$8.5^{d.} \qquad \frac{\overset{d.}{12)8.5}}{}$$

$$14^{s.} \qquad \frac{20)1,4.70\dot{8}\dot{3}}{.73541\dot{6}}$$

You perceive by this arrangement, that you at once place the decimals arising from the first division in the proper situation for the second division, and so on.   Now let us bring 2 .. 14 .. 7 .. 7 (qrs. lbs. oz. dr.) into the decimal of 1 cwt.   First, we write the figures of each denomination directly under each other, and then proceed with the divisions.

$$\frac{16)7.0000}{}$$

$$\frac{16)7.4375}{}$$

$$\frac{28)14.46484375}{}$$

$$\frac{4)\ \ 2.51660156\ \&c.}{.62915039\ \&c.\ =\ \text{decimal of a cwt.}}$$

*Ed.*  But the three first are long division sums, and you háve set them down as if they were short.

*Mrs. D.*  Yes; when these occur you must either do your long division sums in another part of the slate, and copy your result as I have done, or you may break your divisors into more simple ones, the result will be the same (*see* p. 53), whether you divide by 16 (4 × 4), or first by 4, and then the quotient thus obtained by 4. Thus, 16 = 4 × 4, 16 = 4 × 4, 28 = 4 × 7; therefore, the same result will be produced whether we divide by 16, 16, 28, and 4, successively, or whether we divide by 4, 4, 4, 4, 4, 7 and 4, successively—the latter is the better plan.

o

| | |
|---|---|
| drs. | 4)7.00 |
| 7 | |
| oz. | 4)1.7500 |
| 7 | |
| lbs. | 4)7.4375 |
| 14 | |
| qrs. | 4)1.859375 |
| 2 | |
| | 4)14.46484375 |
| | 7) 3.6162109475 |
| | 4) 2.5166015639 &c. |
| | .6291503906 &c. |

Q. 81. Bring into a decimal of 1 lb. troy 6 .. 7. $\overset{\text{oz.} \quad \text{dwts.}}{}$

Q. 82. Bring into a decimal of a week 6 .. 17 .. 35. $\overset{\text{d.} \quad \text{hrs.} \quad \text{min.}}{}$

Q. 83. Bring into the decimal of a yard 2 .. 4. $\overset{\text{ft.]} \quad \text{in.}}{}$

*Mrs. D.* In like manner it may be readily seen that to bring decimal parts of a high denomination into numbers at lower denominations, the same principle is pursued as in the reduction of whole numbers into those of lower denominations. Thus, to bring pounds into shillings we multiply by 20, and therefore, if we multiply .73645 of a pound by 20, we shall have .73045 × 20 shillings = 14.72900 shillings, this .729 × 12 = 8.748 pence, and .748 × 4 = 2.992 farthings, so decimal .73645 of a pound = 14 : 8¾ nearly, because decimal .992 is nearly equal to 1, and therefore, 2.992 are nearly equal to 3 farthings

$$
\begin{array}{r}
.73645 \\
20 \\
\hline
14.72900 \\
12 \\
\hline
8.748 \\
4 \\
\hline
2.992
\end{array}
$$

Now let us bring .6291504 of a cwt. into quarters, pounds, &c.

$$
Ed. \; .6291504 = \overset{\text{qr.}}{2} .. \overset{\text{lb.}}{14} .. \overset{\text{oz.}}{7} .. \overset{\text{dr.}}{7}.0002688
$$

$$
\underline{\phantom{qrs. 2.516601}4}
$$

qrs. 2.5166016

$$
\underline{\phantom{qrs. 2.516601}7}
$$

3.6162112

$$
\underline{\phantom{3.616211}4}
$$

lbs. 14.4648448

$$
\underline{\phantom{lbs. 14.464844}4}
$$

1.8593792

$$
\underline{\phantom{1.859379}4}
$$

oz. 7.4375168

$$
\underline{\phantom{oz. 7.437516}4}
$$

1.7500672

$$
\underline{\phantom{1.750067}4}
$$

dr. 7.0002688

*Mrs. D.* You will remark that this decimal of 1 cwt. exceeds that obtained by our preceding example, where we found that $\overset{\text{qrs.}}{2} .. \overset{\text{lbs.}}{14} .. \overset{\text{oz.}}{7} .. \overset{\text{dr.}}{7}$ were equal to .629150390625 &c. of 1 cwt., which is less than 6291504 by .000000009375, &c. This is so very trifling a difference, that in working the reverse of the sum it might be safely rejected in order that the multiplication might be somewhat abridged : you see by the result that it only produces an excess of .0002688 of a drachm, an error so minute as not to be recognized in the practical application of arithmetic. If we had wished to abridge

o 2

our labour still more, and called our decimal .62915, then this would have been less than

629150390625, &c.

by 0390625, &c.

and our error would have been on the other side: the number of drachms would then have been 6.9886, or .01146 less than 7, which for practical purposes would be no sensible error, and therefore we might well have limited our multiplication to five places of decimals. I have pointed this out to your notice, that you may the better understand the nature of decimals, how they are to be applied to practice, and how they may in all cases be limited so as to be made best available for this purpose.

Q. 84. What number of days, &c. are there in .5673 of a week?

Q. 85. Find the number of feet, &c. in .984 of a yard.

Q. 86. Find the number of pecks, &c. in .7603 of a. bushel.

The principle on which decimal notation is founded rests on the first rudiments of arithmetic, and may be perfectly understood by all who are acquainted with the numeration of whole numbers: the management of decimals to the best advantage, however, requires the exercise of the judgment, and it were vain to multiply rules on the subject, as the pupil, who knows how to use that faculty of the mind, would deem them superfluous; while he who considers arithmetic as a merely mechanical process, would find them at best defective and inefficient.

With rules for shortening operations which depend on particular cases, I shall not therefore perplex you. An easy method of bringing the decimal of a pound into shillings and pence by inspection, however, does not, perhaps, fall under this description. In many business calculations, the conversion of money into decimal parts is much used, and therefore it is desirable to know how to apply this notation with the greatest facility.

Since a shilling is the $\frac{1}{20}$ of $\overset{\pounds}{1}$, it follows that $\overset{s}{1} =$ $\frac{1.00}{20} = \frac{.10}{2} = .05$, and that $\overset{s.}{2}$ are $\frac{2}{20} = \frac{1}{10} = .1$ of $\overset{\pounds}{1}$; and therefore any even number of shillings must be half its number of tenths of $\overset{\pounds}{1}$; and one added to the even number making it an odd number, will be .05 more of $\overset{\pounds}{1}$. Hence any number of shillings being given, half the greatest even number is written in the first place of decimals, and if the number be uneven 5 is added in the the second place. Thus $\overset{s.}{7} = .35$ of $\overset{\pounds}{1}$; $\overset{s.}{18} = .9$ of $\overset{\pounds}{1}$.

Again, $\overset{\pounds}{1} = 20 \times 12 \times 4 = 960$ farthings; therefore every farthing is $\frac{1}{960}$ of $\overset{\pounds}{1}$; if it had been $\frac{1}{1000}$ instead, it is plain that any number of farthings would have consisted of so many thousandths, and have been so many decimal parts of $\overset{\pounds}{1}$. But $\frac{1}{960} - \frac{1}{1000} = \frac{100}{96000} - \frac{96}{96000}$ $= \frac{4}{96000} = \frac{1}{24000}$; and therefore every farthing is $\frac{1}{1000} + \frac{1}{24000}$, or one-thousandth $+ \frac{1}{24}$ of a thousandth, or $001 + \frac{1}{24}$ of .001. Hence we may approximate a decimal of three places of figures with sufficient correctness for most practical purposes. Since 1 farthing $= .001 + \frac{1}{24}$ of .001, it follows that 12 farthings $= .012 +$

$\frac{12}{24}$ of .001, $\overset{\text{far.}}{24} = .024 + \frac{24}{24}$ of .001, and $36 = .036 +$

$\frac{36}{24}$ of 001; therefore when there are more than 12 and less than 36 farthings to be expressed in decimals of £1, the excess of these above the same number of thousandths of £1 will range between $\frac{1}{2}$ and $1\frac{1}{2}$; if then to any number of farthings between 12 and 36 we add 1, and denote them as thousandths of £1, this number will very nearly express the correct decimal, being rather too much when under 24, and rather too little when above that number; in the same manner, if 2 be added to farthings more than 36, there will be a trifling excess, but in no case can the error be as much as .0005. Hence the rule. To bring pence and farthings into decimal parts of £1, reduce them into farthings; and if more than 12 and less than 36 add 1; if more than 36 add 2, and express this number in decimals as thousandth parts.

Let us find by this method what decimal of £1 are $\overset{£}{16} : \overset{s.}{4}\overset{d.}{\frac{1}{2}}$.

> Here $.8 = \frac{1}{2}$ of 16
> $.018 =$ farthings in $4\frac{1}{2}$.
> $\underline{\phantom{..}1}$ for the excess of 12.
> $.819 =$ decimal required.

$19 : 11\overset{d.}{\frac{1}{4}}$.    Here $.9 \phantom{..}= \frac{1}{2}$ of 18.
> $.05 \phantom{..}=$ odd shilling.
> $45 =$ farthings in $11\frac{1}{4}$.
> $\underline{\phantom{..}2}$ for the excess of 36.
> $.997 =$ decimal required.

I have here put down the several steps, that you may the more clearly understand the process. But on seeing

any number of shillings and pence, the decimal by this method at once presents itself to the mind, and with a little practice we shall be able to write them down into decimals as quickly as we could copy the figures. Thus
$1 : 11\frac{3}{4}$ s. d. $= .099 :$ £ $2 ; 5\frac{1}{2}$ s. d. $= .123.$ This is called finding the decimal by inspection. Find in the same manner the decimals of $5 : 7\frac{3}{4}$ s. d. $; 8 : 3\frac{1}{2}$ s. d. $; 9 : 6$ s. d. .

*Ed.* And if we have a decimal of a pound we can, by working the reverse, I suppose, find that by inspection.

*Mrs. D.* Tell me, what are the shillings and pence in .819 of £1 ?

*Ed.* $8 \times 2 = 16 =$ number of shillings; $\dfrac{19 - 1}{4} =$ $4\frac{1}{2}$. So .819 of £1 $= 16 :$ s. $4\frac{1}{2}$ d. .

*Mrs. D.* What are the shillings and pence in .997 of £1 ?

*Ed.* $9 \times 2 = 18$; 9 more than 5; therefore there is 1 more shilling, leaving .047, then $\dfrac{47 - 2}{4} = 11\frac{1}{4}$. So £ .997 $= 19 :$ s. $11\frac{1}{4}$ d. .

*Mrs. D.* Find in the same manner the shillings and pence of $\begin{Bmatrix} .075 \\ .684 \\ .378 \end{Bmatrix}$ of £1.

---

*Mrs. D.* In any compound quantity, it is evident that one denomination is but a fraction of the next higher: thus 1 dwt. is $\dfrac{1}{20}$ of 1 oz.; 1 d. $\dfrac{1}{12}$ of 1 s.; 1 ft. $\dfrac{1}{3}$ of 1 yd.;

$\overset{\text{s.}}{7} : \overset{\text{d.}}{6}$ may therefore be expressed as $7\dfrac{6}{12} = 7\dfrac{1}{2}$, and

brought to an improper fraction $= \dfrac{15}{2}$; and $\dfrac{15}{2}$ of $\overset{\text{s.}}{1}$, or

of $\dfrac{1}{20}$ of $\overset{\pounds}{1} = \dfrac{15}{2 \times 20} = \dfrac{15}{40}$ of $\overset{\pounds}{1}$; therefore $\dfrac{15}{40} = \dfrac{3}{8}$ of $\overset{\pounds}{1}$

truly expresses $\overset{\text{s.}}{7} : \overset{\text{d.}}{6}$. Hence to bring any compound quantity into a fraction of a higher denomination we proceed exactly on the same principle as with whole numbers—divide the number of one denomination by that number in which one of these is contained in the next highest and so on. Now let us bring $\overset{\text{oz.}}{6} : \overset{\text{dwts.}}{12}$ into the fraction of 1 lb. Here $\overset{\text{dwts.}}{12} = \dfrac{12}{20}$ of 1 oz.; therefore $\overset{\text{oz.}}{6} : \overset{\text{dwt.}}{12}$

$= \overset{\text{oz.}}{6}\dfrac{12}{20} = \overset{\text{oz.}}{6}\dfrac{3}{5} = \overset{\text{oz.}}{\dfrac{33}{5}} = \dfrac{33}{5}$ of $\dfrac{1}{12}$ of 1 lb. $= \overset{\text{lb.}}{\dfrac{33}{60}} = \dfrac{11}{20}$ of

1 lb. Express $\overset{\text{s.}}{14} : \overset{\text{d.}}{8\frac{1}{2}}$ in the fraction of $\overset{\pounds}{1}$.

*Ed.* $\overset{\text{d.}}{8\frac{1}{2}} = \dfrac{17}{2} = \dfrac{17}{2}$ of $\dfrac{1}{12}$ of $\overset{\text{s.}}{1} = \dfrac{17}{24}$ of $\overset{\text{s.}}{1}$; $\overset{\text{s.}}{14} : \overset{\text{d.}}{8\frac{1}{2}}$ are

therefore $= 14\dfrac{17}{24} = \dfrac{353}{24}$ of $\overset{\text{s.}}{1} = \dfrac{353}{24}$ of $\dfrac{1}{20}$ of $\overset{\pounds}{1} =$

$\dfrac{353}{24 \times 20} = \dfrac{353}{480}$ of $\overset{\pounds}{1}$.

*Mrs. D.* In the same manner a fraction of a high denomination may be expressed in lower denominations; we have only to reverse our process. Thus $\dfrac{11}{20}$

of 1 lb. troy $= \dfrac{11}{20}$ of 12 oz. $= \dfrac{132}{20} = \overset{\text{oz.}}{6}\dfrac{12}{20}$. Again $\dfrac{12}{20}$

of 1 oz. $= \dfrac{3}{5} = \dfrac{3}{5}$ of 20 dwts. $= \overset{\text{dwts.}}{\dfrac{60}{5}} = \overset{\text{dwts.}}{12}$; therefore $\dfrac{11}{20}$

of 1 lb. $= \overset{\text{oz. dwts.}}{6 : 12}$. Now find what shillings and pence

are $\dfrac{353}{480}$ of $\overset{£}{1}$.

$Ed.$ $\dfrac{353}{480}$ of $\overset{£}{1} = \dfrac{353}{480}$ of 20 shillings $= \dfrac{353}{24} = 14\dfrac{17}{24}$.

Now $\overset{\text{s.}}{\dfrac{17}{24}} = \dfrac{17}{24}$ of 12 pence $= \dfrac{17}{2} = \overset{\text{d.}}{8\tfrac{1}{2}}$; therefore $\dfrac{353}{480}$

of $\overset{£}{1} = \overset{\text{s.}}{14} : \overset{\text{d.}}{8\tfrac{1}{2}}$.

Q. 87. What is the value of $\dfrac{3}{5}$ lb. troy ?

Q. 88. Bring $\overset{\text{oz. dwts.}}{7 : 4}$ to the fraction of 1 lb.

Q. 89. Bring $\overset{\text{s. d.}}{4 : 8}$ to the fraction of $\overset{£.}{1}$.

Q. 90. What is the value of $\dfrac{578}{953}$ of $\overset{£}{1}$ ?

Q. 91. Reduce $\dfrac{5}{6}$ of a penny to the fraction of $\overset{£}{1}$.

Q. 92. Bring $\overset{\text{qrs. lb. oz.}}{2 : 7 : 13}$ to the fraction of 1 cwt.

*Mrs. D.* It is apparent from the foregoing that any compound quantity may be brought into one denomination in three different ways: either by bringing the whole into the lowest denomination; or by expressing the lower denominations in decimal parts of the highest; or lastly, by bringing these into a fraction of the highest. Thus $\overset{£}{3} : \overset{\text{s.}}{14} : \overset{\text{d.}}{8\tfrac{1}{2}} = \overset{£}{3.735} = \overset{£}{3}\dfrac{353}{480}$ : hence it follows, that any calculations involving compound quantities may be worked by three different methods. A thorough knowledge of the nature of numbers united to practice can alone enable us to judge which method in every particular case is most advantageous. In selecting this method, many things are to be taken into consideration, more especially accuracy, expedition, and conciseness; but I would not by any means advise that much time should be lost in endeavouring to discover the very best method which may be pursued. Decision and promptness may arrive at the goal by the longest road, ere yet indecision and deliberation have made choice of a path. Therefore in applying hereafter your knowledge to practice, it were better to take at once a circuitous but well-defined way, rather than to ponder long over the best means of arriving at the result. It is, however, very desirable that you should acquire the ability of readily knowing how to seize immediately on the simplest method, and therefore you cannot do better at present than to exercise yourself in answering various questions by the three different methods. This will enable you to judge for yourself what are the particular questions which each method will best suit, while at the same time you will prove to yourself the correctness of your operations through the agreement of your results obtained by different processes. Here are three examples worked at full length by the three different ways. You will perceive, in the first question, that the first method is the most advantageous; in the second question, the second method is the shortest; and in the third example, the third method is preferable. I have designedly made selections that would produce these results, as striking examples usually give a better insight into knowledge than multiplied rules and precepts.

lb.    oz.    dwt.

A goldsmith bought a bar of gold weighing 6 : 10 : 10,

£.    s.    d.             dwt.

for 251 : 12 : 6. How much did 1 cost at this rate?

## First method.

lb.  oz.  dwts.      £.    s.   d.      dwt.    s.   d.

6 : 10 : 10 cost 251 : 12 : 6 ; so 1 cost 3 : 0$\frac{1}{2}$ and $\frac{2}{5}$ of a far.

$$\frac{12}{\overline{82}}$$
$$\frac{20}{}$$

As $\overline{1650}$   cost

$$\frac{20}{\overline{5032}}$$
$$\frac{12}{\overline{60390}}$$ therefore, 1 dwt.

will cost $\dfrac{60390}{1650} = $  d. $=$

$\dfrac{366}{10} = 36\dfrac{6}{10} = \overset{\text{s. d.}}{3} : 0\frac{1}{2}$ and $\frac{2}{5}$ of a far.

366
4026
12078
60390
1650
330
110
10

## Second method, by Fractions.

lbs.  oz.  dwts.      £.    s.   d.      dwt.    s.   d.

6 : 10 : 10 cost 251 : 12 : 6 ; so 1 costs 3 : 0$\frac{1}{2}$ and $\frac{2}{5}$ of a far.

dwts.

$10 = 10$ of $\dfrac{1}{20}$ of 1 oz. $= \dfrac{1}{2}$ oz.; $10\frac{1}{2} = \dfrac{21}{2}$ of $\dfrac{1}{12}$ of 1 lb.

$= \overset{\text{lb.}}{\dfrac{21}{24}} = \dfrac{7}{8}$, therefore, $\overset{\text{lb. oz. dwts.}}{6 : 10 : 10} = 6\dfrac{7}{8} = \dfrac{55}{8}$ of 1 lb. In

the same way $\overset{\text{d.}}{6} = 6$ of $\dfrac{1}{12}$ of $\overset{\text{s.}}{1} = \overset{\text{s.}}{\dfrac{1}{2}}$; $12\frac{1}{2} = \dfrac{25}{2}$ of $\dfrac{1}{20}$ of

$\overset{£.}{1} = \dfrac{25}{40} = \dfrac{5}{8}$; $\overset{£. \quad s. \quad d.}{so\ 251 : 12 : 6} = 251\dfrac{5}{8} = \dfrac{2013}{8}$; $\overset{\text{dwt.}}{1} = 1$

of $\dfrac{1}{20}$ of $\dfrac{1}{12}$ of 1 lb. $= \dfrac{1}{240}$.   Since $\overset{\text{lb.}}{\dfrac{55}{8}}$ cost $\overset{£.}{\dfrac{2013}{8}}$,

therefore, $\overset{\text{lb.}}{\dfrac{1}{240}}$ will cost $\overset{£}{\dfrac{2013}{8}} \times \dfrac{1}{240} \div \dfrac{55}{8} = \dfrac{2013 \times 8}{8 \times 240 \times 55}$

$= \dfrac{671}{80 \times 55} = \dfrac{61}{80 \times 5} = \dfrac{61}{400}.$

61
20

$4/00) \overline{12/20}$

$3\frac{3}{20}\text{s.} = \overset{\text{s. d.}}{3} : \frac{1\ 2}{2\ 0} = \overset{\text{s. d.}}{3} : 0\frac{1}{2}$ and $\frac{2}{5}$ of a far.

### Third method, by Decimals.

lbs. oz. dwts.   £.   s.   d.   dwt.    s .d.
6 : 10 : 10 cost 251 : 12 : 6; so 1 costs 3 : 0½⅔

$$20)1.00$$

20)10.

$$12)\overline{.050}$$

12)10 500

$$\overline{.00416}$$

6.875 cost 251.625; so .00416 costs $\dfrac{251.625 \times .00416}{6.875}$

183
2013
10065
50325
251625

$251625 \times .00416 = \dfrac{.00416 \times 183}{5}$

6875
1375
275
5½
5

.00416*
183
‾‾‾‾‾
.01250
.33333
.41666
5)‾.76250‾
   £.   s.   d.
.1525 of 1 = 3 : 0½ and ⅔ of a far.

### EXAMPLE 2.

   s.   d.    qrs. lb. oz.
If I pay 17 : 0¾ for 3 : 13 : 8, what must I pay for 50 cwt. ?

---

* The working of this sum shows how recurring decimals may be managed in multiplication. Here .6̇ or .6666, &c. × 3 = 1.9999, &c. = 1.9̇, but 9̇ = 9/9 (see page 123) = 1 ; therefore 1.9̇ = 2 and .6̇ × 3 = 2. Also .6666, &c. × 8 = 5.3333, &c. = 5.3̇.

*First method.*

qrs. lb. oz.     s.   d.     cwt.    £   s.   d.

$3 : 13 : 8$ cost $17 : 0\frac{3}{4}$; so 50 cost $49 : 0 : 0$.

```
 28            12              4
 ──            ───            ───
 37            204            200 qrs.
  6              4             28
 ──            ───            ───
 97 lbs.       819           5600 lbs.
 16                            16
───                          ─────
590                          33600
 97                             56
```

1560 oz. cost 819 far., so 89600 oz. cost $\dfrac{273 \times 2240}{1560}$ 

$$\text{farthings} = \frac{273 \times 2240}{13}$$

```
      273        2240
      819 × 89600
      ────────────
         1560
         520
          13
```

```
         273
        2240
       ─────
       10920
        546
        546
       ─────
13)611520(4)47040
       52    12)11760
       ──    ────────
       91    2/0)98.0
       91    ─────────
      ─────    49..0..0
       ·52
       52
```

*Second method, by Fractions.*

qrs. lbs. oz.    s.   d.     cwt.    £.  s.  d.

$3 : 13 : 8$ cost $17 : 0\frac{3}{4}$, so 50 cost $49 : 0 : 0$    qrs.

lbs oz.    lbs.

$13 : 8 = 13\frac{1}{2}$; equal to $\dfrac{27}{2}$ of $\dfrac{1}{28}$ of 1 qr. $= \dfrac{27}{56}$

and $3\dfrac{27}{56} = \dfrac{195}{224}$ of 1 cwt.

$17 : 0\frac{3}{4} = 17\dfrac{3}{48} = \dfrac{819}{48}$ of $\dfrac{1}{20}$ of $1 = \dfrac{819}{960}$. Therefore,

cwt.

$\dfrac{195}{224}$ costs $\dfrac{819}{960}$, so 50 cwt. cost $\dfrac{819 \times 50}{960} \div \dfrac{195}{224}$

P

$$\frac{819 \times 5 \times 224}{960 \times 195} = \frac{\cancel{819} \times \cancel{224} \times \cancel{5}}{\cancel{960} \times \cancel{195}} = 7 \times 7 = 49$$

### Third method, by Decimals.

qrs. lbs. oz.    s.   d.     cwt.     £. s. d.
3 : 13 : 8   cost 17 : 0¾, so 50 cost 49 : 0 : 0

4) 8.0

4) 2.0

4) 13.5

7) 3.375

4) 3.482142857

$\frac{}{870535714}$ &c. cost .853125, so 50 cost $\frac{.853125 \times 50}{.870535714}$

```
      853125
          50
```

870535714 &c.)42,656.25000.0(49
     34 821 42856

      7 834 821440
      7 834 821426

.0 000 000014 this slight excess, because the whole decimal was not used in the divisor.

A club, consisting of 70 persons, imported 30 casks of wine, for the payment of which each of the subscribers was called upon to contribute 25 : 19 : 9. Each cask should have contained exactly 63 gallons, but 9 out of the 30 casks were found deficient in one eighth of the quantity they should have held. After some time the club was dissolved, and one person to whom they were indebted $518:5:7\frac{3}{4}$ agreed to take out his debt in wine at prime cost. Now, how much wine should he receive? The number of gallons originally imported were $63 \times 30 - \dfrac{63}{8}$ of 9 casks;— to work in whole numbers, we must bring the gallons into $\dfrac{1}{8}$ths, or pints, and therefore, $63 \times 8 \times 30 - 9 \times 63$, will be equal to the aggregate number of pints contained in all the casks.

| £. s. d. | | | £. s. d. |
|---|---|---|---|
| 25 : 19 : 9 | 63 | 63 | $518:5:7\frac{3}{4}$ |
| 20 | 9 | 8 | 20 |
| 519 | 567 | 504 | 10365 |
| 12 | | 30 | 12 |
| 6237 | | 15120 | 124387 |
| 4 | | 567 | 4 |

24948 × 70 will obtain 14553 then 497551 should obtain 518 gallons $2\dfrac{31}{120}$ pints.

Therefore, $\dfrac{14553 \times 497551}{24948 \times 70}$ = required quantity = $\dfrac{497551}{120}$

12,0)49755,1

8)4146$\frac{31}{120}$ pints.

518 gallons, and $2\frac{31}{120}$ pints.

### Second method, by Fractions.

We find the same as in the last, that $\dfrac{14553}{8} =$ whole

number of gallons imported. Then, if $\overset{£.\quad s.\quad d.}{25:19:9} \times 70$

obtain $\dfrac{14553}{8}$, so should $\overset{£.\quad s.\quad d.}{518:5:7\frac{3}{4}}$ obtain $\overset{gals.\quad pts.}{518:2\frac{31}{120}}$

$\overset{d.}{9} = \frac{3}{4}$ of $\overset{s.}{1}$; $19\frac{3}{4} = \dfrac{4 \times 19 + 3}{4} = \dfrac{79}{4}$ of $\overset{s.}{1} = \dfrac{79}{4}$ of $\dfrac{1}{20}$ of $\overset{£.}{1}$

$= \dfrac{79}{80}$ of $\overset{£.}{1}$; $25\dfrac{79}{80} = \dfrac{25 \times 80 + 79}{80} = \dfrac{2079}{80}$.

| ⊙ | | |
|---|---|---|
| 19 | 80 | So $\overset{£.\quad s.\quad d.}{25:19:9} = \dfrac{2079\dagger}{80}$ |
| 4 | 25 | |
| 76 | 2000 | |
| 3 | 79 | |
| 79 | 2079 | |

Again $7\dfrac{3}{4} = \dfrac{31}{4}$ of $\dfrac{1}{12}$ of $\overset{s.}{1} = \dfrac{31}{48}$; $5\dfrac{31}{48} = \dfrac{5 \times 48 + 31}{48} =$

$\dfrac{271}{48}$ of $\dfrac{1}{20}$ of $\overset{£.}{1} = \dfrac{271}{960}$; and $518\dfrac{271}{960} = \dfrac{518 \times 960 + 271}{960} =$

$\dfrac{497551}{960} = \overset{£.\quad s.\quad d.}{518:5:7\frac{3}{4}}.$

| 48 | 518 |
|---|---|
| 5 | 960 |
| 240 | 31080 |
| 31 | 4662 |
| 271 | 497280 |
| | 271 |
| | 497551 |

Therefore, if $\dfrac{2079}{80} \times 70$ obtain. $\dfrac{14553}{8}$ so should $\dfrac{497551}{960}$

obtain 518 gallons $2\dfrac{31}{120}$ pints, $\dfrac{14553}{8} \times \dfrac{497551}{960} \div$

$\dfrac{2079 \times 70}{80} =$ required number of gallons $=$

$$\frac{14553 \times 497551 \times 80}{8 \quad \times 2079 \times 70 \times 960} = \frac{497551}{960}$$

gals.   pints.
960)49755,1(518 : $2\frac{31}{120}$
480

175
96

795
768

271
8

216,8 pints.
192

248 $= \dfrac{248}{960} = \dfrac{62}{240} = \dfrac{31}{120}.$

*Third method, by Decimals.*

We find $\dfrac{9 \times 63}{8} = \dfrac{567}{8} = 70.875$; therefore, if from

$30 \times 63 = 1890$ we take $70.875 = 1819.125 =$ whole number of gallons in all the casks.

£.    s.    d.
$25 : 19 : 9 = 25.9875$ and $518 : 5 : 7\frac{3}{4} = 518.28225$ &c.

Therefore, if 25.9875 × 70 obtain 1819.125, so should

$$518.28225 \text{ \&c. obtain } \frac{1819.125 \times 518.28225}{25.9875 \times 70 \times 10} = 518.2 \text{ \&c.}$$

= 518.28225 &c. gallons = 518 gallons 2.258 pints.

$$\frac{8}{2.25800}$$

Q. 93. On the 21st October, 1828, a Swedish turnip was dug up in Surrey, which weighed 21 lbs., and measured one yard in circumference. The seed which produced it was sown on the 7th of July, and weighed $\frac{1}{14000}$ of an ounce; how many times had it increased its weight; and, assuming that this was augmented uniformly, or, that in equal given times the same increase of positive weight was always produced, how many times the weight of the seed did it increase per minute?

Q. 94. By the steam printing press 2400 papers are printed in an hour; how many are printed in a minute, and how long a time would be required to print 26,963 papers?

Q. 95. The average weight of the cocoons formed by silk-worms is about 29¼ grains each; from 7½ lbs. of these cocoons 10 ounces of fine reeled silk are usually obtained; now, how many cocoons are required to yield 1 lb. of silk; and supposing that the silkworms which produce 7½ lbs. of cocoons, consume 97½ lbs. of mulberry leaves during their whole existence, how many pounds of mulberry leaves are required to feed the silkworms which produce one pound of reeled silk?

Q. 96. The following is the receipt for 160 gallons of soup, which was made at Birmingham in a time of scarcity, to be distributed among the poor:—

| | £. | s. | d. |
|---|---|---|---|
| 141 lbs. meat, which cost.......... | 1 | 5 | 0 |
| 37 quarts peas................. | 0 | 7 | 4 |
| 21 lbs. onions ................. | 0 | 1 | 8 |
| 48 lbs. ground rice.. .......... | 0 | 10 | 0 |
| 12 lbs. salt.......... ........ | 0 | 0 | 0 |
| 6 oz. black pepper............. | 0 | 0 | 10 |
| 2 oz. ground ginger........... | 0 | 0 | 2 |
| 4 oz. cayenne pepper........... | 0 | 0 | 3 |
| Herbs.................... | 0 | 0 | 1 |

Now what did this soup cost per gallon? and wanting to make the same kind of soup on a small scale, I require to know how much of each ingredient I must take to make 2 gallons?

Q. 97. The steam-carriages travel from Liverpool to Manchester, a distance of 32 miles, in 1 hour and 25 minutes, what space of ground do they go over in each minute?

Q. 98. In a very circumstantial detail of the culture and manufacture of sugar in the Masulipatam Circar, we find it stated, that a vissum, or 72,000 square feet of ground, were found to produce 85,140 canes; these canes yielded, on expression, 41,412 lbs. of juice, which produced 300 maunds, or 7200 lbs. of jaggry, or inferior sugar, from which was obtained 19 : 3 : 11 of good marketable sugar. I require to know what number of sugar-canes can, at this rate, be obtained from one acre of land, and likewise the quantity of jaggry and of sugar?

Q. 99. It has been estimated that the manufacturers in the neighbourhood of Manchester are saved 20,000 per annum on the transport of cotton wool from Liverpool since the opening of the rail-road between Manchester and Liverpool in consequence of the less expensive carriage of the material through that means. The rate of carriage of goods on the rail-road is 10$^{s.}$ per ton ; by

canal it used to be 15$^{s.}$ per ton. Assuming this statement to be correct, how many pounds of cotton wool are
sent to Manchester from Liverpool for manufacture in
the course of one year?  The average price of cotton
wool being 8$\frac{1}{4}$$^{d.}$ per pound, what is the whole value of the
raw cotton manufactured into goods at Manchester per
annum?  And suppose a quarter of this quantity to be
made into calico, each square yard of which takes 1085
troy grains of raw material, how many yards of calico
will be thus furnished?

Q. 100. It is stated in Bakewell's Geology that the coal-
beds in South Wales extend over 1200 square miles, and
it is reckoned that one square mile will yield 32,000,000
of tons, after deducting for waste, &c.  Now how long
will this one coal-field alone afford a sufficient supply for
the London market, supposing the consumption to continue at its present rate of 2,014,804 tons per annum?

Q. 101. The consumption of coals in steam-vessels
is usually averaged at 7 lbs. per horse power per hour.
How many bushels of coals does an Edinburgh steam-
packet consume during the passage between London
and Edinburgh, this being accomplished in about 67
hours?  The engines on board the vessel are two of 80
horse power each.  About 82 lbs. of coal measure 1
bushel.

Q. 102. A silk-mill, constructed more than a century
ago at Derby, and which was put in motion by water,
was of so stupendous a size, that at every revolution of
the water-wheel 73,726 yards of raw silk were thrown
(or twisted previous to weaving).  This wheel revolved
three times in a minute; continuing this progress for 12
hours, how much silk would be thrown in that time?

Q. 103. A person, in the enjoyment of an annuity

amounting to $896 : 17^{s.}$, laid by at the end of the year $210^{£.}$, and gave quarterly to the poor $5^{£.}$; how much has he spent, and at what rate per day?

Q. 104. The carriage of a parcel, weighing 2 tons, cost $10^{s.}$ for 6 miles. What should be paid at the same rate for the carriage of 12 tons 17 cwt. for 17 miles?

---

*Mrs. D.* Hitherto, when the price of one thing has been given, you have found the cost of any number of the same things by multiplying the number and the price together: this is the most obvious method, but there is another and a shorter mode of arriving at the same result, and its extensive use has obtained for this mode the characteristic name of PRACTICE. I have bought 3257 lbs. of sugar at the price of $4^{d.}$ for each pound. Now how much must I pay for the whole?

*Ed.* The whole will cost 3257 multiplied by $4^{d.}$, or $3257 \times 4 = 13028$ pence; surely there cannot be a shorter way than this.

*Mrs. D.* Very true, if I were going to pay in pence; but I want to convert these into shillings; so our sum will be $\dfrac{13028}{12}$.

*Ed.* Equal to $1085 : 8^{d.}$.

*Mrs. D.* You will perceive now, that you have been doing two operations when one would have been suffi-cient; you first multiplied 3257 by 4, and then divided by 12, or $\dfrac{3257 \times \cancel{4}}{\cancel{12} \atop 3} = \dfrac{3257}{3} = 1085\tfrac{2}{3}^{s.}$; therefore if you had at once divided by 3 you would have had less trouble.

*Ed.* Yes, to be sure, I might have cancelled.

*Mrs. D.* If 1 lb. had cost 1$^{s.}$, 3257 lbs. would have cost 3257$^{s.}$; and since 4$^{d.}$ is $\frac{1}{3}$ of 1$^{s.}$, it follows that at 4$^{d.}$ per lb. they will cost $\frac{1}{3}$ of 3257$^{s.}$, and we should thus state and work the question in practice.

$$4^{d.} \text{ is } \frac{1}{3} \text{ of } 1^{s.} \frac{3257 \qquad \text{price at } 1^{s.} \text{ per lb.}}{1085:8 \quad . \quad . \quad 4^{d.}}$$

Therefore, when the price is a certain number of pence which are contained in 12 a whole number of times, that is to say, when 12 is a multiple of this, it will be easier to divide by a number equal to 12 divided by the price, instead of first multiplying by the price, and then dividing by 12. Thus, 2, 3, 4, and 6, are factors of 12, and therefore, if the sugar had cost 2d. per lb., it would have been $\frac{2}{12}$ or $\frac{1}{6}$ of 1$^{s.}$—if 3$^{d.}$, it would have been $\frac{3}{12}$ or $\frac{1}{4}$ of 1$^{s.}$, and if 6$^{d.}$ it would have been $\frac{6}{12}$ or $\frac{1}{2}$ of 1$^{s.}$.

When any number is contained in another number a whole number of times, the former is usually called the aliquot part of the latter; therefore, all factors of a number are its aliquot parts: 2$^{d.}$, 3$^{d.}$, 4$^{d.}$, and 6$^{d.}$, are aliquot parts of 12$^{d.}$, or of 1$^{s.}$. In the same manner 1$\frac{1}{2}$ = 6$^{far.}$, is the aliquot part of 48$^{far.}$, or is $\frac{1}{8}$ of 1$^{s.}$.

Now, if the price of our sugar were 5$^{d.}$ per lb. instead of 4$^{d.}$, a fourth part of the cost at 4$^{d.}$ per lb. will be the cost at 1$^{d.}$ per lb., and these two prices added together will give the whole cost at 5$^{d.}$  Our sum would then stand thus—

4$^{d.}$ is the $\frac{1}{3}$ of 1$^{s.}$    3257    price at 1$^{s.}$ per lb.

1$^{d.}$ is the $\frac{1}{4}$ of 4$^{d.}$    $\overline{1085 : 8^{d.}}$ . . 4$^{d.}$

             271 : 5   . . 1$^{d.}$

$\overline{5^{d.}}$ . . . . $\overline{1357 : 1}$ price at 5$^{d.}$ per lb.

In like manner, if the price were 10$^{d.}$ per lb., we should find the price at 6$^{d.}$, and at 4$^{d.}$, and add these together—

6$^{d.}$ is $\frac{1}{2}$ of 1$^{s.}$    3257    price at 1$^{s.}$ per lb.

4$^{d.}$ is $\frac{1}{3}$ of 1$^{s}$    $\overline{1628 : 6}$ . . 6$^{d.}$

$\overline{10}$          1085 : 8   . . 4$^{d.}$

          $\overline{2714 : 2}$ . $\overline{10}$

The same principle of course extends when the price is beyond 1$^{s.}$  If 3257 are at 4$^{s.}$ per lb., then 4$^{s.}$ being equal to $\frac{4}{20}$ or $\frac{1}{5}$ of 1$^{£.}$, the cost will be $\frac{1}{5}$ of the cost at 1$^{£.}$, or $\frac{3257}{5}$ and the statement will be

4$^{s.}$ is $\frac{1}{5}$ of 1$^{£.}$    3257$^{£.}$    at 1$^{£.}$ per lb.

          $\overline{651 : 8^{s.}}$    4$^{s.}$

In like manner, if the price be any other aliquot part or parts of 1$^{£.}$, we may pursue a similar process. For example, 2710 at 6 : 8. Here 6$^{s.}$ : 8$^{d.}$ is exactly $\frac{1}{3}$ of 1$^{£.}$, being 80$^{d.}$ and $\frac{80}{12 \times 20} = \frac{80}{240} = \frac{1}{3}$, therefore,

6 : 8$^{s. \, d.}$ is $\frac{1}{3}$ of 1$^{£.}$    2710    price at 1$^{£.}$

          $\overline{903 : 6 : 8}$ . . 6 : 8$^{s. \, d.}$

If the price were $\overset{\text{s. d.}}{7:4}$, or $\overset{\text{s. d.}}{6:8} + \overset{d.}{8}$, it would be 1 tenth more; since $\overset{\text{s. d.}}{6:8}$ are $\overset{d.}{80}$, and therefore, $\overset{d.}{8}$ is contained 10 times in $\overset{\text{s. d.}}{6:8}$. If the price were $\overset{\text{s. d.}}{11:8}$, then $\overset{\text{s. d.}}{11:8} = \overset{\text{s.}}{5} + \overset{\text{s. d.}}{6:8}$, would be $\frac{1}{4}$ and $\frac{1}{3}$ of $\overset{\mathcal{L}.}{1}$. Hence, the reason is made sufficiently manifest of the following rule, which comprises the whole of what is called practice. First find the most suitable aliquot part of the next denomination, then, if this be not the whole price, find other aliquot parts of the same, or of the aliquot part used, and proceed thus till the whole of the price is taken; divide successively, and add the results. A little ingenuity is sometimes required in taking those aliquot parts, which will make the process the most short and simple, but practice will soon make you expert in this matter. It is scarcely necessary to add, that care must be taken in the divisions to select the proper dividends; if you understand the principle on which you proceed, you cannot possibly make a mistake in regard to these. We will now work one or two examples stated with more brevity than the preceding, but I think with sufficient clearness for practice.

What is the price of 2510 cwt. at $\overset{\text{s. d.}}{14:7\frac{1}{4}}$?

| | £. |
| --- | --- |
| | 2510 price at 1. |
| s. d.    £. s. d. | |
| $10:0 \ \frac{1}{2}$ of $1:0:0$ | 1255 |
| $4:0 \ \frac{1}{5}$ of $1:0:0$ | 502 |
| $0:6 \ \frac{1}{8}$ of $0:4:0$ | 62:15 |
| $0:1 \ \frac{1}{6}$ of $0:0:6$ | 10: 9:2 |
| $0:\frac{1}{4} \ \frac{1}{4}$ of $0:0:1$ | 2:12:3$\frac{1}{2}$ |
| $14:7\frac{1}{4}$ | 1832:16:5$\frac{1}{2}$ |

$$\overset{\pounds.\;\;s.\;\;d.}{2710 \text{ lbs. at } 2:3:7\tfrac{1}{4},} \text{ what is the cost?}$$

| £. s. d. | 2 |
|---|---|
| 2 : 0 : 0    2 | 5420 |
| 0 : 2 : 0 $\frac{1}{10}$ | 271 |
| 0 : 1 : 0  $\frac{1}{2}$ | 135 : 10 |
| 0 : 0 : 6  $\frac{1}{2}$ | 67 : 15 |
| 0 : 0 : 1$\frac{1}{2}$ $\frac{1}{4}$ | 16 : 18 : 9 |

$$2 : 3 : 7\tfrac{1}{2} \qquad \pounds5911 : 3 : 9$$

Q. 105. Find what is the cost of 7291 at 10$\frac{3}{4}$ (d.)?

Q. 106. 9872 at 8$\frac{3}{4}$ (d.)?

Q. 107. 3715 at 9 : 4$\frac{1}{2}$ (s. d.)?

Q. 108. 2710 at 19 : 2$\frac{1}{2}$ (s. d.)?

Q. 109. 2517 at 3 : 15 : 2$\frac{1}{4}$ (£. s. d.)?

Sometimes the process will be found more simple, if, instead of adding prices together, we subtract one from another; but this entirely depends on the nature of the question.

Thus, 7972 at 11$\frac{3}{4}$ (d.) Here the price of each is a shilling all but one farthing: therefore, 7972 − 7972 (far.) will be the answer.

| 7972 at 1 (s.) | 4)7972 (far.) |
|---|---|
| 166 : 1 at $\frac{1}{4}$ | 12)1993 |
| 2,0)780(5 : 11 | 166 : 1 |
| 390 : 5 : 11  Price at 11$\frac{3}{4}$ (d.) | |

*Mrs. D.* In books designed for teaching arithmetic, it is usual to give a number of rules for different calculations arising out of commercial transactions: these

Q

can all be solved by the simple application of rules which have already been explained. It may, however, be as well briefly to notice some of the more important mercantile usages which require the aid of arithmetic. INTEREST takes here a most conspicuous place, and therefore I shall first explain the meaning of this term. Interest is a certain price paid for the use of a sum of money: thus, if a tradesman borrow $\overset{£.}{100}$ for one year, and if he pay back, at the expiration of that time, not only the $\overset{£.}{100}$ he borrowed but $\overset{£.}{5}$ in addition, this $\overset{£.}{5}$ is called the interest upon the $\overset{£.}{100}$ borrowed; and whatever the sum of money borrowed may be, the interest is always reckoned at the rate charged per cent., that is to say, for each hundred: thus $\overset{£.}{5}$ for every hundred is called 5 per cent.; $\overset{£.\ \ s.}{4:10\ 4\frac{1}{2}}$ per cent.; $\overset{£.\ \ s.}{7:5\ 7\frac{1}{4}}$ per cent.; and so on.

*Ed.* But I cannot see why the tradesman should have borrowed the money at all if he were to lose $\overset{£.}{5}$ by it.

*Mrs. D.* It is of great advantage in trade to have the use of money, and therefore for that advantage people are willing to pay an equivalent price. Perhaps, instead of losing, the tradesman gained by the transaction. He did not borrow the $\overset{£.}{100}$ to put them away in a chest, and pay them back with interest at the end of the year; if he had done so, he would indeed have been unwise. Suppose, however, that he laid this money out in goods, which he sold before the end of the year at a high profit, he could then afford to pay $\overset{£.}{5}$ out of this profit.

Thus money is lent or laid out at various rates of interest, according to the agreement entered into between the contracting parties.

*Ed.* Yes, now I understand : if a person can lay out money to a very great advantage, he is of course willing to pay very high interest for the use of this money.

*Mrs. D.* The existing laws of this country, however, set a limit to the interest which may be demanded ; 5 £. per cent. is this limit ; to take a higher rate of interest is called usury, which is punishable by law.

*Ed.* Is not this a very odd law ?

*Mrs. D.* It was, I believe, made for the protection of young spendthrifts, and prodigal heirs ; that in raising money, they might not be victims to the extortion of those who are always ready to take advantage of the necessities of others. It however not only proves wholly inadequate, but increases the evil sought to be prevented ; while the operation of this law is very pernicious in mercantile transactions. A much better protection to youth would be found in a good moral education, teaching forethought, prudence, and high principles of integrity. But let us return to the arithmetical consideration of interest.

If $373:4:6$ be lent, for which $4$ per cent. interest, £. s. d.                            £.

or $4$ for every $100$, is to be paid, you will be able readily to calculate the interest on the whole sum. £.    £.

*Ed.* It is nothing but a common Rule of Three sum.

*Mrs. D.* True : if $4$ be paid for every $100$, $\dfrac{4}{100} = .04$ £.                                    £.    $\dfrac{4}{100}$

$=$ the interest for every $1$. £.

Now $373:4:6 =$ by inspection $373.225$ ; therefore £. s. d.

$373.225 \times .04 = 14.929 = 14:18:7 =$ interest required. £.            £.    £. s. d.

When we say at such a rate per cent., without defining any time, that rate per annum is always understood.

The money lent is called the principal; the sum of the principal and the interest at the end of the time is called the amount.

If a person borrow money, and if he pay the interest regularly at the stipulated times, it will be considered that he retains in his hands simply the sum of money originally borrowed; the interest thus accruing is called simple interest. But if he do not pay this interest at the end of the first period, it is clear that he will now have the use of the principal and interest, for the whole of which he should pay interest at the end of the next period; and if the debt still remain unpaid, he will now have the principal, the interest of the first period, and the increased interest of the second, for all of which he should pay interest at the end of the third period; and so on, the debt continuing to accumulate with an accelerating rate of increase. The interest thus constantly augmenting is called compound interest.

We will first consider simple interest, when it is for more or for less than one year. For this an example in each will be found sufficient.

What is the simple interest on $563 : \overset{\pounds.}{7} : \overset{s.}{6}$ at $3\frac{1}{2}$ per cent. for $5\frac{1}{4}$ years? $563 : \overset{\pounds.}{7} : \overset{s.}{6} = 563.275 \times .035 \left(\dfrac{3.5}{100}\right)$ $=$ interest for 1 year; therefore $563.275 \times .035 \times 5.25 (5\frac{1}{4}) =$ interest for $5\frac{1}{4}$ years.

$$563.275$$
$$035$$
$$\overline{\phantom{000}}$$
$$2816375$$
$$1689825$$
$$\overline{\phantom{000}}$$
$$19.714625$$
$$5.25$$
$$\overline{\phantom{000}}$$
$$98573125$$
$$39429250$$
$$98573125$$
$$\overline{\phantom{000}}$$

£.   s.  d.

$$103.50178125 = 103 : 10 : 0\tfrac{1}{4}$$

In many business transactions money is often lent for less than a year, sometimes only for a few days, and sometimes for one or more years and an odd number of days, the calculations are then rather more tedious.

For example, what is the interest on 175 : 8 : 3 (£. s. d.) at 5 per cent. for 57 days? Now, one day being $\dfrac{1}{365}$ of a year,

57 days are $\dfrac{57}{365}$ of a year, and therefore, the interest for one year being multiplied by $\dfrac{57}{365}$ will give the interest for 57 days.

$$175 : 8 : 3 = 175.4125 \times .05 \times \frac{57}{365} = \frac{175.4125 \times .05 \times 57}{365}$$

$$= \frac{175.4125 \times .57 \ (.01 \times 57)}{73}$$

$$175.4125$$
$$.57$$
$$\overline{\phantom{000}}$$
$$12278875$$
$$8770625$$
$$\overline{73)99.985125}(1.369 = £1 : 7 : 4\tfrac{3}{4}$$
$$73$$
$$\overline{26.9}$$
$$219$$
$$\overline{\phantom{00}508}$$
$$438$$
$$\overline{\phantom{00}705}$$

When the interest is for a mixed number of years and days, that is to say, when the number of days is no aliquot part of a year, it must be found for the years and days separately. These comprise every case of questions in simple interest.

Compound interest may be found exactly in the same manner as simple interest, the process only being longer.

If it be required to find the compound interest of £370 for 3 years at 5 per cent. then,

|  | £. | £. | s. | d. |
|---|---|---|---|---|
| The principal = | 370 | | | |
| Interest for first year } = 370 × .5 = | 18.5 | 18 : | 10 : | 0 |
| Second year's principal = | 388.5 | | | |
| Interest for second year } = 388.5 × .05 = | 19.425 | 19 : | 8 : | 6 |
| Third year's principal = | 407.925 | | | |
| Interest for third year } = 407.925 × .05 = | 20.39625 = | 20 : | 7 : | 11 |
| | | 58 : | 6 : | 5 = inter$^t$. |

£. s. d.
428.32125 = 428 : 3 : 5 = amou$^t$

When the interest has been accumulating for several years, it is evident that the above will be a very tedious

process, for which reason it is seldom or never applied to practical purposes. The following is a better method:
—If 1$^{£.}$ amount to a certain sum at the end of a given time, it is evident that 2,$^{£.}$ calculated at the same rate of interest, will amount to double that sum in the same time; 3,$^{£.}$ three times, and so on: therefore, 370$^{£.}$ multiplied by the amount of 1$^{£.}$ at 5 per cent. for 3 years, will give the amount of 370 for that time; and, in general, the amount at compound interest of any sum for any number of years, is that sum multiplied by the amount of 1$^{£.}$ for that time at the same rate of interest. The manner of finding the amount of 1$^{£.}$ for any time is thus :—Let us suppose that 1$^{£.}$ will amount to 2*$^{£.}$ at the end of the first year, then 2$^{£.}$ will amount to 2 × 2 in the same time; 4, or 2 × 2, will amount to 4 × 2 or 2 × 2 × 2, in the same time, therefore, the amount of 1$^{£.}$ in the first year, being 2, the amount in the second year will be 2 × 2, or the amount at the end of the first year multiplied by the amount of 1$^{£.}$ in one year; in the same manner, at the end of the third year, the amount will be 2 × 2 × 2, the amount of 1$^{£.}$ for one year continually multiplied into itself as many times as the number of years. Thus, if 1$^{£.}$ amount to 1.05 at the end of one year, at the end of the 2nd year

it will be .. .. .. .. 1.05 × 1.05
at the end of the 3rd .. .. 1.05 × 1.05 × 1.05
at the end of the 4th .. .. 1.05 × 1.05 × 1.05
&c. &c. &c. &c. &c. &c.

When a number is thus multiplied continually into

---

* This is an extravagant assumption, which is put merely to make the principle more apparent.

itself, the product is called the power of that number, and the number of times it is multiplied into itself is called the index of that power:—thus, $1.05 \times 1.05$ is called the second power of 1.05; $1.05 \times 1.05 \times 1.05$ third power of 1.05, and these may be expressed with more brevity by the use of the index; thus, $\overline{1.05}|^2$ denotes the second power of 1.05, and means that 1.05 is to be multiplied by 1.05; $\overline{1.05}|^3$ denotes the third power, and $\overline{1.05}|^{20}$ denotes the 20th power. Now let us find the third power of 1.05, which, multiplied by 370, will give the amount of that principal for 3 years.

| | |
|---|---|
| 1.05 | $1.157625 = \overline{1.05}|^3$ |
| 1.05 | 370 |
| 5.25 | 81033750 |
| 105 | 3.472875 |
| 1.1025 | amount of 370 } in 3 years $= 428.321250 = £428 : 6 : 5$ |
| 1.05 | 370 |
| 55125 | whole interest $= \overline{58 : 6 : 5}$ |
| 11025 | |

$1.157625 = \overline{1.05}|^3$

If from the amount the principal 370 be taken, it gives the accumulation of interest during the three years.

But the calculation of compound interest for a number of years is, even conducted in this manner, a very tedious process for practical purposes. It is evident, however, that if the amount of $\overset{£.}{1}$ at every period is known, the difficulty at once vanishes, and the compound interest for any number of years on any given sum may be readily and promptly found.

Tables have, therefore, been constructed of the amount of $\overset{£.}{1}$ for different numbers of years at different rates of interest. Here is a small one which will be found applicable to most practical purposes.

*The Amount of £1. in any number of Years at different rates of Interest.*

| Years. | 3 per cent. | 3½ per cent. | 4 per cent. | 4½ per cent. | 5 per cent. |
|---|---|---|---|---|---|
| 1 .. | 1.0300 | 1.0350 | 1.0400 | 1.0450 | 1.0500 |
| 2 .. | 1.0609 | 1.0712 | 1.0816 | 1.0920 | 1.1025 |
| 3 .. | 1.0927 | 1.1087 | 1.1249 | 1.1412 | 1.1576 |
| 4 .. | 1.1255 | 1.1475 | 1.1669 | 1.1925 | 1.2155 |
| 5 .. | 1.1593 | 1.1877 | 1.2167 | 1.2462 | 1.2763 |
| 6 | 1.1941 | 1.2293 | 1.2653 | 1.3023 | 1.3401 |
| 7 .. | 1.2299 | 1.2723 | 1.3159 | 1.3609 | 1.4071 |
| 8 .. | 1.2668 | 1.3168 | 1.3686 | 1.4221 | 1.4775 |
| 9 .. | 1.3048 | 1.3629 | 1.4233 | 1.4861 | 1.5513 |
| 10 .. | 1.3439 | 1.4106 | 1.4802 | 1.5530 | 1.6289 |
| 11 .. | 1.3842 | 1.4600 | 1.5395 | 1.6229 | 1.7103 |
| 12 .. | 1.4258 | 1.5111 | 1.6010 | 1.6959 | 1.7959 |
| 13 .. | 1.4685 | 1.5640 | 1.6651 | 1.7722 | 1.8856 |
| 14 .. | 1.5126 | 1.6187 | 1.7317 | 1.8519 | 1.9799 |
| 15 .. | 1.5580 | 1.6753 | 1.8009 | 1.9353 | 2.0789 |
| 16 .. | 1.6047 | 1.7340 | 1.8730 | 2.0224 | 2.1829 |
| 17 .. | 1.6528 | 1.7947 | 1.9479 | 2.1134 | 2.2920 |
| 18 .. | 1.7024 | 1.8575 | 2.0258 | 2.2085 | 2.4066 |
| 19 .. | 1.7535 | 1.9225 | 2.1068 | 2.3079 | 2.5270 |
| 20 .. | 1.8061 | 1.9898 | 2.1911 | 2.4117 | 2.6533 |

It is sometimes useful, having the principal and the rate of interest given, to know in what time the interest on this principal will amount to a certain sum.

Find the interest on the principal for one year, then the whole amount of interest divided by the interest for one year, will, it is evident, give the time in which the given amount of interest will accrue at simple interest.

For example—in what time will the simple interest of 556 amount to 66 : 14 : 4¾ £. s. d. at the rate of 4 per cent. per annum ?

Here 556 × .04 = 22.24 = interest for one year, and

$$\frac{66:14:4\frac{3}{4}}{22.24} = \frac{66.72}{22.24} = 3 \text{ years} = \text{time in which the in-}$$

terest will amount to $66:14:4\frac{3}{4}$.

In what time will the simple interest on $397:9:5$
amount to $31:6$ at $3\frac{1}{2}$ per cent. per annum?

$$\frac{31.5}{397.471 \times .035}$$

### Miscellaneous Questions in Interest.

Q. 110. What is the simple interest of $576:2:7$ for $7\frac{1}{4}$ years, at $4\frac{1}{2}$ per cent. per annum?

Q. 111. What is the interest on $2768$ for 96 days at 4 per cent.?

Q. 112. In what time will the interest on $6437$ amount to $150$, at the rate of 5 per cent.?

Q. 113. What is the amount at compound interest of $372$, accumulating at 5 per cent. interest for 7 years?

Q. 114. How long a time will elapse before the simple interest, reckoned at $3\frac{1}{4}$ per cent. on $953$ will amount to 267?

Q. 115. If I lay out 2573 at compound interest at $4\frac{1}{2}$ per cent. for 14 years, to how much will it then amount?

Insurance is a branch of commercial arithmetic which has a very extensive application. By means of this rule we compute the amount of all those contracts under which one party engages for a certain rate of payment to make good to another party certain possible losses to which the latter is more or less exposed. Insurances are principally made against the dangers of the seas, and accidents by fire, and also to secure, by means of certain periodical payments made during life, the receipt of a stipulated sum to a person's representatives after his death.

But little explanation is required for the elucidation of computations connected with this branch of contract, and which partake greatly of the nature of commission.

Indeed one class of commercial insurances, which are made to an exceedingly great extent,—the insurance of debts,—and to which the term *del credere*, borrowed from the Italian, has been applied, is in some cases so confounded with the principle of commission (although really and essentially different therefrom both in their nature and results), that the two charges are consolidated, and the allowance which is made under the name of commission includes not only the payment for services performed, but the premium in consideration of which the party making the charge agrees to answer for the punctual payment of the amount upon which it is calculated.

It is common, in effecting marine insurances, to *cover* the amount of the invoice or sum which is the subject of the insurance ; in other words, to secure, in the event of loss, the payment of such a sum as will reimburse to the merchant the money paid for the goods, together with all the expenses attending their shipment, including commissions, and the premium paid for the insurance itself and the charges attendant upon recovering the loss.

Suppose a merchant has shipped, on board a vessel bound to Calcutta, goods, for which, with the freight and
£.
charges of shipment, he has paid 5240, what sum must be insured so as to yield this amount in the event of

loss, after the premium of insurance and all commission are deducted? Assuming the premium to be at the rate of 55 shillings per cent., stamp duty 5 shillings per cent., commission for effecting the insurance ¼ per cent., and on settling and recovering the loss, 2½ per cent. These together are 6 £. per cent. It is therefore clear that only 94 £. will be recovered towards replacing the sum of 5240 £ out of every 100 £. insured, and consequently the sum insured must bear the same proportion to 5240 £. that 100 £. bears to 94 £., or for every 94 £. contained in 5240 £., 100 £. must be insured; therefore $\dfrac{5240 \times 100}{94}$ = 5575,* £. the sum which should be insured.

---

Commission is a certain per-centage allowed to an agent or merchant for transacting business. Brokerage is an allowance of a certain per-centage to a person called a broker, for assisting merchants in procuring or disposing of goods. The merchant acts for correspondents residing abroad or in the country—the broker under the direction of parties residing on the spot. Thus the correspondent of a merchant consigns goods to him of the value of 754 £. : 16 s., for the proper management of the sale of which he proposes to pay 2½ per cent.; to what will this amount?

A broker charges ¼ per cent. to the merchant for selling these goods; to what will his brokerage amount?

*Ed.* These are exactly the same as questions in common interest.

754 £. : 16 s. = 754.8 £. × .025 = 18.87 £. = 18 £. : 17 s. : 4¾ d. = commission.

---

* Insurances are never made for broken sums of shillings and pence.

$\overset{\textit{£.}}{754} : \overset{\textit{s.}}{16} = \overset{\textit{£.}}{754.8} \times .0050 = \overset{\textit{£.}}{3.774} = \overset{\textit{£.}}{3} : \overset{\textit{s.}}{15} : \overset{\textit{d.}}{5\frac{3}{4}} =$ brokerage.

Q. 116. What is the brokerage at $\frac{1}{2}$ per cent. on sales amounting to $\overset{\textit{£.}}{2572} : \overset{\textit{s.}}{6} : \overset{\textit{d.}}{4}$?

Q. 117. What is the commission at 5 per cent. charged to a correspondent on a consignment of goods producing $\overset{\textit{£.}}{5367} : \overset{\textit{s.}}{17}$?

In the business transactions of two parties, if the one agree to pay the other a certain sum of money at the end of a year, or any other stated time, and he wish to discharge his debt immediately, it would not be just that he should, at the present time, pay the whole of the money that is not due until the stipulated period.

*Ed.* Certainly not; for the other party, instead of himself, would then have the advantage of the use of the money during the time.

*Mrs. D.* Suppose the debt is $\overset{\textit{£.}}{100}$, to be paid at the end of the year, and that he can borrow money at 5 per cent., how much out of the $\overset{\textit{£.}}{100}$ should be allowed for prompt payment? Since $\overset{\textit{£.}}{100}$ would at that rate amount to $\overset{\textit{£.}}{105}$, it follows that, if the sum had been $\overset{\textit{£.}}{105}$, $\overset{\textit{£.}}{5}$ should be deducted if the debt were immediately discharged. And if $\overset{\textit{£.}}{5}$ be deducted for $\overset{\textit{£.}}{105}$, it follows that $\overset{\textit{£.}}{\frac{5}{105}}$ should be deducted for every $\overset{\textit{£.}}{1}$; and, for $\overset{\textit{£.}}{100}$,

$$\frac{500}{105} = \frac{100}{21} = 4.7619 = \overset{\textit{£.}}{4} : \overset{\textit{s.}}{15} : \overset{\textit{d.}}{2\frac{3}{4}}.$$

The sum allowed for prompt payment is called discount, and this method of computing it is evidently cor-

R

rect; but, in commercial transactions, discount is reckoned in a more simple manner, and the interest for the
given time is computed instead of the discount: thus the
discount allowed on 100 (£.), due at the end of the year at
5 per cent., is 5 (£.) instead of 4 : 15 : 2¾ (£. s. d.), which is, in fact,
obtaining for money a higher rate of interest than 5 per
cent. For if for 100 (£.), payable at the end of a year, 95 (£.)
is paid at present, that sum put out at 5 per cent. interest will amount, for that time, to 95 + 4.75 (£.) (95 ×
.05) = 95 + 4 : 15 (£. £. s.) = 99 : 15 (£. s.); and therefore, if the
man who receives the 95 (£.) at present were to lend this
at 5 per cent., he would, at the end of the year, find a
deficiency of 5 (s.) in his 100 (£.).

*Ed.* Then the man who has got money to pay his
debt at present is wise to discharge it at once, since he
gains five shillings by the transaction.

*Mrs. D.* This question involves many intricacies of
business, which have nothing to do with the mere arithmetical computation of discount and interest. But the
profit arising from discounting debts, or of lending money on debts not due until certain future periods, is
considered sufficiently advantageous to make this a con-
siderable branch of mercantile business.

---

*Mrs. D.* Equation of payments is the finding of a time
to pay at once several debts due at different times, so
that no loss shall be sustained by either the creditor or
debtor. For example:—A merchant has goods con-
signed to him from his correspondent abroad. Some of
these he sells to receive 250 (£.) at the end of 3 months;

£.

some to receive 470 at the end of 6 months; and some

£.

to receive 340 at the end of a year and a half. Now at the end of what period of time must he charge himself with the whole debt, so that the interest accruing on the sums which are overdue may be counterbalanced by the discount on the sums which are not yet due?

The sum due at the end of the first period, if not paid till the last period, will have the interest accruing on it during the intermediate time. The sum due at the second period, if not paid till the last, will likewise have the interest accruing upon it during the interval between the second and last period; and so on. Now these several interests added together will give the whole interest if all the money were to be paid at the last period. But this would not fulfil the intended purpose, which is to discover a precise intermediate time, whereat the interest due upon the portions payable before that time would amount to the same sum as the discount receivable upon the portions payable after that time. By calculating interest upon the different portions, from the various periods of payment up to the day when the last sum is due, we have found what amount of principal and interest would be due if the whole debt were to be discharged at that period. To fulfil the intended purpose and annul the interest, we must ascertain what number of days' interest upon the entire principal sum will equal the aggregate interest calculated upon the individual sums; and anticipating by that number of days the time at which the last payment will be due, we ascertain precisely the period whereat the interest due upon the portions forborne is equal to the discount receivable upon the portions anticipated; in other words, we have discovered the equation of payment. Thus the interval between the first and last payment in this example is the

R 2

difference between 3 months and 18 months, or 15 months, or 1.25 year the interest of 250 £. for that time at 5 per cent. is equal . . . . . $250 \times .05 \times 1.25 = 15.625$
The interval between the .
  second and last period
  equal to $18 - 6 = 12$
  $= 1$ year; the interest
  for 470 for that time $= 470 \times .05 \qquad = 23.5$
Due last payment . . . . . . 340 $\qquad\qquad \overline{39.125}$
$\qquad\qquad£1060 =$ whole principal.

Now (*see* p. 177) the time in which 39.125 will be the interest obtained on 1060 £. at 5 per cent. per annum, is equal to $\dfrac{39.125}{1060 \times .05} = \dfrac{39.125}{53} = .7382$, which, taken from 1.5, or a year and a half, time of last payment, equal to $1.5 - 7382 = .7618$ of a year, which, multiplied by 365, give the number of days from the present time, at which the aggregate sums should be paid.

It has been remarked, that "no rule in arithmetic has been the occasion of so many disputes as that of equation of payments. Almost every writer upon this subject has endeavoured to show the fallacy of the methods made use of by others, and to substitute a new one in their stead." I think, however, no fallacy can be discovered in the above method of proceeding, since it is not only deduced from strict reasoning on the subject, but its truth can be made still further manifest by direct proof. For, let us suppose that each sum is paid at the appointed time, and that it is employed until the period of the last payment. It will be found that the interest upon the whole sum, calculated from the period when I have shown it should be payable, will amount to precisely the same sum, and therefore the period assigned is the only true one which will answer the conditions of the question.

Try the following examples :—

Q. 118. A merchant sells goods for his correspondent at different times, for which he is to receive 52 : 7 : 6 *£. s. d.* at the end of 4½ months, 80 : 10 *£. s.* at the end of 3½ months, and 76 : 2 : 6 *£. s. d.* at the end of 5 months; what is the equated time to pay the whole, reckoning money at 5 per cent.?

Q. 119. A. owes B. 1200, *£.* the payments for which are to be made as follow :—200 *£.* immediately, 560 *£.* in 7 months, 270 *£.* in 14 months, and the remainder at the end of 18 months; but A., wishing to liquidate the debt at one payment, he requires to know the period at which he should pay the whole, reckoning money at the rate of 3 per cent. interest.

---

*Mrs. D.* By the application of the Rule of Three, all questions in the buying or selling of stocks may be determined.

*Ed.* What do you mean by stocks?

*Mrs. D.* Stock was a term originally used to signify the capital of public companies; their stock being another term for their actual wealth or capital, and in that sense properly applied. The word is now, however, chiefly applied to denote the public funds, which really mean, not the *funds*, but the *debts* of the nation ; and therefore, without explanation, the term cannot convey an accurate idea to the mind. In consequence of this misapplication of terms, uninformed people usually entertain erroneous ideas on the nature of the National Debt, considering it rather as a deposit or treasure, and a sign of national wealth, than as an evidence of poverty.

*Alfred.* But when it is said, such a person has so much money in the stocks, or in the funds, does not this mean, that he is actually possessed of so much wealth which he can realize and convert into money at any moment of time he may think proper : are not the funds then real tangible property ?

*Mrs. D.* The fund, the capital really entitled to be so characterised, was originally borrowed by Government at various periods, to meet the exigencies of the time being, and has long since been swallowed up and lost to the nation, leaving behind it an obligation to furnish with an equivalent perpetual annuity such individuals or their representatives as from time to time have parted with proportions of this capital. Thus, a debt has been incurred at different times, by Government, to the amount of 346,640,505 of pounds, called Consolidated Annuities, and the public faith is pledged for the payment of 3 per cent. per annum, to those who advanced the money, or others who have purchased from them any proportion of this debt, with the advantages annexed thereto.

*Ed.* So then, when we purchase stock, we buy a debt; how can that make us richer, mother?

*Mrs. D.* Not a debt, but the annuity attached to that debt, and given as an equivalent or in payment of it.

*Alfred.* But if the nation cannot pay the debt, how can it pay the annuity ?

*Mrs. D.* By far the greater part of the taxes raised in this country are applied to the purpose of paying the public annuitant, who buys the stock having full security in the faith and honesty of the nation, which *must* fulfil the obligations it has incurred.

The amount of the Consolidated Annuities or Consols of which I have spoken, is not the only debt which has been contracted by the nation; many loans have been raised, and other stock has been created, which have different denominations, arising from the manner in

which they have been formed: it would take too much
time at present to explain to you why they have received
their respective names, and the inquiry would lead us too
far from our present subject, which is the buying and
selling of stock.

The whole public debt is now between seven and
eight hundred millions of stock, for which from £3 to
£4 per cent. per annum are paid, making the whole
amount of more than twenty-seven millions per annum
received by the public creditors.

*Alfred.* When did the nation incur so tremendous a
debt?

*Mrs. D.* This funding system did not commence till
after the Revolution, in the year 1688: for the few first
years, sums were borrowed for short periods, and par-
tially repaid. By degrees the debt has reached its
present enormous amount: it most rapidly increased
from the last half of the past century.

Let us now, however, come to the practical part.
When a person buys stock, it is transferred to his name
from that of the seller: his name is inscribed in the books
kept at the Bank of England as a public creditor for the
amount purchased, and he, therefore, becomes entitled
to the annuity annexed thereto, which is paid, on application at the Bank, in half-yearly dividends. There are
dealers in stock as well as in any other articles of trans-
fer, and therefore there is always a market where stock
can be bought and sold, it fluctuating in price according
to the demand, and other disturbing causes, which also
occasion one particular stock to be sometimes dearer
than others.

Q. 120. I want to invest 675 money in the 3 per
cent. consols, and find that for every 100 pounds of stock
I must pay $91\frac{3}{4}$ (or 91 : 15, or 91.75). How much
stock shall I be able to purchase?

*Ed.* Dividing 91.75 by 100 we have .9175 for the cost of £1 stock, so 675 × .9175 = answer.

Q. 121. A person wishes to buy stock which will yield an income of 35 : how much money must he lay out to accomplish this in 3 per cent. stock, the price of which is 92¼ per 100. Since for every 100 we get 3 $\dfrac{35 \times 100}{3}$ will be the amount of stock required, and there-fore $\dfrac{35 \times 92.125}{3} =$ money, which will purchase this amount of stock.

Q. 122. Having 5763 which I wish to lay out, I find that the stock yielding 3 per cent. is 90¼, and that yielding 3½ per cent. is 97¾ : in which stock will it be most to my advantage to invest my money, and what income shall I obtain in either case?

Q. 123. In 1812, during the war, the price of stocks was very low; that of 3 per cent. consols was at one time only at 54, at which price 3747 money was invested in them; three years afterwards, this stock was again sold, when consols were at 72, how much more money was obtained, and to how much more would it have amounted if the stock had not been sold till the present time (1835), when its price is at 92?

———

*Mrs. D.* I think I have now, my dear boy, nearly explained to you all the rules and their various applications which are requisite to be known in commercial arithmetic. Barter—Profit and Loss—Fellowship—are all so simple in themselves, and are all so completely questions which may be resolved merely by the Rule of Three, that it is quite unnecessary to offer you any ex-

planation, or give you any separate lessons on these
rules.

One other rule in this branch of the subject remains
to be slightly noticed; but I think you will be able
readily to solve the questions which it involves without
much assistance from me.

ALLIGATION shows how to find the mean price of any
mixture of several things, of different quantities, and
bearing different prices, and on the contrary, having the
price of the mixture, to discover what should be the
quantities used in its composition of things bearing different prices. The first is very simple, and requires nothing but an example to make it sufficiently apparent.

A maltster mixes together 30 quarters brown malt, at
28 per quarter; 46 quarters pale malt, at 30 per quarter; and 24 quarters of high dried malt at 25 per quarter. What is the value of this mixture per quarter?

Now 30 qrs. at 28 will cost 30 × 28 =    840
$\qquad$ 46 ...... 30 ...... 46 × 30 = 1380
$\qquad$ 24 ...... 25 ...... 24 × 25 =   600

Therefore 100 qrs. of the mixture will cost .. 2820; and
$\dfrac{2820}{100}$ = 28.2 = 1 : 8 : $2\frac{1}{4}$ = price per quarter.

*Ed.* This is indeed easy to be understood without one
word of explanation. Will you give me another question of the same kind?

*Mrs. D.* Q. 124. In order to improve the quality of
some home-made wine, which cost 4 per gallon, I mixed
in a cask, containing 33 gallons of this, 2 gallons of
brandy, at 31 per gallon, and 8 gallons of foreign wine,
at 17 per gallon. What is the price per gallon of the
whole mixture?

Q. 125. Of what fineness is that gold which is made by melting 7 oz. of gold of 22 carats fine, 12½ oz. of 21 carats fine, and 17 oz. of 19 carats fine?

*Mrs. D.* Now let us endeavour to discover the reverse of these questions, and when the prices of several things are given, to find what quantities of each should be used to form a mixture of a given price. For example:—a grocer has tea at 16 per lb. and at 9 per lb.; what quantity of each must he take to produce a mixture worth 10. The difference of the highest price and the mean price will be the number of pounds of the lowest price; and the difference of the mean price and the lowest price will give the number of pounds of the highest price, which, together, will make a mixture at the rate of value of the mean price: thus—

$$16 - 10 = 6 = \text{number of lbs. at } 9$$
$$10 - 9 = 1 = \ldots\ldots\ldots\ldots \text{ at } 16$$

which, together, will make a mixture at 10 per lb. For $\overline{16 - 10} \times 9$ or $16 \times 9 - 10 \times 9 = $ cost of $\overline{16 - 10}$ lbs. at 9 per lb.; and $\overline{10 - 9} \times 16$ or $10 \times 16 - 9 \times 16 = $ cost of $10 - 9$ lbs. at 16 per lb.; and these added together will give the cost of the whole number of pounds when mixed together, or of $16 - \cancel{10} + \cancel{10} - 9 = \overline{16-9}$ lbs. Therefore $10 \times 16 - \cancel{9} \times \cancel{16} + \cancel{9} \times \cancel{16} - 9 \times 10 = $ cost of $16 - 9$ lbs. $= 10 \times 16 - 9 \times 10 = \overline{16 - 9} \times 10 = $ cost of $16 - 9$ lbs.; and since $\overline{16 - 9} \times 10 = $ cost of mixture of this number of lbs., it follows that 10, the required price, is the cost of 1 lb. of the same. Now the manner of analysing this rule does not at all depend on the numbers here given as examples; and it is evident, if any other numbers whatever were used, provided the mean price were an intermediate number between the other two, that the truth of the rule would be equally apparent. In like manner, if three or more things are to be mixed together, the same rule and the same reasoning applies. Thus, if a grocer wished to form a mixture of tea worth 10$^{s.}$ per lb., not only of qualities at 16$^{s.}$ and 9$^{s.}$, but also at 14$^{s.}$, then the mixture at 9 and 14 would be, from the rule, $14 - 10 = 4$ lbs. at 9$^{s.}$, $10 - 9 = 1$ lb. at 14$^{s.}$, and these, added to the other mixture of 16$^{s.}$ and 9$^{s.}$, will give 1 lb. at 16$^{s.}$, 1 lb. at 14$^{s.}$, and $6 + 4 = 10$ at 9$^{s.}$, for a mixture worth 10$^{s.}$ per lb.

If there were 4 or more things of different prices to be mixed together, say at 16$^{s.}$, 14$^{s.}$, 9$^{s.}$, and 8$^{s.}$, to make a mixture at 10$^{s.}$, then the quantities may be found of a mixture between 14$^{s.}$ and 8$^{s.}$, or $14 - 10 = 4$ lbs. at 8$^{s.}$,
$10 - 2 = 2$ lbs. at 14, and the quantities of the whole mixture, at the price of 10$^{s.}$, will therefore be

        1 lb. at 16$^{s.}$
        2 lb. at 14
        6 lb. at 9
        4 lb. at 8

But if, instead of finding the respective quantities at 16$^{s.}$ and at 9$^{s.}$ of the mixture, and the respective quantities at 14$^{s.}$ and 8$^{s.}$ of the mixture, we had found the requisite quantities of $\overset{s.}{16}$ and $\overset{s.}{8}$ to form the mean mixture, and the requisite quantities at $\overset{s.}{14}$ and $\overset{s.}{9}$ to form a mixture at the same price, it is evident the conditions of the question would be perfectly answered, and that

$$16 - 10 = 6 \text{ lbs. at } \overset{s.}{8}$$
$$10 - \phantom{0}8 = 2 \text{ lbs. at } 16$$
$$14 - 10 = 4 \text{ lbs. at } \phantom{0}9$$
$$10 - \phantom{0}9 = 1 \text{ lb. } \text{ at } 14$$

would likewise form a mixture worth $\overset{s.}{10}$ per lb.

Hence it is shown that these questions admit of various answers, the number of these increasing according to the number of things of different prices used.

Q. 126. How much sugar at $\overset{d.}{4}$, at $\overset{d.}{6}$, and at $\overset{d.}{11}$ per lb. must be mixed together, so that the composition formed by them may be worth $\overset{d.}{7}$ per lb.

Q. 127. A goldsmith has gold of 17, 18, 22, and 24 carats fine. How much must he take of each to make it 21 carats fine?

# PART FOURTH.

## CHAPTER I.

ANY series of numbers having the difference between the first and second numbers the same as the difference between the second and third, and so on, are said to be in arithmetical progression. Thus, 2, 4, $\overset{(2+2)}{6}$, $\overset{(2+2+2)}{8}$, &c., and 1, 5, $\overset{(1+4)}{9}$, $\overset{(1+4+4)}{13}$, &c., are series of numbers in arithmetical progression. The numbers which form the series are called the terms of the progression. Now, if we had such a series 2, 4, 6, 8, 10, 12, 14, &c., continued to 100 terms, and we wished to know the sum of all these terms added together, how should we proceed to discover this?

*Ed.* Add all the numbers together, I suppose; but it would make a very long addition sum.

*Mrs. D.* True, it would indeed be a formidable row of figures; let us, therefore, consider the formation of the series, and endeavour to discover a shorter road to the result. For this purpose we will investigate progressions of fewer terms, and when we have once found the principle, we shall be able to apply this to a larger number of terms. Since the difference of the first and second terms is equal to the difference of any other two consecutive terms, it follows that the second exceeds the first or the first exceeds the second, by as much as the last exceeds the last but one, or as the last but one exceeds the last, that the difference of the second and third is the same as the difference of the second and third

S

from the last, and so on : it therefore follows, that in any arithmetical series $\overset{1}{1},\ \overset{2}{3},\ \overset{3}{5},\ \overset{4}{7},\ \overset{5}{9},\ \overset{6}{11},\ \overset{7}{13},\ \overset{8}{15}$, or $\overset{1}{16},\ \overset{2}{13},\ \overset{3}{10},\ \overset{4}{7},\ \overset{5}{4}$, the sum of the first and last term equal the sum of the second and last but one, or of any other two terms equally distant from the two extremes : thus, $\overset{1}{1} + \overset{8}{15} = \overset{2}{3} + \overset{7}{13} = \overset{3}{5} + \overset{6}{11} = \overset{4}{7} + \overset{5}{9}$, the excess of one term being always equal to the deficiency of the other term. In the second series, where the number of terms are odd, $\overset{1}{16} + \overset{5}{4} = \overset{1}{13} + \overset{4}{7}$, and 10 the middle term being 3 more than 7, and 3 less than 13, it follows, that $10 \times 2$ are the same as $7 + 13$, or that $7 + 3 + 13 - 3 = 7 + 13 = 10 \times 2$. Now, since the sum of the extremes is always equal to the sum of any two terms equidistant from the extremes, and if the number of terms be odd, the middle term is equal to half the sum of any of these pairs, it follows that the sum of the whole number of terms is equal to the sum of the extremes multiplied by half the number of terms : thus, the sum of the first series is $\overline{1 + 15} \times \frac{8}{2} = 16 \times 4 = 64$, and the

sum of the second series $= \overline{4 + 16} \times \frac{5}{2} = \frac{20 \times 5}{2} = 50$. Hence, the first and last terms, and the number of terms being given, the sum of the whole number of terms may be found. The first term of an arithmetical progression is 3, the last term 700, and the number of terms 100, what is the sum of the terms?

*Ed.* This is indeed easily answered, $\frac{\overline{3 + 700} \times 100}{2} =$

$703 \times 50 = 35150$.

*Mrs. D.* Q. 128. How many strokes does a clock strike in 12 hours?

Q. 129. What debt can be discharged in a year by weekly payments in arithmetical progression, the first payment being $\overset{s.}{1}$, and the last or 52nd payment $\overset{£. \; s.}{5:3}$?

Q. 130. The first term is 5, the last term 21, and the number of terms 9; required the sum of the series?

*Mrs. D.* If the lowest and highest terms and the number of terms of an arithmetical series be given, the common difference may be found. Since the highest term is made up of the lowest term, and the continual addition of the common difference, it follows that the 2nd term equal 1st term + or − the common difference; the 3rd term = 1st term + or − the com. diff. × 2; 4th term = 1st term + or − the com. diff. × 3, and the highest term equal to the lowest term + com. diff. × by the number of terms less 1. Thus, in the series $\overset{1}{1}, \overset{2}{3}, \overset{3}{5}, \overset{4}{7}, \overset{5}{9}, = 1, 1 + 2, 1 + 2 + 2,$ $1 + 2 + 2 + 2, 1 + 2 + 2 + 2 + 2$, the last term $= 1 + 2 \times \overline{5-1} = 1 + 8 = 9$. Again, $9 - 1 = 2 \times \overline{5-1} = 2 = \dfrac{9-1}{5-1}$. Hence, if the difference of the first and last term be taken, and this be divided by the number of terms less 1, the quotient will be the common difference. If the first term, the last term, and the common difference be given, we can, by the converse of the preceding, find the number of terms. For, since the difference of the extremes divided by the terms less 1, gives the common difference, the difference of the extremes will be equal to the terms less 1, multiplied by the common difference; and therefore, the difference of the extremes divided by the common difference, will give the number of terms less 1. Thus, $\dfrac{9-1}{5-1} = 2, \& 9 - 1 = \overline{5-1} \times 2$ $\& \dfrac{9-1}{2} = 5 - 1$, and so, if to the difference of the extremes divided by the common difference 1 be added, the result will be the number of terms.

Hence, in an arithmetical progression, we have to take into consideration

1. The first, or lowest term    Abbreviated, F.
2. The last, or highest term         L.
3. The number of terms             N.
4. The common difference          D.
5. The sum of all the terms         S.

Any three of which being given, the other two may be found. The following is a summary of all we have already proved by the preceding investigation :—

$$S = \overline{F + L} \times \frac{N}{2}$$

$$D = \frac{L - F}{N - 1}$$

$$N = \frac{L - F}{D} + 1$$

$$F^* = L - D \times \overline{N - 1}$$

$$L = F + D \times \overline{N - 1}$$

Q. 131. The first term is 7, the last term 31, the number of terms 13; required the sum of the series, and the common difference?

Q. 132. The last term is 31, the first term 7, the common difference 2; required the number of terms?

Q. 133. The last term is 31, the common difference 2, the number of terms 13; required the first term?

Q. 134. The first term is 7, the common difference 2, the number of terms 13; required the last term?

---

* F is also equal to $\dfrac{S}{N} - \dfrac{D \times \overline{N - 1}}{2}$, which is deduced from above.

Q. 135. A certain debt can be discharged in one year by weekly payments in arithmetical progression, the first payment being $\overset{s.}{1}$, and the last $\overset{£. \; s.}{5:3}$; what is the common difference of the terms?

Q. 136. A person travelling into the country went 3 miles the first day, and increased every day by 5 miles, till at last he went 58 miles in one day, how many days did he travel?

Q. 137. A man is to receive $\overset{£.}{360}$ at 12 several payments, each to exceed the former by 4, what are the first and last payments?

Q. 138. The first term is 6, the number of terms 20, the common difference 8; required the last term?

---

*Mrs. D.* You are now, I think, perfectly familiar with arithmetical progression, and we will therefore turn to the consideration of GEOMETRICAL PROGRESSION, or of numbers which increase regularly by multiplication instead of addition.

We will first, however, notice GEOMETRICAL PROPORTION. Four numbers are said to be in geometrical proportion when the first bears the same proportion to the second · as the third bears to the fourth, that is, when the first is contained as many times in the second as the third is contained in the fourth, or the second is contained as many times in the first as the fourth is in the third. Thus 2, 6, 18, 54, are four numbers in geometrical proportion, because $\frac{6}{2} = \frac{54}{18}$, or 6 contains 2 the same number of times as 54 contains 18; and 24, 12, 6, 3, are four numbers in geometrical proportion, because $\frac{24}{12} = \frac{6}{3}$, or 12 is contained as many times in 24 as 3 is in 6.

Three numbers are said to be in geometrical proportion when the first bears the same proportion to the second as the second bears to the third: thus 2, 6, 18, are three numbers in geometrical proportion, because $\dfrac{6}{2} = \dfrac{18}{6}$ or 2 is contained in 6 as many times as 6 is contained in 18. The first and last terms of these proportions are called the extremes, and the middle terms are called the means. When four numbers are in *continued* geometrical proportion, the three first are likewise in geometrical proportion, but four numbers may be in proportion without answering to this condition: 2, 3, 10, 15, are four numbers in proportion; that is, $\dfrac{3}{2} = \dfrac{15}{10}$, or 2 is contained as many times in 3 as 10 is contained in 15; in this latter case the proportion is said to be *discontinued*. Four numbers in proportion are written thus: as

3 : 9 : : 27 : 81
7 : 8 : : 14 : 16

which is read, as 3 is to 9 so is 27 to 81
7 is to 8 so is 14 to 16.

The first is in continued proportion, the second in discontinued proportion. Three numbers in geometrical proportion are expressed thus: as 3 : 9 : : 9 : 27, and may be considered like four numbers in proportion, the 2d and 3d terms being alike. Now since, from the definition of proportion, the second term divided by the first term is always equal to the fourth term divided by the third, it follows that the first term multiplied by the fourth term is equal to the second multiplied by the third term: for as 7 : 8 : : 14 : 16; therefore $\dfrac{8}{7} = \dfrac{16}{14} = 8 \times 14 = 16$ × 7, or the product of the means is equal to the product of the extremes. Hence if any three numbers be given, a fourth proportional to them may be found; such as, this 4th number shall bear the same proportion to the 3d, as the 2d bears to the 1st; for since the product of the extremes is equal to the product of the means, one of the extremes will be equal to the product of the means divided by the other extreme, or $8 \times 14 = 16 \times 7 = \dfrac{8 \times 14}{7} = 16$. Let it be required to find a number having the same proportion to 9 as 7 bears to 3, or otherwise let 3, 7, and 9, be three numbers to which a fourth proportional is required.

*Ed.* Here $\dfrac{7 \times 9}{3} = \dfrac{63}{3} = 21$ will be the number required.

*Mrs. D.* And it will be as $3 : 7 :: 9 : 21$. You will now be able to understand that all sums in the Rule of Three resolve themselves in this: to find a fourth proportional to three numbers given. Thus if 3 yards cost $\overset{\text{\tiny F.}}{2}$, what will 12 cost? Since 3 yards cost $\overset{\text{\tiny s.}}{2}$, 1 yard will cost $\dfrac{1}{3}$ of 2 or $\dfrac{2}{3}$; and 12 yards will cost $12 \times \dfrac{2}{3} = \dfrac{12 \times 2}{3} = 8$; and therefore, since 8 is obtained by the product of two numbers divided by a third, these four numbers will be in proportion, or as $3 : 2 :: 12 : 8$, or 3 bear the same proportion to the price 2 as 12 bear to the price 8; and this result, it is evident, does not in any way depend on the particular numbers here used as an example. The Rule of Three, therefore, is truly the rule of proportion, or, as it is called in arithmetical books, " The Golden Rule, which teacheth by three numbers given to find out a fourth in such proportion to the third as the second is to the first."

*Q. 139. A cargo of goods is to be insured in which A.

£.      s.            £.     s.

has ventured 5647 : 13, and C. 4563 : 4, the insurance

£.   s.   d.

comes to 376 : 6 : 6, how much ought each to pay of this ?

*Q. 140. Three persons, A., B., and C., freighted a
ship with 340 tuns of wine; A. loaded 110 tuns, B. 97,
and C. the rest. In a storm, the seamen were obliged
to throw overboard 85 tuns; how much must each person sustain of the loss?

*Q. 141. D., E., and F., hold a piece of ground in

£.    s.   d.

common, for which they are to pay 36 : 10 : 6. D. puts
in 23 oxen 27 days, E. 21 oxen 35 days, and F. 16
oxen 23 days; what is each man to pay of the said
rent?

Q. 142. The planet Mercury makes one revolution
round the sun in 87 days 23 hours, and Venus in 224
days 17 hours; how many revolutions will they each
make while the earth is making $7\frac{1}{2}$ revolutions, reckon-

days  hrs.

ing each of these 365  6, or one year? Likewise, what
proportion does one of each of their years bear to one of
ours, reckoning their year to be completed in one of
their revolutions?

Q. 143. The mean distance of Mercury from the Sun
is 37 millions of miles, of Venus 68, of the Earth 95;
what are their relative distances reckoned in the mean
distance of the Earth from the Sun?

Q. 144 If Alfred runs three times as fast as Edmund,
and Edmund is 20 yards before him, how many yards
will they each have run before the one overtakes the
other? Since A. goes 3 yards while E. goes 1, it follows that for every yard E. goes, A. will gain 2 upon

---

* These are questions in " Fellowship," which are readily answered by the rule of Proportion.

him; but he has to gain 20 upon E before he can come up with him; therefore, as $2 : 1 :: 20 : \dfrac{20}{2} = 10$, the number of yards E. has to run before he is overtaken, and A. will therefore run $10 + 20$ in the same time.

Q. 145. The hour and minute hands of a clock are together between the hours of 7 and 8. What o'clock is it at that time?

Q. 146. A courier was sent express with dispatches to overtake an embassy before it arrived at its destination. He travelled 9 miles an hour, night and day; the embassy progressed very slowly, going on an average 50 miles a day. The distance of the place of destination from the nearest sea-port was 265 miles; the courier arrived at the sea-port 4 days after the embassy had left it. Did he overtake it before arriving at the end of the journey, and if so, how long did he take in accomplishing his purpose?

Q. 147. Two persons are obliged to be at a certain hour of the day in a place a certain number of miles distant. One travels on foot, and goes at the rate of 2 miles an hour; another on horseback, and goes at the rate of 7 miles an hour. They both set' out from the same spot; the pedestrian started 9 hours before the other, and they both arrive exactly at the same time at the place of destination. What is the distance?

---

*Mrs. D.* Any series of numbers, the terms of which gradually increase or decrease by a constant multiplication or division, is said to be in geometrical progression. Thus 3, 9, 27, 81, 243, 729, &c., and 32, 16, 8, 4, 2 are geometrical progressions, where the terms of the first series are formed by the continual multiplication by 3, and the second by the continual division by 2. This constant multiplier or divisor is called the ratio.

*Ed.* We shall not, I think, be able to find the sum of a geometrical, as readily as we found that of an arithmetical, progression.

*Mrs. D.* Not quite ; but with a little contrivance the process may be simplified very much.

Let the geometrical progression 2, 4, 8, 16, 32, 64 be given to find the sum of all the terms, or the sum of the series; multiply each of the terms by the ratio, in this case 2, and then we shall have another progression, which will, it is evident, be as many times the first series as the number expressed by the ratio : thus the ratio being 2, the sum of the second series will be twice the first, or $\overline{2 + 4 + 8 + 16 + 32 + 64} \times 2 = 4 + 8 + 16 + 32 + 64 + 128$ : now if the first series be taken from the second, $2 + 4 + 8 + 16 + 32 + 64$, it is evident that $128 - 2$ will be the result, since the 5 last terms of the first are like the 5 first terms of the second, and these terms of the one being taken from those of the other, nothing will remain, and there will only be the first term of the first series to be taken from the last term of the second series, or $128 - 2$; and it is evident the same reasoning will apply to any other series : thus 2, 6, 18, 54, 162 multiplied by 3, the ratio, equal to 6, 18, 54, 162, 486, and the first series being taken from the second leaves $486 - 6$. Now (since the second series is formed of the first multiplied by the ratio) if the first be taken from the second, there remains as many times the sum of the first series as the number expressing the ratio less one; and therefore, if this result be divided by the ratio less one, it will give the sum of the series : this is, in the first case, $\dfrac{128 - 2}{2 - 1} = 126$, and in the second $\dfrac{486 - 6}{3 - 1} = \dfrac{480}{2} = 240$.

Hence the rule, multiply the last term by the ratio; from this product subtract the first term, and divide by the ratio less one.

The first term of a geometrical progression is 1, the last term 65536, and the ratio 4; required the sum of the series?

$$Ed. \quad \frac{65536 \times 4 - 1}{4 - 1} = \frac{262144 - 1}{3} = 87381.$$

$$\begin{array}{c} 65536 \\ \underline{\quad 4 \quad} \quad 3) \\ 262144 - 1 = 262143 \\ \overline{\qquad 87381} \end{array}$$

*Mrs. D.* You will not, I think, need more than one other example to make you sufficiently familiar with the rule.

Q. 148. The first term is 2, the last term 8192, and the ratio 2; what is the sum of the series?

---

*Mrs. D.* Any term of an increasing geometrical progression is equal to the product of the first term and the ratio multiplied into itself as many times as the number of terms less one. This is evident from the definition of the progression, wherein it is said the terms increase by a constant and uniform multiplication, as

$$\overset{(2 \times 2)}{2,} \quad \overset{(2 \times 2 \times 2)}{4,} \quad \overset{(2 \times 2 \times 2 \times 2)}{8,} \quad \overset{}{16,} \quad \&c.;$$ therefore, the first term and the ratio being given, any other term assigned may be found.

Thus, the 1st term is 2, and the ratio 2, required the 13th term? Here the first term 2 multiplied by the $13-1$, power of the ratio will be the 13th term. Or $2 \times \overline{2}|^{12} = 13$th term. Now, since

$$2 \times 2 \times 2 \times 2 \times 2 \times 2 = 64 \,\&$$
$$64 \times 2 \times 2 \times 2 \times 2 \times 2 \times 2 = 64 \times 64$$

it follows, that 64 is the 6th power of 2, and that $64 \times 64$ is the 12th power of 2, and therefore $\overline{2|}^6 \times 2^6 = \overline{2}|^{6 \times 2} = \overline{2}|^{12}$, or the product of 2 multiplied by itself 6 times, and 2 multiplied by itself 6 times, will be the product of 2 multiplied by itself 12 times; and in general, the 12th power of any number is equal to the 6th power multiplied by 2. In the same way we may break the continual multiplication of any number in any manner which will best suit our convenience; so that we multiply 2 twelve times into itself, it makes no difference whether we take the product of $\overset{(2 \times 2 \times 2)}{8} \times \overset{(2 \times 2 \times 2 \times 2) \times}{16} \times$ $\overset{(2 \times 2 \times 2 \times 2)}{32}$ or of $\overset{(2 \times 2 \times 2 \times 2 \times 2)}{32} \times \overset{(2 \times 2 \times 2 \times 2 \times 2) \times}{32} \times \overset{(2 \times 2)}{4}$ so that the sum of the indices be equal to 12; and $\overline{2}|^5 \times \overline{2}|^7 \times \overline{2}|^2 = \overline{2}|^3 \times \overline{2}|^4 \times \overline{2}|^5 = \overline{2}|^6 \times \overline{2}|^6 = \overline{2}|^{12}$ &c. In like manner $\overline{3}|^{23} = \overline{3}|^9 \times \overline{3}|^9 \times \overline{3}|^5 = \overline{3}|^7 \times \overline{3}|^7 \times \overline{3}|^7 \times \overline{3}|^2 = \overline{3}|^{10} \times \overline{3}|^{10} \times \overline{3}|^3$ &c.; and the same may be shown of any other number, or any other power whatever. Now, to apply this to our last example, bring 2 to the 12th power.

*Ed.* $\overline{2}|^{12} = 2\overline{2}|^6 \times \overline{2}|^6 = 64 \times 64 = 4096.$

*Mrs. D.* And, therefore, the 13th term of the geometrical progression, the first term of which is 2, and the ratio 2, is $= 2 \times \overline{2}|^{12} = 2 \times 4096 = 8192.$

Q. 149. The first term of a geometrical series is 1, the ratio 3, and the number of terms 17; required the last term, and the sum of the series?

To those who have never given their attention to this subject, the rapid increase of the value of the terms is matter of astonishment: thus, we have found that the 13th term, or 2, multiplied into itself 13 times, amounts to 8192, and of course, when the ratio is greater, the increase is more rapid. Many curious questions have, in consequence, been invented on the supposition of the superior knowledge of one party practising on the norance of another party. One or two of these well-known problems I have copied for your consideration; but do not, unless you feel quite inclined to enter into the calculation, trouble yourself with their solution.

Q. 150. Two persons having a dispute about the price of a horse, the man who wished to dispose of it said he would be willing to receive in payment only 1 farthing for the first nail in his shoes, 3 farthings for the second, 9 farthings for the third, tripling the price of every nail to 32, the number of nails in his four shoes, the purchaser readily agreed to give this price; what money was he called upon to pay?

Q. 151. One Sessa, an Indian, having first discovered the game of chess, showed it to his Prince Shehzam, who was so delighted with the invention, that he bid him ask what he would require as a reward for his ingenuity; upon which Sessa requested that he might be allowed one grain of wheat for the first square on the chess-board, two for the second, and so on, doubling continually to 64, the whole number of squares : now, supposing a pint to contain 7680 of these grains, and one quarter, or 8 bushels, to be worth $1 : 7 : 6$, it is required to find what will be the value of all the corn?

*Alfred.* These questions are certainly very curious and ingenious, and the investigation of both arithmetical and geometrical progressions is very interesting.—Do they, however, lead to any practical result?

*Mrs. D.* But very rarely, if ever, in mere arithmetical calculations; and an inquiry into their properties is of little use, unless it is our intention to carry our flight still farther into the region of mathematics. These may be called the flowers of arithmetic, like those in the vegetable world which, though they may not contribute to the actual nourishment of our frame, charm us by their

T

beauties, and serve more powerfully than the merely useful, to attract us to the examination of the wonderful works of nature, and to fascinate us with its beauties. So the surprising powers of numbers are better shown, and their study is made more inviting, by the consideration of this branch of arithmetic, than perhaps by that of any other of more practical utility. Permutation is another of these flowers of arithmetic, and to this I shall call our pupil's attention in our next lesson.

In the meantime you may, perhaps, be amused by the following speculation.

Q. 152. According to some experiments, it has been found that one stem of the hyosciamus produces more than 50,000 seeds ; but if we admit the number to be only 10,000, and each of these produced a plant the second year, and the produce of all the plants alike prolific was sown the third year and so on; allowing the space of one foot to each plant, what space of the surface of the earth would the produce of the original stem occupy at the end of the fourth year, the whole surface of the earth being 198,943,750 square miles ?

------

## CHAPTER II.

*Mrs. D.* Permutation is the showing in how many different ways any given number of things may be placed with respect to each other. For example : Emily, who is now sitting on the right of you, can change her position and sit on the left of you, and therefore you can assume two different positions with regard to each other. Now if Alfred comes and sits by you and he remains in his place while you two are mak-

ing your changes—these will be two. Now let Emily take
Alfred's place, and you and he make the two changes;
lastly you take the quiet place, and let your brother
and sister change about. You three have now made
two changes three times, or 3 × 2 = 6 changes. In
the same manner, if I were to place myself at your
side, you among yourselves could make 2 × 3 changes;
then I joined with two of you could make 2 × 3 changes,
each of us sitting in the quiet place while the other 3
were making their 2 × 3 changes; it follows therefore
that we could altogether make 2 × 3 × 4 changes; and
in the same manner it may be shown that 5 persons can
make 2 × 3 × 4 × 5 changes; and so on, the number
of changes which can be made of any number of things
is therefore the continual product of the natural numbers 1 × 2 × 3 × 4 × 5, &c., up to the given number.

*Ed.* Do let us try these changes. Come, mother, it
is now your turn to move.

*Mrs. D.* I would rather send a representative to
make all these permutations for me. It will suit my
indolence better to call ourselves A, B, C, D, and fancy
our movements on paper; this will be quite as convinc-
ing, at least to one of our senses.

| | | | |
|---|---|---|---|
| A B C D | B A C D | C B A D | D A B C |
| A B D C | B A D C | C B D A | D A C B |
| A C B D | B C A D | C A B D | D B A C |
| A C D B | B C D A | C A D B | D B C A |
| A D C B | B D C A | C D A B | D C A B |
| A D B C | B D A C | C D B A | D C B A |

*Mrs. D.* Now you will have no difficulty in answering the following questions :—

Q. 153. How many changes may be rung upon 12
bells, and how long would they be ringing but once

T 2

over, supposing 10 changes might be rung in a minute
and the year to contain 365 days 6 hours?

Q. 154. How many changes may be made of the
words in the following sentence:—

The study of arithmetic strengthens the powers of the
mind?

*Mrs. D.* Now let us endeavour to find out how many
changes can be made of any number of different things
by taking a given number of quantities at a time. Here
are A, B, C, D; what changes can be made out of
them, taking them two by two?

| A B | B A | C A | D A |
| A C | B C | C B | D B |
| A D | B D | C D | D C |

If A be put the first letter, its combination with each of
the others will make 3 changes; in like manner if B
be taken first, its combination with each of the others
will make 3 changes, and when each of the other letters
is taken first, there will be likewise 3 changes; but
there are here 4 letters, therefore there will be 4 × 3
changes; and if there be five things, A, B, C, D, E, the
changes which can be made out of them, taking them two
by two, will, by pursuing the same reasoning, be found to
be 5 × 4 changes; and in general whatever number there
be, the changes which can be made out of them, taking
them two by two, will be that number multiplied by
that number less one. When 3 out of 5 are to be taken
together, then the two first letters, A B, in combining
with each of the others in turn, will make 3 changes.

| A B C | A C B | A D B | A E B |
| A B D | A C D | A D C | A E C |
| A B E | A C E | A D E | A E D |

In like manner A C, as first letters, will make 3

changes; A D, as first letters, will make three changes;
and A E, as first letters, will make 3 changes; making
4 × 3, the whole number of changes which can be
made of 3 out of 5 when A is the first letter; but there
are five letters which may each in its turn be made the
first letter, and therefore the whole number of changes
which can be made of 3 out of 5 will be 5 × 4 × 3. In
like manner it may be shown, that when there are any
number of different things out of which any other
number is to be taken at a time, the number of changes
will always be equal to the continual multiplication of
the terms of a series, the first term of which is equal to
the whole number of things given, and the remaining
terms decreasing progressively by one, the number of
terms being equal to the number of things which are to
be taken at one time. Thus if 12 different things be
given, out of which 5 are to be combined together at
each time, the changes which may be made are $12 \times 11$
$\times 10 \times 9 \times 8 = 9504$.

Q. 155. How many changes may be rung with 3 bells
out of 8 ?

Q. 156. There are 20 toll-keepers in one trust; 2 of
these are always at one turnpike. Now suppose it is so ar-
ranged that the same two men come together as little as
possible, how many changes may be made before 2 men
find themselves together again?

*Ed.* You know that in my box of portraits every face
is divided into three parts, and the whole are so contrived
that the combination of any three of these, that is to
say, any head, nose, and chin, put together at hazard,
will form a face. There are 28 of each of these parts,
and it is said on the cover of the box that 21952 different faces may be made from these. Now I want you

T 3

to teach me how to find out whether this be a correct statement.

*Mrs. D.* Let us find out the principle on which we should proceed to make the calculation, by using a smaller number. Thus, if we have two sets of things, A, B, and a, b, one of each to be combined together, A first joined to a, and then to b, will make 2 changes, and B joined to a, and then to b, will likewise make 2 changes, and therefore there will be 2 × 2 changes. If there be 3 of 3 kinds, A, B, C, a, b, c, in like manner there will be 3 × 3 changes ; and in general, if there be any the same number of two kinds of things, the number of changes which can be made by putting together one of each will be the number of one kind of thing multiplied by itself, or the 2nd power of that number.

Aa Ba Ca
Ab Bb Cb
Ac Bc Cc

Now, if there be the same number of 3 different kinds of things, A, B, C, a, b, c, *a, b, c,* here A can be added to one of each of the other two kinds, through all the combinations made among the things of these two kinds. In like manner, B can join them in all their changes ; so if there be 2 of each kind, the number of changes will be 2 × 2 × 2; if 3, the number of changes will be 3 × 3 × 3; and in general, whatever like number there be of each different kind, the changes which may be made will be shown by the 3rd power of that number. If there be 4 or more different kinds, it is readily seen that on the same principle the number of changes will be the number of things of one kind multiplied into itself as many times as there are different kinds of things.

In this box of portraits there are 28 pieces of 3 different kinds, and therefore the number of changes which can be made will be $\overline{28}|^3 = 21952$. So the cover of the box gives correct information.

Q. 157. Now suppose each of the portraits were divided into 4 pieces, and only 9 of every kind were taken, what would be the number of changes?

Again, if instead of having them divided into equal sets, you had 28 of one, 15 of another, and 8 of another; now since 8 of each of two kinds will give 8 × 8 changes, or the first kind multiplied by the number in the second kind, therefore if there be 15 of the second kind, there will be 15 × 8 changes, and these repeated with each of the 28 of the third kind will give 28 × 15 × 8 = whole number of changes. In the same manner this may be shown with any other numbers, and therefore generally the number of changes will always be equal to the product of the number of each kind multiplied continually together.

Q. 158. There are 3 arms to a telegraph; one expresses units, the other tens, and the other hundreds. Each of these can be placed in 6 different positions. It is required to find out how many different words can be expressed by each combination denoting one particular word?

I will not farther enlarge on this subject, although there is yet much to be shown concerning the doctrine of permutations, combinations, &c., since any farther investigation at present may perhaps appear misplaced. The application of this doctrine is of very extensive use in some branches of mathematics, but in treating merely of arithmetic, it would not be consistent to enter more fully on what belongs more peculiarly to a higher stage of mathematical inquiry.

### Chapter III.

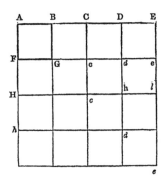

*Mrs. D.* I believe I need not explain to you that a rectangle is a four-sided figure, having all the angles right angles, and that a square is a rectangle having all its sides equal, as A B F G. If A B = to 1 yard, then the surface of the square A G = 1 square yard. If A B = 1 inch, then the square A G = 1 square inch; and speaking generally, if the line A B be expressed by 1 or unity, the square A G is expressed by 1 or unity, and is called a square contained under the line A B. Now if A B be continued to C, so that B C = A B, then the square under A C, or A C c H, will have the small squares C G, &c. of which it is formed all equal to A G, and their number will be equal to 2 × 2 = 4. If A C be continued to D, so that C D = C B = A B, then the square under the whole line A D, or A D d h, will contain 3 × 3 squares, each equal to A G. Thus 1 square yard contains 3 × 3 = 9 square feet. In the same way if D E be produced to E, making D E = C D, we shall have 4 squares = A G 4 times repeated, or 16, and in like manner it may be shown that the square of a line, expressed by any number will contain as many small squares contained under that part of the line denoting unity, as the number multiplied by itself, or as the second power of that number. Thus 1 square foot, or a square contained under a line of 12 inches, is equal to or contains 12 × 12, or 144 square inches. A square contained under any line is likewise called that line square. Thus 3 × 3 feet is called 3 feet square.

The rectangle A C c F, contained under the lines A C and A F, is, it is seen, equal to the 2 squares A G and G E, or two squares under A B, expressed by unity; so A D $d$ F = 3 squares, A E e F = 4 squares. Again, the rectangle A H h D = 3 × 2 squares, A H $l$ E = 4 × 2 squares; therefore, in general terms, the rectangle contained under sides, expressed by any two numbers, is the product of these two numbers, or the surface of the rectangle contains this product of squares expressed by unity. Thus the rectangle under two lines, the one being 6 yards and the other 7 yards in length, will contain 6 × 7 = 42 square yards, or 42 × 9 square feet, or 42 × 9 × 144 square inches, and this is usually expressed 6 yards by 7.

If, instead of whole numbers, the sides of the rectangle be expressed by mixed or fractional numbers, the surface they enclose will still be truly expressed by multiplying the two sides together.

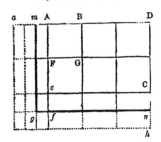

Let A D $=$ 3 and C D $=$ 2, then 2 $\times$ 3 $=$ rectangle A D C $c$; now if A $m$ be taken, any part, say $\frac{1}{3}$ of A B, or its equal A $a$ and C $n$ be taken, any part, say $\frac{1}{2}$ of A B, or its equal C $h$, then the rectangle under D $m=$ 3 $\frac{1}{3}$, and D $n=$ 2 $\frac{1}{2}$, will be truly expressed by 3 $\frac{1}{3}$ $\times$ 2 $\frac{1}{2}$ $=$ 6 $\frac{2}{3}$ $+$ $\frac{3}{2}$ $+$ $\frac{1}{6}$, or $\frac{10}{3}$ $\times$ $\frac{5}{2}$ $=$ 8 $\frac{2}{6}$. For $m$ F $=$ $\frac{1}{3}$ of the square $a$ F, or its equal A G; and therefore $m$ $c$ is equal to $m$ A $\times$ A $c=\frac{1}{3}$ $\times$ 2 $=$ $\frac{2}{3}$ of A G. In like manner C $n$ is equal to $\frac{1}{2}$ A G; and therefore $c$ $f$ (C $n$) $\times$ C $c$ (A D) $=$ $\frac{1}{2}$ $\times$ 3 $=$ $\frac{3}{2}$ of A G and $c$ $g=$ $m$ A $\times$ $f$ $c=$ $\frac{1}{3}$ $\times$ $\frac{1}{2}$ $=$ $\frac{1}{6}$ of A G; therefore the whole rectangle $m$ $n$ is equal 6 $+$ $\frac{2}{3}$ $+$ $\frac{3}{2}$ $+$ $\frac{1}{6}$ $=$ 8 $\frac{1}{3}$, or 2 $\frac{1}{2}$ $\times$ 3 $\frac{1}{3}$ $=$ D $m$ $\times$ D $n$.

Therefore, in general, whether in integers or fractions, the square of a number is its 2nd power, and the rectangle of two numbers is equal to their product.

Q. 159. What is the square of 347?

Q. 160. What is the rectangle contained under 59 and 87?

Q. 161. What part of an acre is a piece of ground contained under 4 feet by 20?

Q. 162. In a piece of ground, 15 feet square, I transplanted young cabbages, in rows 20 inches apart, and at intervals of fifteen inches. How many plants were required to fill this space?

Q. 163. A room 27 feet wide and 31 long is to be covered with carpeting ¾ of a yard wide. What quantity must be obtained for this purpose?

---

*Mrs. D.* You already know that a solid square is called a cube, that is to say, a cube is a rectangular solid, having each of its six sides a square. Any square 1 inch thick could therefore be cut into solid or cubic inches, equal in number to the square of the side;

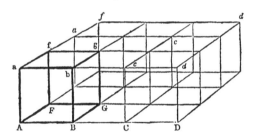

thus if the side be 2 = A C, there will be 2 × 2 = 4 solid inches; if the side be 3 = A D, there will be 3 × 3, or 9 solid inches, and so on. Now let us place on this square of an inch thick another equal square of the same thickness;

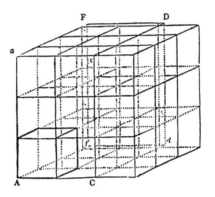

then if the side of the square be equal to only two inches, these two squares so placed will form a cube, and will contain 2 × 2 × 2 cubic inches. If the side of the square be 3, and we place another equal square of the same thickness on the other two, then the three squares will form a cube, and will contain 3 × 3 × 3 cubic inches, and in like manner it can be shown that the cube of a line expressed by any number will contain as many smaller cubes expressed by unity as the number multiplied into itself twice, or as its 3rd power.

It may likewise be readily seen that the solid content of any rectangular solid, A C D F is equal to the rectangle A $d$, multiplied by the height A $a$, or equal A C × C $d$ × A $a$, and therefore is equal to the length, breadth, and height multiplied into each other.

What is the cube of 59?

*Ed.* 59 × 59 × 59.

```
       59
      ___
      531
      295
     ____
     3481
       59
    _____
    31329
    17405
   _____
   205379
```

*Mrs. D.* An engineer wished to know how many gallons of water can be contained in a boiler, the breadth of which is = 18 inches, the length = 80, the height = 48. The number of gallons of water contained in each cubic foot are $6\frac{1}{4}$.

Here is the calculation made in the common way, and the result is quite correct :—

```
           18
           80
         _____
         1440
           48
        _____
        11520
         576
      _____
    12)69120
      _____
    12)  5760
      _____
    12)   480
         _____
          40
         6.25
         _____
          250
```

Now, why did he do all this, and how would you an-swer the question?

*Ed.* Here are 18 × 80 × 48 to obtain the solid content in inches, this product is divided by 12 × 12 × 12
to bring the cubic inches into cubic feet, and then this
result is multiplied by 6¼ to find the quantity of water.

$$\text{Hence } \frac{\cancel{18} \times \cancel{80} \times \cancel{48} \times 6.25}{\cancel{12} \times \cancel{12} \times \cancel{12}} = 40 \times 6.25 = 250 \text{ gals.}$$

*Mrs. D.* You see cancelling has here much simplified
our process.  Now, answer the following questions :—

Q. 164.  What number of cubic yards are there in a
solid cube, the side of which measures 4 feet ?

Q. 165.  I require a cistern which will be capable of
containing 320 gallons of water, but I am limited to
space, and can allow only 3½ feet for its length, and 2½
feet for its breadth : now, what height must it be to contain that quantity of water ?

———

*Mrs. D.* By considering the formation of squares
and cubes, we may often facilitate the working of our
calculations on this subject, while the investigation is a
preliminary, almost necessary to the proper understanding of the method of evolving, or undoing our work.

*Ed.* But we already know how these numbers are
obtained by multiplication, and, therefore, are fully acquainted with their formation, while it is not very difficult to undo our work, if we divide by the same number
with which we had previously multiplied.

*Mrs. D.* Notwithstanding this, we will proceed with
our inquiry, and I think that you will soon discover and
acknowledge its utility.

Let us take any number, 37 for example, to find its
square.   Now, 30 + 7 = 37, therefore, 37 × 37 =
$\overline{30 + 7} \times \overline{30 + 7}$ = 30 × 30 + 30 × 7 + 30 × 7 +

$7 \times 7 = 30 \times 30 + 2 \times 30 \times 7 + 7 \times 7$. In like manner, if we take 23 or $30 - 7$; $23 \times 23 = \overline{30 - 7}$ $\times \overline{30 - 7} = 30 \times 30 - 30 \times 7 - 30 \times 7 + 7 \times 7 = 30 \times 30 - 2 \times 30 \times 7 + 7 \times 7$.

$$30 \times 30 = 900$$
$$2 \times 30 \times 7 = 420$$
$$7 \times 7 = \underline{\phantom{0}49}$$
$$37 \times 37 = \overline{1369}$$
$$30 \times 30 = 900$$
$$2 \times 30 \times 7 = \underline{420}$$
$$480$$
$$7 \times 7 = \underline{\phantom{0}49}$$
$$23 \times 23 = \overline{529}$$

Now it is evident that this conclusion does not in any way depend on the particular numbers here used, and that any other two numbers might have been operated upon in a similar manner: therefore the square of the sum of any two numbers is equal to the squares of each of the numbers, plus twice their product; and the square of the difference of any two numbers is equal to the squares of the numbers, minus twice their product.

Again, the cube of $37 = \overline{30 + 7}^3 = \overline{30 + 7}^2 \times$ $\overline{30 + 7} = \overline{30 \times 30 + 2 \times 30 \times 7 + 7 \times 7} \times \overline{30 \times 7}$ $= 30 \times 30 \times 30 + 2 \times 30 \times 30 \times 7 + 30 \times 7 \times 7$
$$+ \quad 30 \times 30 \times 7 + 2 \times 30 \times 7 \times 7 + 7 \times 7 \times 7$$

Cube of $37 = \overline{30 + 7}^3 =$
$$\overline{30 \times 30 \times 30 + 3 \times 30 \times 30 \times 7 + 3 \times 30 \times 7 \times 7 + 7 \times 7 \times 7}$$

The cube of $23 = \overline{30 - 7}^3 = \overline{30 - 7}^2 \times \overline{30 - 7} =$ $\overline{30 \times 30 - 2 \times 30 \times 7 + 7 \times 7} = 30 \times 30 \times 30 - 2 \times 30 \times 30 \times 7 + 30 \times 7 \times 7$
$$- \quad 30 \times 30 \times 7 + 2 \times 30 \times 7 \times 7 - 7 \times 7 \times 7$$
$$\overline{30 \times 30 \times 30 - 3 \times 30 \times 30 \times 7 + 3 \times 30 \times 7 \times 7 - 7 \times 7 \times 7} =$$
$\overline{30 - 7}^3 =$ cube of 23.

$$30 \times 30 \times 30 = 27000 \qquad 30 \times 30 \times 3 = 27000$$
$$3 \times 30 \times 30 \times 7 = 18900 \qquad -3 \times 3 \times 30 \times 7 = -18900$$
$$3 \times 30 \times 7 \times 7 = \phantom{0}4410 \qquad 3 \times 30 \times 7 \times 7 = \phantom{0}4410$$
$$7 \times 7 \times 7 = \phantom{00}343 \qquad -\phantom{0}7 \times 7 \times 7 = -\phantom{00}343$$
$$37|^3 \qquad = \overline{50653} \qquad 23|^3 \qquad = \overline{12167}$$

And as this reasoning does not depend on the numbers
here used, it follows that the cube of the sum of any two
numbers is equal to the sum of their cubes, plus three
times the square of the first, multiplied by the second,
and plus three times the square of the second, multiplied
by the first; and the cube of the difference of any two
numbers is equal to the difference of their cubes, minus
three times the square of the first, multiplied by the
second; plus three times the square of the second, multiplied by the first.

*Ed.* It is easier, however, to find the squares and cubes
by common multiplication than by this method.

*Mrs. D.* I will show you how the consideration of
squares and cubes under these forms may be made of
practical application. Let us find the square and the
cube of 59. Then $59 = 60 - 1$, so $\overline{59}|^2 = \overline{60-1}|^2$ and
$59|^3 = \overline{60-1}|^3$

$$\overline{60}|^2 = \phantom{0}3600 \qquad \overline{60}|^3 = \phantom{0}216000$$
$$-2 \times 60 \times 1 = -120 \qquad -3 \times \overline{60}|^2 \times 1 = -\phantom{0}10800$$
$$\overline{1}|^2 = \phantom{000}1 \qquad 3 \times 60 \times \overline{1}|^2 = \phantom{0000}180$$
$$\overline{59}|^2 = \overline{60 - 1}|^2 = \overline{3481} \qquad -\overline{1}|^3 = -\phantom{00000}1$$
$$\overline{59}|^3 = \overline{60 - 1}|^3 = \overline{205379}$$

Now, tell me the square and cube of 999?

*Ed.* Here $999 = 1000 - 1$, and therefore,
$$\overline{999}|^2 = \overline{1000 - 1}|^2 \;\&\; \overline{999}|^3 = \overline{1000 - 1}|^3$$

$$\overline{1000}|^2 = 1,000,000 \qquad \overline{1000}|^3 = 1,000,000,000$$
$$-2 \times 1000 \times 1 = -\phantom{0}2000 \qquad -3 \times \overline{1000}|^2 \times 1 = -3,000,000$$
$$1|^2 = \phantom{0000000}1 \qquad 3 \times 1000 \times 1 = \phantom{000000}3000$$
$$\overline{999}|^2 = \overline{1000 - 1}|^2 = 998001 \qquad 1|^3 = \phantom{00000000}-1$$
$$\overline{999}|^3 = \overline{1000 - 1}|^3 = 997,002,999$$

This is certainly a much shorter way than multiply-ing the number into itself.

*Mrs. D.* Yes; squares and cubes may be very easily worked mentally in this way, and with a little practice a person will acquire a great facility in answering such questions. In like manner, to find the product of two or more numbers, we may break them into parts, which will very much reduce the labour of multiplication, and oftentimes enable us to work apparently difficult sums in our minds with very little exertion. This, however, I have already shown you a long time back (p. 56). I will give you another example at present. Multiply 999 by 945.

*Ed.* $999 = 1000 - 1$; therefore $945000 - 945 = 944055 = 999 \times 945$.

*Mrs. D.* Now let us multiply 345 by 879. Here $345 = 69 \times 5$, and $69 = 70 - 1$; multiplying by 10 and dividing by 2 produce the same result as multiplying by 5; therefore $345 \times 879 = 70 - 1 \times 4395 \left( \dfrac{8790}{2} \right)$ $= 307650 - 4395 = 303255$.

Q. 166. Find the 2nd and 3rd power of 789?

Q. 167. What are the square and cube of 591?

Q. 168. Given 293 and 567, to find their product?

---

The consideration of the formation of cubes and squares teaches us how to find from given cubes and squares their side, or, as it is called, their root: thus 3 is the square root of 9, and the cube root of 27, and the finding of this is called the extraction of the root, or evolution. When the number given, from which the

root is to be extracted, has been formed by the multiplication of a number into itself, this evolving is not a
very difficult operation; we will therefore first consider
numbers of this nature which are called perfect or rational squares and cubes.   For this purpose let us still
further examine the formation of square and cube numbers, looking back to any of the squares and cubes we
have by this method produced.   Thus we have found
$37^2 = 1369$; and therefore 37 is the square root of
1369.   In analysing a square or cube, we shall be enabled to make the different steps more distinct if, instead
of denoting the values of the figures by calling them as
usual units, tens, hundreds, &c., we say 1st, 2nd, 3rd,
&c. figures, our explanation will likewise be consider-
ably abridged if we point off the figures into what are
called periods, by putting a mark over every second
figure in the squares, and over every third figure in the

cubes, beginning from the place of units;—thus $1\overset{.}{3}6\overset{.}{9}$

and $50\overset{.}{6}5\overset{.}{3}$—the utility of this arrangement will be made
sufficiently apparent as we proceed.

   If we break any square number into its parts, for ex-

ample 1369, (*see* p. 219), we shall find that the 1st figure
must always be the units of the square of the 1st figure
of the root: in this case $7 \times 7 = 4/9$: the 2nd figure consists of the units of twice the product of the 1st and 2nd
figures of the root plus the tens of the square of the
1st figure: in this case $2 \times 3 \times 7 = \underline{4/2} + 4$ (the tens
of $7 \times 7$), and the last period is equal to the square of
the last figure of the root plus the tens of twice the product of the last and last but one figure of the root (in
this case the tens of twice the product of the 1st and
2nd figures): therefore the last period in this case =

$3 \times 3 + 4$ (the tens of $2 \times 3 \times 7$). If the square root consists of 3 places of figures, for example 437, then breaking it into $400 + 37$ its square $= \overline{400 + 37}|^2$

$$\overline{400}|^2 = 160000$$
$$2 \times 400 \times 37 = 29600$$
$$\overline{37}|^2 = 1369$$

$$\overline{400 + 37}\,^2 = \overline{437}|^2 = 1\dot{9}09\dot{6}9$$

we shall find on inspection that the observations I have just made equally apply to this number: the 1st and 2nd figures are evidently produced in the same manner as in the last, or as in the square of 37, and the last period is equal to the square of the 3rd figure of the root + the tens of twice the product of the 3rd and 2nd figures of the root, increased by the excess of the other numbers beyond the 1st and 2nd periods of figures; the last period in this case, therefore, $4 \times 4 + 3$ (the tens of $2 \times 4 \times 3$, &c.)

In the same manner, if we consider the cube of any number, for example 50653, we find that the 1st figure (*see* p. 220) expresses the units of the cube of the 1st figure of the root: in this case $7 \times 7 \times 7 = \underline{34}/3$, the 2nd figure consists of the units of three times the product of the 2nd figure into the square of the 1st figure plus the tens of the cube of the 1st figure in this case ($3 \times 3 \times 7 \times 7 = \underline{44}/1 + 4$ (tens of $3/4/3$); and the last period is the cube of the last figure of the root plus the tens of 3 times the product of the square of the last figure of the root into the last but one figure of the root, increased by the excess of the other numbers beyond the other periods: in this case $3 \times 3 \times 3 + 23$ (tens of $3 \times 3 \times 3 \times 7 +$, &c.).

If the cube root consists of 3 places of figures, for example 437, then $\overline{437}|^3 = \overline{400 + 37}|^3$, or $\overline{430 + 7}|^3 =$ 83453453;

| | |
|---|---|
| $\overline{400}|^3 = 64,000,000$ | $\overline{430}|^3 = 79507000$ |
| $3 \times \overline{400}|^2 \times 37 = 17\ 760\ 000$ | $3 \times \overline{43}|^2 \times 7 = 3882900$ |
| $3 \times 400 \times \overline{37}|^2 = 1\ 642\ 800$ | $3 \times 43 \times \overline{7}|^2 = 63210$ |
| $\overline{37}|^3 = 50\ 653$ | $\overline{7}|^3 = 343$ |
| $83,453,453$ | $83453453$ |

and as it has been shown in the square root, so it may be shown here, that a cube of three or any other number of periods is formed on exactly the same principle: in this case the last period equal to $4 \times 4 \times 4 + 19$ (tens of $3 \times 4 \times 4 \times 3 +$, &c.), and in the same way the two last periods $=$ the cube of the 2 last figures $+$ tens of the next period, in this case $\overline{43}|^3 + 3946$ (tens of $3 \times \overline{43}|^2 \times 7 +$, &c.).

Having obtained this data, we may easily show how it is practically useful. As a preliminary step, however, you must first make for yourself, and examine

*A Table of the Squares and Cubes of the Nine Digits.*

| Numbers. | Squares. | Cubes. |
|---|---|---|
| 1 | 1 | 1 |
| 2 | 4 | 8 |
| 3 | 9 | 2 \| 7 |
| 4 | 1 \| 6 | 6 \| 4 |
| 5 | 2 \| 5 | 12 \| 5 |
| 6 | 3 \| 6 | 21 \| 6 |
| 7 | 4 \| 9 | 34 \| 3 |
| 8 | 6 \| 4 | 51 \| 2 |
| 9 | 8 \| 1 | 72 \| 9 |

You will observe that the four figures preceding 5 make the units of their squares the same as the four figures succeeding 5, the like figure denoting the units receding from each side of 5 in a regular order easily remembered. Therefore, when we have a perfect square given us to find its root, we know immediately, on seeing the 1st figure, that the 1st figure of the root must be one of two numbers. Thus, if the 1st figure of a square number be 4, the 1st figure of its root will be either 8 or 2, because the units of the square of each of these are 4; if the first figure of the square be 6, the 1st figure of its root is 6 or 4; if 9, the 1st figure of the root is 7 or 3, and so on.

All the cubes of the 9 digits have their units different, and, in an arrangement with which you may quickly become familiar, the cubes of 8 and 2, 7 and 3, have merely their units reversed, and all the other units of the cubes are the same as their cube roots. Therefore, on seeing a perfect cube, we can, without a moment's hesitation, name the first figure of its root: thus, if the 1st figure of a cube number be 4, we know the 1st figure of its root is 4; if 7, we know the 1st figure of its root is 3, and so on.

Again, the greatest square or cube contained in the last period of a square or cube is the root of the last figure of the root: since this last period has been shown to be the square or cube of the last figure in the root, the square or cube of this figure cannot, it is evident, be more than the greatest square contained in the last period, neither can it be less, since the whole square or cube number must always be less than the $\overline{\text{last fig.} + 1}^2$, or $\overline{\text{last fig.} + 1}^3$, that is to say $\overline{437}^2$ less than $\overline{500}^2$, and $\overline{437}^3$ less than $\overline{500}^3$.

Now I feel that I have been conducting you over a

long wearisome path where even no difficulties have appeared to call your energies into action, and while tracing our course you may perhaps have been unmindful of the leading truths which I have wished to establish : let us therefore draw up a summary of these.

In all perfect squares consisting of 3 periods,—

1st. The 1st figure expresses the units of the square of the 1st figure in the root.

2nd. The 2nd figure consists of the units of twice the product of the 2nd and 3rd figure of the root increased by the tens of the square of the 1st figure of the root.

3rd. The last period is the square of the 3rd figure of the root increased by the tens of twice the product of the 3rd and 2nd figure + the excess of the other numbers above the two first periods.

4th. The figure preceding the last period, together with its tens contained in the last period, express twice the product of the 2nd and 3rd figure of the root + tens of the preceding number; therefore this number divided by twice·the 3rd figure of the root will give the 2nd figure of the root.

In all perfect cubes consisting of 3 periods,—

1st. The 1st figure expresses the units of the cube of the 1st figure in the root.

2nd. The 2nd figure consists of the units of 3 times the product of the 2nd figure of the root into the square of the 1st figure of the root, plus the tens of the cube of the 1st figure in the root.

3rd. The last period is the cube of the 3rd figure of the root, increased by the tens of 3 times the product of the square of the 3rd figure of the root, into the 2nd figure of the root, plus the excess of the other numbers above the two first periods.

4th. The figure preceding the last period, together

with its tens contained in the last period, express 3 times the square of the 3rd fig. × by the 2nd fig. of the root + tens of the other numbers of the period—therefore this number divided by 3 times the square of the 3rd figure of the root will give the 2nd figure of the root.

All these things being premised, we at length come to the application.

A perfect square $11\overset{.}{6}9\overset{.}{6}\overset{.}{4}$ being proposed, let us find its root. Here the units of the square root of 4 are either 8 or 2. In the first case $2 \times 2 = 4$, add no tens to the 2nd fig.; and in the second case, $8 \times 8 = 64$, have 6 tens, which must be taken from the 2nd fig. to leave the units of $2 \times$ 1st $\times$ 2nd fig. of root; therefore, if the 1st fig. of the root be

2, then $2 \times 2 \times$ 2nd fig. of root has the units 6.
8, then $2 \times 8 \times$ 2nd fig. of root has the units 0.

The greatest square in 11 (the last period) equal $9 = 3_1^2$; $11 - 9 = 2 =$ tens of $2 \times 3 \times$ 2nd fig.: this 2nd fig. cannot therefore be more than 4, or otherwise these tens would be more than 2; and if the 2nd fig. be 4, then $2 \times 2 \times 4$ has the units 6, and since the 2nd fig. cannot be more than 4, and no number below $4 \times 2 \times 2$ will have the units 6, and no fig. $\times 2 \times 2$ can have the units 0, it follows, that the 2nd fig. can be no other than 4 to answer both the requisite conditions, therefore,

$\overset{3d\,2d\,1st}{3\,\cdot 4\,\ 2}$ is the square root of $11\overset{.}{6}9\overset{.}{6}\overset{.}{4}$.

Given $3283\overset{..}{29}$ to find its square root.
$$9 = \text{units of } \overline{3}_1^2 \text{ or } \overline{7}_1^2$$
If 3, then $2 \times 3 \times$ 2nd fig. of the root has the units 2
If 7, then $2 \times 7 \times$ 2nd fig. of the root   ..   .. 8
for $\overline{7}_1^2 = 49 \& 4 + 8$ have the units 2.

$32-25 \ (\overline{5}\vert^2) = 7 =$ tens of $2 \times 5 \times$ 2nd fig. : this 2nd fig. must therefore be 7, because these tens + the last figure of the 2nd period are found by the product of $2 \times 5 \times$ 2nd fig., increased by excess of tens of the preceding figure, and since $2 \times 5 = 10$ is contained 7 times in 78, it follows, that it cannot be more than 7, neither can it be less, because 32 is much nearer the next square 36 than 25 ; and 5 and 6, the next lower numbers, will not, it is evident, make the 2nd fig. 2 or 8 ;—therefore, 7 must be the 2nd fig., and $2 \times 3 \times 7$ has the units 2 ; therefore, 3 must be 1st figure and the square root $=$

3d 2d 1st

5  7  3.

Now let us try another with abbreviations : taking it for granted that you comprehend what has gone before, we will not repeat explanations, but confine ourselves to what is necessary for the actual operations.

Given 600625 to find its square root.

Here the units of the 1st fig. of the root equal 5 ;

$60 - 49 \ (\overline{7}\vert^2) = 11$, and $\overset{\text{T}}{110}$ divided by $2 \times 7 = 14$

3d 2d 1st

give $7 =$ 2nd fig., therefore, 7 7 5 $=$ square root required.

Q. 169. Given 246016 to find its square root.

Q. 170. Given 358801 to find its square root.

It is much easier to find the cube root in this way by inspection, than the square root, since we have never any doubts of the 1st figure. For example, let us find the cube root of the perfect cube $40001688$. Here $8 =$ cube of $2 =$ 1st fig. of root. Then $3 \times \overline{2}|^2 \times$ 2nd fig. has the units 8; $3 \times \overline{2}|^2 = 12$, which multiplied by 4 or by 9 will give the units 8. The nearest cube to 40 is $27 = \overline{3}|^3$; now, if the second fig. were 9, the last period would be much nearer to the next cube to 27, which is 64, than to 27, but it is nearer to 27 than 64, and therefore, the 2nd fig. must be 4, and the whole cube root will be 3 4 3.

<sup>3d 2d 1st</sup>

Given $188132517$ to find its cube root. Here 27 $=$ cube of three $=$ 1st fig. of root, therefore, $3 \times \overline{3}|^2 =$ $27 \times$ 2nd fig. has the units 9, because 2 (the tens of 27) and 9 are 11, but the only figure multiplied by $2/7$ which will make the units of their product 9, is 7, therefore $7 =$ 2nd figure. And the nearest cube to 188 is $\overline{5}|^3$, therefore, $5 =$ 3rd figure, and the whole root $= 5\ 7\ 3$.

<sup>3d 2d 1st</sup>

Given $465484375$ to extract the cube root. Here $125 =$ cube of 5 $=$ 1st fig. of root, therefore, $3 \times \overline{5}|^2 \times$ 2nd fig. of root has the units 5, because 2 (the tens of $1/2/5$) and 5 $= 7 =$ 2nd figure of cube. $343 = \overline{7}|^3 =$ nearest cube to 465.

Now any odd number multiplied by $3 \times \overline{5}|^2$ will have the units 5, and therefore, in this case, and only in this case, when the 1st fig. of the cube is 5, we must subtract the nearest cube from the last period, to determine by this remainder what the second fig. of the root should be. Here $465 - 343 = 122 =$ tens of last fig. of 2nd period, but these tens and the last figure of 2nd period $= 1224 = 3 \times \overline{7}|^2 \times$ 2nd fig., but 7 is the odd number

x

which, multiplied by 147 $(3 \times \overline{7}^{|2})$, will produce its tens the nearest to 122; or $\dfrac{1224}{147}$ has the quotient 7, and therefore 7 is $=$ 2nd fig., because 465 is much nearer to the next cube 512 than to 343, and therefore the 2nd fig. cannot be less than 7, and the whole cube root $=$

<sup>3d 2d 1st</sup>
7 7 5.   Although I have gone through the whole of the multiplications to explain to you the method, they need in reality be only in part performed in the mind, and a little practice will give a wonderful celerity in discovering what figures will produce the given tens or units. All the necessary operations are gone through with great rapidity. If you try two or three, you will soon find that very little intellectual effort is called for, and that what appears so formidable in repetition passes through the mind with a quickness which only those who have performed it can conceive.

Try the following easy example without writing it down :—what is the cube root of 329939371 ?

*Ed.* The 1st fig. of the root must be 1, and therefore, 3 × 1 × 2nd fig. has the units 7; now, 9 is the only figure which multiplied by 3 gives the units 7, and therefore, 9 $=$ 2nd fig.; 216 $= \overline{6}^3$ the nearest cube in 329 ;—

<sup>3d 2d 1st</sup>
therefore, the three numbers 6 9 1.

*Mrs. D.* Q. 171. What is the cube root of 277167808?
Q. 172. Find the cube root of 103161709.
Q. 173. What is the cube root of 20346417?

*Ed.* I like this finding of the cube root in my head, or, as you call it, mentally—the process appears so very difficult, and yet, in fact, requires little or no mental exertion. But is it useful?

*Mrs. D.* I think not practically so—because there seldom can occur such a question in the application of arithmetic to useful purposes. It is, however, a good exercise to the mind, while it familiarizes us with the nature of figures, shows us in part the power we have over numbers, and may perhaps lead us still farther to the knowledge of that power—moreover, this simple process is usually supposed to be an astonishing and unexplained working of the mind. The finding of the cube roots of perfect cubes was among the questions answered by Zerah Colburn, the American boy, who was exhibited some years back as possessing wonderful powers of calculating. It is more than probable that the method here given was used by him, since by this method any person, with a little practice, may be enabled to furnish an answer with almost as much promptitude as was shown by this child. When a number was proposed to him which was not a perfect cube, he failed in giving a correct answer, and when the units of the cube were 5, it was a chance whether the 2nd fig. of his root were right: thus, he apparently did not take the trouble to determine this with certainty from the consideration of the last period.

*Ed.* Did he not explain his manner of proceeding?

*Mrs. D.* No; he either could not or would not. It is hitherto an unexplained phenomenon of the human mind, how some untaught children should be so extraordinarily gifted, as to perform mentally and apparently by intuition, operations in arithmetic with a quickness of result wholly unattainable and inexplicable to those most conversant in numbers.

This is, however, quite a digression; let us return to our squares and cubes.

*Ed.* How can we always discover whether a number be a real square or cube?

*Mrs. D.* In many cases it is not possible to know

x 2

this on inspection. But there are some hints which may be found useful in discovering those numbers which cannot possibly be perfect squares or cubes. In squares, the first figure can never be 2, 3, 7, or 8, since no figure multiplied into itself will produce those units. When the first figure is 1, 4, 5, or 9, then the 2nd figure must be an even digit; and when the first figure is 6, then the 2nd fig. must be an odd digit, because 2 × 1st fig. of root × 2nd fig. root, is, it is evident, always an even number whatever the 1st and 2nd figure may be.

In cubes, when the 1st fig. is 1, 3, 7, or 9, then the 2nd fig. may be any number whatever; when the 1st fig. is 2 or 6, the 2nd must be odd; when the 1st is 4 or 8, the 2nd must be even; and when the 1st fig. is 5, the 2nd must be either 2 or 7; all this is evident from considering that the units of 3 times the square of the 1st fig. of the root into the 2nd fig. of the root + tens of the cube of the 1st fig. is equal to the 2nd fig. of the cube.

There is another property of cube numbers, which I once hoped would have facilitated the extraction of the roots of numbers in general, but I have not yet been able to apply it to any practical utility; it is, however, simple and pretty. Every perfect whole cube, minus its cube root, is equal to the continued product of three consecutive numbers, whereof the cube root is the middle term, and this product is always divisible by 6.

For example, $37 \times 37 \times 37 - 37 = 36 \times 37 \times 38$; because $36 \times 37 \times 38 = \overline{37 - 1} \times 37 \times \overline{37 + 1} = \overline{37 \times 37 - 37} \times \overline{37 + 1} = 37 \times 37 \times 37 - 37 \times 37 + 37 \times 37 - 37$: the two middle terms being alike, the one plus and the other minus destroy each other, leaving $37 \times 37 \times 37 - 37$ formed from $36 \times 37 \times 38$, which is therefore equal $\overline{37}^3 - 37$; and this, it is evident, does not depend on the particular figures here employed; therefore the first part of our position is established.

Now any whole number whatever, being divided by 2, is exactly divided, or leaves 1 as a remainder; therefore 1 of any two consecutive numbers is always divisible by 2. Again, any whole number whatever, being divided by 3, is either exactly divided or leaves 1 or leaves 2 as a remainder; and therefore one of any 3 consecutive numbers is divisible by 3: it follows thence that the continued product of any 3 consecutive numbers must be divisible by 2 and by 3, since 1 out of these numbers is divisible by 2 and 1 by 3; therefore the whole product is divisible by 2 × 3 or 6, and therefore every whole cube number minus its root is divisible by 6.

*Mrs. D.* We have hitherto been amusing ourselves with the consideration of perfect squares and cubes;— we have now to pursue our investigations upon numbers the roots of which cannot exactly be extracted, that is, when no number can be found which multiplied into itself to form a square, and twice into itself to form a cube, will produce the given number.

Thus let it be required to find the side of a square which contains exactly 5 square feet, or, in other words, let us extract the square root of 5. Now what steps shall we take to obtain this result?

*Ed.* This is a very difficult question. The side should be 2 and a bit more, but I do not think it is possible to find any number which, multiplied into itself, will have exactly 5 for the product.

*Mrs. D.* Very true, it is not possible; but we may approximate so very near to the number as to cause no perceptible error. Thus we know the length of the side

x 3

must be between 2 and 3—the first too little, the other too much, as the square of 2 is 4 and the square of 3 is 9. It is therefore 2 and something more. Now the question is, what is this something?

To discover this, let us take the square of $2 = 4$ from 5, and convert the remaining 1 into hundredths by adding 2 noughts. Now if 5.00, or $4 + 1.00$ be a square number, this 1.00 should, from the formation of the square of two numbers, be equal to the product of $2 \times 2 \times$ by the figure sought, plus the square of that figure; we find that $\dfrac{10}{2 \times 2} = 2 \overset{*}{+}$; and therefore that the number sought cannot be more than 2; neither in this case, it is evident, can it be less, and therefore 2 = figure sought (p. 219).

Perhaps, however, it will be better to work the sum in length first, and explain the different steps afterwards.

$$
\begin{array}{rll}
 & & 5(2.236068 \\
\overline{20|^2} = 400 & & 4 \\
2 \times 2.0 \times .2 = .80 \} & & \overline{1.00} \\
.2 \times .2 = .04 \} = & & .84 \\
\overline{+2.2|^2} = \overline{4.8400} & & .1600\| \\
2 \times 2.2 \times .03 = .1320 \} & & .1329 \\
\overline{.03|^2} = 9 \} & & \\
{}^\circ\, \overline{.2.23|^2} = \overline{4.972900.} & & 027100^{\S} \\
2 \times 2.23 \times .006 = 026760 \} & & \\
\overline{.006|^2} = 36 \} & = & .026796 \\
\overline{2.236|^2} = \overline{4.9996960000} & & .0003040000 \\
2 \times 2.236 \times .00006 = 2683200 \} & & .0002683236 \\
\overline{.00006|^2} = 36 \} & & \\
\overline{2.23606|^2} = \overline{4.9999643236} & & .0000356764 \\
\end{array}
$$

We find as above that $\overline{2.2|^2} = \overset{+}{4}.84$, therefore $5. = \overline{2.2|^2} + \overset{\|}{.16}$. To make our sum more exact, we must

---

* This + means + the remainder.

add two more noughts to our remainder, that we may have another figure of the next denomination in the root; and proceeding the same way as before, we find $\dfrac{.160}{2.2 \times 2} = 3 + =$ figure sought. Complete the square and we find as above that $5 = \overline{2.23}|^2 + 027\overset{\circ}{1}$, and adding 2 more noughts to obtain another figure in the root of the next denomination in the same way we find $\dfrac{.02710}{2.23 \times 2} = 6 +$, and continuing our work as above we find $5 = \overline{2.236}|^2 + .000304$.

*Ed.* Well, I see we shall never get the exact side of our square, and so we had better be contented with this trifling error.

*Mrs. D.* Let us see if we cannot make it still more trifling. Adding two more noughts, we find $\dfrac{0003040}{2.236 \times 2}$ $= \dfrac{3040}{4472}$.

*Ed.* And here we cannot go on because 3040 is less than 4475, and therefore 4472 is contained no times in 3040, and has 3040 as a remainder.

*Mrs. D.* True; but we can put nought to show there is no figure in that denomination in the root, and let us add two more noughts. Then $\dfrac{304000}{44720} = 6 +$ and completing the square we have $5 = \overline{2.23606}|^2 + 00000356764$. Then adding two more noughts $\dfrac{3567640}{2.23606 \times 2} = \dfrac{3567640}{447212}$ $= 8$ nearly, and therefore $5 = \overline{2.236068}|^2$ minus a very slight error.

Now it is evident that if this number, instead of being 5, had been 5000000000000, we should have proceeded exactly the same, and our answer would have been 2236068; therefore, in the same manner as we have extracted the square of these units, by bringing the figures into decimals, so we could work in whole numbers, bringing down two figures of the number instead of adding two noughts. For example, let us extract the square root of 7864037; and here, after what I have already said, it will be unnecessary to explain every step; what we do will be sufficiently seen and understood in the working.

(No. 1.)

$\overset{\displaystyle \cdots}{7864037} (2804.289 +$

$\overline{2}|^2$ nearest sqre to 7 is .. 4

excess of 786 over 400 .. 386

$\qquad\qquad 2 \times 20 \times 8 .. 32$ $\qquad\qquad\qquad \dfrac{38}{2 \times 2} = 8 +$

$\qquad\qquad\qquad \overline{8}|^2 .. \ 64$

$\qquad\qquad$ excess .. $\overline{24037}$ $\qquad\qquad \dfrac{24}{28 \times 2} = 0 +$

$\qquad 2 \times 2800 \times 4 = 22400$

$\qquad\qquad\qquad \overline{4}|^2 = \ \ 16$ $\qquad\qquad \dfrac{2403}{*280 \times 2} = 4 +$

$\qquad\qquad$ excess .. $\ 1621.00$

$\quad 2 \times 28040 \times .2 = \ 112160$ $\qquad \dfrac{16270}{2804 \times 2} = \dfrac{16270}{5608\dagger} = 2 +$

$\qquad\qquad\qquad .\overline{2}|^2 = \qquad 4$

$\qquad\qquad$ excess .. $\ 4993600$ $\qquad \dfrac{499360}{28042 \times 2} = \dfrac{499360}{56084} = 8 +$

$\ 2 \times 280420 \times .08 = \ 4486720$

$\qquad\qquad\quad .\overline{08}|^2 = \qquad 64$ $\qquad \dfrac{5068160}{560856} = 9 +$

$\qquad\qquad$ excess .. $\ .050681600$

$2 \times 2804280 \times .009 = .05047714$

$\qquad\qquad\quad .\overline{009}|^2 = \qquad 81$

$\qquad\qquad$ excess .. $\ \overline{.000204479}$

Therefore $7864037 = \overline{2804.289}|^2 + .000204479.$

(No. 2.)

7864037(2804.289 +
4
```
 48 | 386
  8 | 384
```
```
*5604 |    24037
    4 |    22416
```
```
†56082 |    162100
     2 |    112164
```
```
560848 |    4993600
     8 |    4486784
```
```
5608569 |    50681600
      9 |    50477221
```
```
                 204479
```

You perceive that the operations performed, though many, are simple. I have purposely omitted one step in obtaining the last figure to show you that it is unnecessary to express this in the working; for 280428 × 2 is the same as 280420 × 2 + 8 × 2, so 28042 × 2 the same as 28040 × 2 + 2 × 2, so 2804 × 2 the same as 2800 × 2 + 2 × 2, and so on, it being evidently unnecessary every time to multiply the whole number by 2. Now you see and perfectly understand all the steps, the manner of setting down the working may be more commodiously performed as in No. 2, where you will readily understand that 384 = 2 × 20 × 8 + 8 × 8 = 48 × 8, and that 48 + 8 = 56 = 2 × 28, and so on.

Q. 174. Find the square root of 37485938.

Q. 175. What is the square root of 498?

Q. 176. There are 4 acres of ground divided into 3 equal squares; what is the side of these equal squares?

Q. 177. A person has a piece of ground 97 yards by 76 ; his neighbour had the same space of ground allotted to him, but his was a square piece. I desire to know what is the side of this square?

In extracting the cube root of any number we proceed on the same principle as the square root, by evolving the work supposed to have been done.

This is of course rather a more complicated process, since the involving of the cube requires more operations than involving the square.

Let us find the nearest cube root to 567893.

$$\overline{80}|^2 = 6400$$
$$2 \times 80 \times 2 = 320$$
$$\overline{2}|^2 = 4$$
$$\overline{82}|^2 = 6724$$
$$3$$
$$\overline{82}|^3 \times 3 = 20172$$
$$.8$$
$$3 \times \overline{82}|^2 \times .8 = 16137.6$$
$$\overline{82.0}|^3 = 6724.00$$
$$2 \times 820 \times .8 = 131.20$$
$$.8|^2 = 64$$
$$\overline{82.8}|^2 \quad 6855.84$$
$$3$$
$$3 \times \overline{82.8}|^2 \times .01 = 205.6752$$
$$\overline{82.80}|^2 = 6855.8400$$
$$2 \times 82.80 \times .01 = 1.6560$$
$$.01|^2 = 1$$
$$\overline{82.81}|^2 = 6857.4961$$
$$3$$
$$3 \times \overline{82.81}|^2 \times .001 = 20.5724883$$

$$\overline{80|}^3 = 512000$$

567893(82.8111 +
512

$$3 \times \overline{80|}^2 \times 2 = 38400$$
$$3 \times 80 \times \overline{2|}^2 = 960$$
$$\overline{2|}^3 = 8$$
$$=$$

55893
39368

∥        $*\overline{82|}^3 = 551368$

16525.000

$$3 \times \overline{820|}^2 \times .8 = 16137600$$
$$3 \times 820 \times \overline{.8|}^2 = 157440$$
$$\overline{.8|}^3 = 512$$
$$=$$

16295.552

$$\dagger \, \overline{82.8|}^3 = 567663.552$$

229.448000

$$3 \times \overline{82.80|}^2 \times .01 = 205.675200$$
$$3 \times 82.80 \times \overline{.01|}^2 = 2484$$
$$\overline{.01|}^3 = 1$$
$$= 205.700041$$

$$\ddagger \, \overline{82.81|}^3 = 567869252041000$$

23.747959000

$$3 \times \overline{82.810|}^2 \times 1 = 20572488300$$
$$3 \times 82.810 \times \overline{1|}^2 = 248430$$
$$\overline{1|}^3 = 1$$
$$= 20.572736731$$

$$\S \, \overline{82.811|}^3 = 567889.824777731$$

3.175222269000

You may, I think, readily trace and understand all that is here put down. The nearest cube in the last period we find $512 = \overline{8|}^3$. Now, the next fig.' of the root cannot be more than 2, because, when 512 is deducted from the last period, the remainder $= 55$, the tens of the last fig. in the next period, and $3 \times \overline{8|}^2 = 192$ is not contained more than twice in 558, let us complete the cube of 82 (see the work *). Then $567893 = (\overline{82|}^3) \, 551368 + 16525$. To find the decimal parts of the root we must add 3 noughts, or another period to our remainder; $3 \times \overline{82|}^2 = 20172$, and $\dfrac{165250}{20172} = 8 \, +$, therefore the next fig. cannot be more than 8; let us complete the cube (see the work*), and we find 567893

---

* For the various workings see preceding page.

$= (82.\overline{8}|^3)$ 567663.552 + 229.448. Proceeding exactly in the same manner, we find the next fig. is 1, and completing our cube, 567893 is now $= \ddagger (82.\overline{81}|^3)$ 567869.$\overline{2}$52041 + 23.7479, &c. Again the next fig. is 1, and 567893 is $= \S (82.81\overline{1}|^3)$ 567889.824, &c. + 3.175, &c. The next figure we find will again be 1, and we need not continue the process any farther.

One more example worked without explanation will be sufficient. Given 5929741 to find its root.

$$5929741(181$$
$$1$$

$$\overline{10}|^3 = 1000 \qquad \qquad 4929$$

$$\left.\begin{array}{l} 3 \times \overline{10}|^2 \times 8 = 2400 \\ 3 \times 10 \times \overline{8}|^2 = 1920 \\ \overline{8}|^3 = \phantom{00}512 \end{array}\right\} = \qquad 4832$$

$$\overline{18}|^3 = 5832 \qquad \qquad 97741$$

$$\left.\begin{array}{l} 3 \times \overline{180}|^2 \times 1 = \phantom{0}97200 \\ 3 \times 180 \times \overline{1}|^2 = \phantom{0000}540 \\ 1|^3 = \phantom{00000}1 \end{array}\right\} = 97741$$

$$\overline{181}|^3 = 5929741 \qquad 0000$$

[5,000,000 much nearer to the next cube 8,000,000 $(200^3)$ than to 1,000,000; therefore, the next figure is probably very high, and $\dfrac{49}{3 \times \overline{1}|^3}$ may be 9 +, but 3 × $\overline{10}|^2 \times 9 + 3 \times 10 \times \overline{9}|^2 + \overline{9}|^3$ more than 4929, therefore try 8.]

Q. 178. Purchased 35867 cubic feet of granite in the form of 6 equal cubes, required the side of each cube.

You will no doubt find this extracting the cube root rather a laborious process: it may be somewhat shortened, bu the reason of the rule given for this purpose depends on a knowledge of algebra; when you become acquainted with that—the next branch in mathematics—you may apply it to abridging the work of evolution : till then, if ever you go this road, you must be content to take the longest way, for I am unwilling, at the close of our lessons in arithmetic, to depart from the law we established for ourselves throughout our course—To find a reason for every rule before applying it to practice.

# ANSWERS

TO

# EXAMPLES AND QUESTIONS.

## PART I.

Ex. (1), Page 31, .. Ans. 57,501,082,128.
(2), .. .. .. 20,219,658,470.
(3), .. .. .. 39,823,335.
(4), .. .. .. 6,144,647,960
(5), .. .. .. 126,068,942,240.
(6), .. 39, .. 11,101,823, and 4 rem.
(7), .. .. .. 131,087,888, and 115 rem.
(8), .. .. .. 54,324,751, and 723 rem.
(9), .. .. .. 27,325,925, and 23 rem.
(10), .. .. .. 365,151, and 390 rem.

Q. 1, Page 46, .. Ans. 677 miles.
Q. 2, .. .. .. .. 3967 sheep, and after all the sales were effected, 1972 left.
Q. 3, .. .. .. .. 72 years of age, and (in 1835) he had been dead 131 years.
Q. 4, .. .. .. .. 169 years (1835).

Q. 5, Page 46, .. Ans. 21,408 lives lost.

Q. 6, .. 47, .. .. 792,820 letters in first; 454,252 in second; 345 pages, 13 lines, 13 letters difference in first; 207 pages, 7 lines, 29 letters, difference in second.

Q. 7, .. .. .. .. 866,908 packages imported; 831,458 retained for home consumption.

Q. 8, .. .. .. .. 3471 shillings.

Q. 9, .. .. .. .. 12 shillings.

Q. 10, .. .. .. .. 147 men.

Q. 11, .. .. .. .. 48 shillings.

Q. 12, .. .. .. .. 6 shillings.

Q. 13, .. .. .. .. 144,023 quarters.

Q. 14, .. .. .. .. 6 lbs. for each, and 130 to be still farther divided between them.

---

## PART II.

Ex. (11), Page 50, .. Ans. 102.

(12), .. .. .. .. 13.

(13), .. .. .. .. 75.

(14), .. .. .. .. 112.

(15), .. .. .. .. 60.

(16), .. .. .. .. 110.

(17), ·· .. .. .. 59.

Q. 15, Page 61, .. Ans. $39\frac{2}{6}\frac{1}{3}\frac{3}{1}$ trees.

Q. 16, .. 62, .. .. $2461\frac{1}{4}$ pounds.

Q. 17, .. .. .. .. 783 yards.

244    ANSWERS TO EXAMPLES AND QUESTIONS.

Q. 18, Page 64, ..   Ans. Given.
Q. 19, .. .. .. ..   16 days.
Q. 20, .. .. .. ..   175½ acres.
Q. 21, .. 65, .. ..   8442 gallons.

Ex. (18), Page 75, ..   Ans. 1782 = 11 × 3 × 3 ×
                             3 × 3 × 2.
    (19), .. .. .. ..     729 = 3 × 3 × 3 × 3
                          × 3 × 3.
    (20), .. .. .. ..     1001 = 13 × 11 × 7.
    (21), .. .. .. ..     343 = 7 × 7 × 7.
    (22), .. .. .. ..     3584 = 7 × 2 × 2 ×
                          2 × 2 × 2 × 2 × 2
                          × 2 × 2.
    (23), .. 76, .. ..   1080 = 5 × 3 × 3 ×
                          3 × 2 × 2 × 2.
    (24), .. .. .. ..   851 = 37 × 23.
    (25), .. .. .. ..   323 = 17 × 19.
    (26), .. .. .. ..   273 = 13 × 7 × 3.

Q. 22, Page 78, ..   Ans. 27.
Q. 23, .. .. .. ..   16, 8, 4, and 2.
Q. 24, .. .. .. ..   3.
Q. 25, .. .. .. ..   2 and 4.

Ex. (27), Page 85, .. ..   Ans. 1⎫
    (28), .. .. .. .. ..     4⎬ = simplest form.
    (29), .. .. .. .. ..     6⎭

Q. 26, Page 86, ..   Ans. Given.
Q. 27, .. .. .. ..   6 bushels of coals.
Q. 28, .. .. .. ..   £640.
Q. 29, .. .. .. ..   140 cwt.
Q. 30, .. .. .. ..   £48.

Ex. (31), Page 89, ..   Ans. $\frac{27}{8}$.
   (32), .. ..  ..   ..   $4\frac{2}{11}$.
   (33), .. ..  ..   ..   $\frac{117}{10}$.
   (34), .. ..  ..   ..   $\frac{165}{15}$.

Q. 31, Page 91, ..  Ans. $\frac{3}{17}$.
Q. 32, .. .. ..   ..   $\frac{1}{3}$.
Q. 33, .. 92, ..   ..   $\frac{55}{64}$.
Q. 34, .. .. ..   ..   $\frac{3}{4}$.
Q. 35, .. .. ..   ..   $\frac{9}{13}$.
Q. 36, .. 94, ..   ..   $\frac{72}{143}$.
Q. 37, .. .. ..   ..   $\frac{63}{80}$.
Q. 38, .. .. ..   ..   $\frac{247}{340}$.
Q. 39, .. 96, ..   ..   $\frac{440}{792}$, $\frac{216}{792}$, and $\frac{603}{792}$.
Q. 40, .. .. ..   ..   $\frac{195}{240}$, and $\frac{144}{240}$.
Q. 41, .. .. ..   ..   $\frac{248}{279}$, and $\frac{144}{279}$.
Q. 42, .. 100 ..   ..   $1\frac{20}{1001}$.
Q. 43, .. 101 ..   ..   $10\frac{12}{80}$.
Q. 44, .. .. ..   ..   $\frac{26}{63}$.
Q. 45, .. .. ..   ..   $3\frac{46}{63}$.

Ex. (35), Page 102,   ..   Ans. $\frac{30}{143}$.
   (36), ..  ..   ..   ..   $\frac{9}{31}$.
   (37), ..  ..   ..   ..   Given.
   (38), ..  ..   ..   ..   $3\frac{12}{35}$.
   (39), .. 105   ..   ..   $\frac{8}{11}$.
   (40), ..  ..   ..   ..   $1\frac{19}{26}$.
   (41), ..  ..   ..   ..   $7\frac{57}{80}$.

Q. 46, Page 105,   ..  Ans. Given.
Q. 47, ..  ..   ..   ..   Given.
Q. 48, .. 106,  ..   ..   2 acres, $1\frac{1}{3}$ acre, 1 acre,
                        $\frac{4}{3}$ acre.

Q. 49, Page 106, .. Ans. D's $\begin{cases} \text{share} = 143\frac{7}{8}. \\ \text{gain} = 31\frac{7}{7}\frac{7}{7}. \end{cases}$

E's $\begin{cases} \text{share} = 215\frac{2}{3}. \\ \text{gain} = 47\frac{8}{3}\frac{9}{7}. \end{cases}$

F's $\begin{cases} \text{share} = 287\frac{1}{8}. \\ \text{gain} = 63\frac{7}{7}\frac{8}{7}. \end{cases}$

Q. 50, .. .. .. .. He sold $\frac{3}{6}\frac{8}{5}$, and had remaining $\frac{2}{6}\frac{7}{5}$.

Q. 51, .. 107, .. .. $3\frac{1}{1}\frac{5}{6}$ days.

Q. 52, .. .. .. .. $2\frac{1}{1}\frac{8}{3}\frac{2}{1}$ days.

Q. 53, .. .. .. .. $6\frac{3}{8}$ days.

Q. 54, .. .. .. .. Given.

Q. 55, Page 112, .. .. 450.5828.

Q. 56, .. .. .. .. 4899.1205.

Q. 57, .. .. .. .. 9155.873255.

Q. 58, .. .. .. .. 262.854889.

Q. 59, .. 116, .. .. 17168.588.

Q. 60, .. .. .. .. .008295.

Q. 61, .. .. .. .. 60664.821069.

Q. 62, .. 118, .. .. 89.129179, &c.

Q. 63, .. .. .. .. .082677, &c.

Q. 64, .. .. .. .. 694.39384, &c.

Ex. (42), Page 121, .. .0304871951, &c.

(43), .. .. .. .$\dot{8}$.

(44), .. 124, .. $\frac{471}{550}$.

(45), .. .. .. $\frac{8449}{11100}$.

---

## PART III.

Q. 65, Page 135, .. Ans. £61 : 2 : $4\frac{3}{4}$.

Q. 66, .. .. .. .. 31,556,928 seconds.

Q. 67, .. .. .. .. 8 miles, 5 feet, 46 yards, 2 feet.

Q. 68, Page 135, ..    Ans. 71680 plants.
Q. 69, .. 136, .. ..   4 tons, 12 cwt , 1 qr.
Q. 70, .. .. .. ..   $\frac{13}{29376}$ drachms, avoir., or $\frac{11375}{940032}$ grains troy; and $82\frac{7882}{113372}$ eggs weigh 1 gr., and each worm weighs $2\frac{6}{9}$ dr. avoir.
Q. 71, .. 139, .. ..   £256 : 4 : 11¼.
Q. 72, .. .. .. ..   5 tons, 2 cwt., 1 qr., 11 lb., 13 oz.
Q. 73, .. .. .. ..   303 acres, 2 roods, 39 poles.
Q. 74, .. 140, .. ..   8 cwt., 2 qrs., 23 lbs., 12 oz., 13 dr.
Q. 75, .. .. .. ..   6 days, 1 hour, 57 min.
Q. 76, .. 142, .. ..   £279 : 10.
Q. 77, .. .. .. ..   126 cwt.
Q. 78, .. 143, .. ..   8 cwt. 3 qr. 10 lb. 8 oz. 12 dr.
Q. 79, .. . .. ..   £1 : 16 : 7¼ $\frac{220}{763}$.
Q. 80, .. .. .. ..   1 hour, 52 min. 26$\frac{2}{73}$ sec.
Q. 81, .. 146, .. ..   .52916 of 1 lb. troy.
Q. 82, .. .. .. ..   .961805 of 1 week.
Q. 83, .. .. .. ..   .7 of a yard.
Q. 84, .. 148, .. ..   3 days, 23 hours, 18 min., 23$\frac{1}{25}$ sec.
Q. 85, .. .. .. ..   2 feet, 11$\frac{53}{125}$ inches.
Q. 86, .. .. .. ..   3 pecks and 2$\frac{300}{625}$ gills.
Q. 87, .. 153, .. ..   7 oz., 4 dwts.
Q. 88, .. .. .. ..   $\frac{3}{8}$ of 1 lb.
Q. 89, .. .. .. ..   $\frac{7}{30}$ of £1.
Q. 90, .. .. .. ..   12s. 1½d. and $\frac{324}{953}$ of 1 far.
Q. 91, .. . .. ..   $\frac{1}{280}$ of £1.
Q. 92, .. .. .. ..   $\frac{1024}{1792}$ of 1 cwt.
Q. 93, .. 162, .. ..   4,704,000 times, and 30 $\frac{180}{150}$ times per minute.

Q. 94, Page 162,  Ans. 40 in a minute, and $11\frac{1468}{2400}$
          hours to print that number.

Q. 95,  ..  ..  ..  2880 cocoons and 156 lbs.
          leaves.

Q. 96,  ..  ..  ..  $3\frac{2}{5}d.$ per gal. Proportions of
          ingredients for 2 gallons :—

          lbs. oz. drs.
          1 : 12 : $3\frac{1}{5}$ of meat.
          $3\frac{7}{10}$ gills of peas.
          oz. dr.
          4 : $3\frac{1}{5}$ of onions.
          9 : $9\frac{3}{5}$ of ground rice.
          2 : $6\frac{2}{5}$ of salt.
           $1\frac{1}{5}$ of pepper.
           $\frac{3}{5}$ of ginger.
           $\frac{4}{5}$ of Cayenne pepper.

Q. 97,  ..  163,  ..  3 furlongs and $2\frac{19}{11}$ yards.

Q. 98,  ..  ..  ..  51509.7 sugar-canes.
          4,356 lbs. jaggry.
          cwt.   oz.
          12 : 0 : 0 : 14.64 of sugar.

Q. 99,  ..  ..  ..  179,200,000 raw cotton.
          £6,160,000 value.
          289,032,258 yards cotton.

Q. 100,  ..  164,  ..  19058 years and $11\frac{55393}{503701}$
          months.

Q. 101,  ..  ..  ..  $915\frac{5}{41}$ bushels of coals.

Q. 102,  ..  ..  ..  159,248,160 yards of silk.

Q. 103,  ..  ..  ..  £666 : 17s., and at
          £1 : 16 : $6\frac{1}{4}\frac{331}{365}$ rate per day.

Q. 104,  ..  165,  ..  £9 : 2 : $0\frac{1}{2}$ cost of carriage.

Q. 105,  ..  169,  ..  £326 : 11 : $6\frac{1}{4}$.

Q. 106,  ..  ..  ..  £359 : 18 : 4.

Q. 107,  ..  ..  ..  £1741 : 8 : $1\frac{1}{2}$.

Q. 108,  ..  ..  ..  £2602 : 14 : 7.

Q. 109,  ..  ..  ..  £9462 : 6 $11\frac{1}{4}$.

Q. 110, Page 178, Ans. £187 : 19 : 3.

Q. 111, .. .. .. £29 : 2 : 5.

Q. 112, .. .. .. 170.1103 days.

Q. 113, .. .. .. £523 : 8 : 9¾.

Q. 114, .. .. .. 8 years 1.7 days.

Q. 115, .. .. .. £4764 : 18 : 9.

Q. 116, .. 181, .. £12 : 17 : 2¾.

Q. 117, .. .. .. £268 : 7 : 10.

Q. 118, .. 185, .. 4 months and 8.8952 days, reckoning 30 days to one month.

Q. 119 .. .. .. 8 months and 29 days.

Q. 120, .. 188, .. Given.

Q. 121, .. .. .. Given.

Q. 122, .. .. .. By investing in the 3½ per cent. stock £14 : 15 : 4¼ per annum will be gained. £206 : 6 : 11¼ income in 3½ per cent. stock. £191 : 11 : 6¾ income in 3 per cent, stock.

Q. 123, .. .. .. £1249 more money obtained. Stock at 54 bought with £3747 equal £6938 : 17 : 9¼. Stock; which sold at 72 = £4996; and at 92 = £6383 : 15 : 6½.

Q. 124, .. 189, .. 7s. 8$\frac{4}{13}$d. per gallon.

Q. 125, .. 190, .. 20.2602 carats fine.

Q. 126, .. 192, .. 1 lb. of each kind.

Q. 127, .. .. .. 3 at 22, 1 at 18, 4 at 24, and 3 at 17; or, 4 at 22, 1 at 17, 3 at 24, and 3 at 18.

## PART IV.

Q. 128, Page 194, Ans. 78 strokes.

Q. 129, .. .. .. £135 : 8.

Q. 130, .. .. .. 117 = sum of series.

Q. 131, .. 196, .. 247 = sum of series, and 2 = com. diff.

Q. 132, .. .. .. 13 = number of terms.

Q. 133, .. .. .. 7 = first term.

Q. 134, .. .. .. 31 = last term.

Q. 135, .. .. .. 2 = com. diff.

Q. 136, .. 197, .. 12 days.

Q. 137, .. .. .. 8 first term, 52 last term.

Q. 138, .. .. .. 158 = last term.

Q. 139, .. 200, .. A. should pay £208 : 2 : 11.
                C.    £168 : 3 : 7.

Q. 140, .. .. .. A.'s loss = $27\frac{1}{8}$ tuns.
                B.'s .. $24\frac{1}{4}$
                C.'s .. $33\frac{1}{4}$.

Q. 141, .. .. .. D. should pay £13 : 3 : $0\frac{1}{4}$.
                E.    15 : 11 : $6\frac{1}{4}$.
                F.    7 : 15 : $11\frac{1}{2}$.

Q. 142, .. .. .. Mercury makes 31.144, &c. revolutions in $7\frac{1}{8}$ of our years, and Venus makes 12.1908, &c. revolutions in the same time. The year of Mercury is to one of ours in the proportion of 2111 to 8766, and that of Venus 5393 to 8766.

Q. 143, .. .. .. The proportion of the mean distances of the Earth and of Mercury from the Sun

is as 1 to $\frac{87}{95}$, or, as 1 to
389473, &c. Of the Earth
and of Venus as 1 : $\frac{68}{95}$, or,
as 1 : .715789473, &c.

Q. 144, Page 200, Ans. Given.

Q. 145, .. 201, .. 38 : 10$\frac{10}{14}$ after 7 o'clock.

Q. 146, .. .. .. The courier overtook the
embassy 4.75904 miles
short of its destination, in
1 day, 4 hours, 54 minutes,
and some seconds.

Q. 147, .. .. .. Distance 25$\frac{1}{2}$ miles.

Q. 148, .. 203, .. 16382 = sum of terms.

Q. 149, .. 204, .. 43046721 = last term,
64570081 = sum of series.

Q. 150, .. 205, .. £965,114,681,693 : 13 : 4.

Q. 151, .. .. .. £51,603,745,730,286 : 15.

Q. 152, .. 206, .. At the end of the 4th crop
there will be
10,000,000,000,000,000
plants, and since the surface
of the earth is 198,943,750
square miles, equal
5,546,233,440,000,000 sq.
ft.; it follows, that the produce of one plant at the end
of 4 years, would cover
much more than the surface
of the whole earth, allowing
one square foot per plant.

Q. 153, .. 207, .. 479,001,600 changes, which
can be rung once over in 91
years, 22 days, and 2 hours.

Q. 154, .. 208, .. 3628800 changes.

Q. 155, .. 209, .. 336 changes.

Q. 156, Page 209, Ans. 380 changes.

Q. 157, .. 211, .. 6561 changes.

Q. 158, .. .. .. $\overline{6|}^3 + 3 \times \overline{6|}^2$; the first number being the combinations the 3 arms together can make, and the second their combination taken two by two, the whole sum equal $216 + 108 = 324$.

Q. 159, .. 215, .. 123409 = square.

Q. 160, .. .. .. 5133 = rectangle.

Q. 161, .. .. .. $\frac{2}{1089}$ of an acre.

Q. 162, .. .. .. 108 plants.

Q. 163, .. .. .. 124 yards.

Q. 164, .. 218, .. $2\frac{10}{27}$ cubic yards.

Q. 165, .. .. .. $6\frac{66}{245}$ feet high.

Q. 166, .. 221, .. $800 - \overline{11|}^2 = 622{,}521.$
$800 - \overline{11|}^3 = 491{,}169{,}069.$

Q. 167, .. .. .. $600 - \overline{9|}^2 = 349{,}281.$
$600 - \overline{9|}^3 = 206{,}425{,}071.$

Q. 168, .. .. .. $\overline{300 - 7} \times 567 = 166{,}131.$

Q. 169, .. 228, .. 496 = square root.

Q. 170, .. .. .. 599 = square root.

Q. 171, .. .. .. 652 = cube root.

Q. 172, .. .. .. 469 = cube root.

Q. 173, .. .. .. 273 = cube root.

Q. 174, .. .. .. 6122.576 &c. = square root.

Q. 175, .. .. .. 22.3159 &c.

Q. 176, .. .. .. 241.088 &c. feet equal side of square.

Q. 177 .. .. .. 85.8603 &c. yards equal side of square.

Q. 178 .. 240, .. 18.14838 &c. = cube root.

London: Printed by W. CLOWES and SONS, Stamford Street.

For EU product safety concerns, contact us at Calle de José Abascal, 56–1°,
28003 Madrid, Spain or eugpsr@cambridge.org.

www.ingramcontent.com/pod-product-compliance
Ingram Content Group UK Ltd.
Pitfield, Milton Keynes, MK11 3LW, UK
UKHW010343140625
459647UK00010B/781